CREATIVE CONNECTIONS

CREATIVE CONNECTIONS

Literature and the Reading Program
Grades 1-3

MARY LOU OLSEN
Fullerton School District
Fullerton, California

LIBRARIES UNLIMITED, INC.
Littleton, Colorado
1987

LIBRARIES UNLIMITED, INC.
P.O. Box 263
Littleton, Colorado 80160-0263

Library of Congress Cataloging-in-Publication Data

Olsen, Mary Lou, 1937-
    Creative connections.

    Bibliography: p. 221
    Includes indexes.
    1. Basal reading instruction. 2. Children--
United States--Books and reading. I. Title.
LB1050.36.047 1987   028.5'35   87-29665
ISBN 0-87287-651-9

DEDICATED IN APPRECIATION

To the hard-working, caring staff of Acacia School,
Fullerton School District, Fullerton, California.

Georgia Menges, Principal

1985-1987 Staff Members

Nancy Rice	Janet Langford	Charlotte Arnwine
Diane Evans	Cheryl Dunn	Jean Moss
Tracy Thompson	John Roseman	Mitchi Mitobe
Andrea Robson	Linda Lockwood	Bette Parke
Sara Bell	Gloria Furuken	Beverly Falconer
Rebecca Thompson	Zita Michalski	Barbara Nelson
Letha Pletcher	Ann Siebert	Pat Bertsch
Sharon Hauger	Cheryl Heredia	Adrienne Knoll
Roberta Landsman	Kathy Wiser	Karen Dreng
Rose Marie Lloyd	Leslie Pertrovich	

With thanks to the teachers who allowed me to
"do my thing with kids."

And with love to 500 kids at Acacia School who
"did their thing with me."

CONTENTS

Grade Two
INTRODUCTIONS

Through Giants of Sea and Land

Of Bear Friends

From a Menu of Stories

Grade Three
EXTENSIONS

Of Information

Into the Animal Kingdom

Out of the Pages of History

AN INTRODUCTION
Literature and the Reading Program

Children's literature is the connection, conduit, or cable to a child's world of learning. Literature is first introduced by parents singing lullabies to their babies and later amusing them with Mother Goose rhymes. These oral introductions to children's literature are followed with a delightful selection of picture books.

Adults are role models for children and fortunate is the child whose model reads and enjoys books, especially children's books. Reading is a lifelong habit that needs to be nourished and allowed to flower.

Reading Program Criteria

Reading should not be taught in isolation. Reading is an expansive subject and should include activities beyond mechanical skills and decoding. It is a smooth, planned integration of rich vocabulary words, resonant oral language, cognitive development, and aesthetic experiences that meld together to form a satisfying whole. A reading program should be diamond-like, all facets included, and each a part of the magnificent whole.

Creative Connections: Literature and the Reading Program is written to support and extend the basal reading programs being used in schools. A reading teacher guides students in acquiring certain mechanical skills. The teacher should combine those skills and expand the learning through an integrated literature program. Included in this introductory material are correlations to the Ginn Reading Program, Harcourt Brace Jovanovich Bookmark Reading Program, and the Scott Foresman Reading Program: An American Tradition. Literature selections in *Creative Connections* enhance basal reading programs through a wide variety of curricular activities in the basic subjects of reading and mathematics, in addition to social studies, health, science, music, and art. Two reading lists, theme and curriculum, in each unit suggest books that correlate with the title unit.

Literature Units Field-Tested with Students

Materials for this book were developed and field-tested during a 2-year literature teaching assignment at Acacia School, Fullerton School District, Fullerton, California. Upon entering the classroom, there was usually an undercurrent of sound and a visual stir of excitement among students. Something special was going to happen! Students knew what the instructor expected—that all would need to participate and exhibit a high level of performance, and that new learning materials were to be presented during each literature lesson.

Curriculum integration in subject content areas is not an *idealistic* goal, but a *realistic* teaching practice that can be used to empower students to take charge of their own learning activities. Critical thinking skills are consistently developed within the scope of the literature unit and the accompanying content subjects through the implementation of Benjamin Bloom's Cognitive Taxonomy of learning.

Student Anecdotes

Literature is so powerful that its effects are sometimes overlooked. Some anecdotes about students who were challenged through the study of literature demonstrate this.

One Mexican-American student in a bilingual class asked the school media specialist to help him find books illustrated with the pointillism technique after an introduction to Susan Jeffer's *Hansel and Gretel* and her pointillism art style. That student will not remember all the things he learned in class, but he'll always be interested in "dot art" because he sought out examples of it in other books. Except through a literature lesson, that student's education plan probably would never have included an art lesson involving that technique.

A student with many discipline problems was very interested in stories of knights and dragons. Privately he would ask about the book selected for study the next week. He wanted to check out a library copy in order to be prepared in advance for the class discussion. His beaming face and intense eyes showed his enthusiasm for books.

Another student chose to send her holiday greeting card made in art class to the literature specialist as a personal thank-you for lessons in literature.

Still another student, long grown-up, recalled the summer that she spent reading myths for an assignment and of still retaining notes about the gods and goddesses written on an index card.

A teacher shared the comments made by a parent regarding her fourth grade son's literature class. He had been introduced to Thomas Locker's *Where the River Begins*. While shopping in a local bookstore he found a Locker book and proceeded to tell his mother about the Hudson River style of the artist and to point out examples through landscapes and cloud formations.

Children enjoy multisensory experiences through literature. They can prepare an "alligator pie," plan an imaginary wedding reception for King Babar and his bride, Celeste, design and sew "Where the Wild Things Are" monster pillows, create Sequoyah's "Talking Leaves" in clay, and select a nutritious meal for a "Very Hungry Caterpillar" from the basic 4 food groups.

Suggested Use of Creative Connections

Grade 1

Integrate a literature unit title or a supplementary book title once a week during the language arts instruction program.

Add a weekly activity that can be enjoyed during the appropriate content area instruction period.

Grade 2

Choose 2 titles, 1 literature unit title and 1 supplementary book, from the theme reading or curriculum connections reading lists each week. Teach the materials as a part of the language arts program.

Integrate 1 reading activity weekly in addition to 1 or 2 subject content activities.

Grade 3

Choose a literature unit and integrate it into curriculum instruction throughout the day in addition to basal reader instruction.

Encourage students to write, share, and critique their products with other students, and to edit the products after discussion.

Integral Parts of a Literature Unit

The format of materials in this book is as follows:

- Bibliographic information (author, illustrator, publisher, and date) is presented.

- *Suggested Grade Level* and *Classification* are designations relating to *Recommended Readings in Literature, Kindergarten through Grade 8*, a California State Department of Education document listing 1,200 literature titles suitable for exploration by students. *Classification* is the type of material, such as picture book, historical fiction, or poetry.

- *Student Objectives* are expected student behaviors stated in terms of Bloom's Cognitive Taxonomy of learning. Developmental steps in the hierarchy of learning are knowledge, comprehension, application, analysis, synthesis, and evaluation.

- *Synopsis* is a brief summary of the story.

- *About the Author-Illustrator* is an information capsule to be used as background information to support the unit.

- *Selected Additional Titles* are other materials published by the author and/or illustrator. Titles written by an author-illustrator are listed as "by the author," those illustrated by an author-illustrator are listed as "by the illustrator," and those both written and illustrated by an individual are listed as "by the author-illustrator."

- *Model Lessons* are structured lessons designed to be taught in approximately 20 minutes on different days; they are introductions to the literature unit. Total integration of the literature across the curriculum is possible with lesson presentations taught in 20-45-minute time periods several times weekly.

- *Computer* and *Instructional Materials Connections* are sources of supplementary student materials to enhance and enrich the lesson.

- *Library Media Center Connections* are optional activities to connect the school library media center and the instructional program, as well as links to curriculum and reference skills through a planned program of integrated lessons.

- *Theme Reading Connections* is a presentation of additional books to complement the unit. *No attempt has been made to ascertain the availability of books; some books that are out-of-print have been included because of their importance and relationship to the unit.* Many out-of-print books are still available through the children's room of public libraries and in school libraries.

- *Activities to Connect Literature and Curriculum* is an integrated approach to curricular activities designed to relate directly to subject content areas by using literature as the instructional vehicle.

- *Guided Reading Connections across a Curriculum Rainbow* provides a comprehensive selection of student readings to enrich the unit study.

- *Enriching Connections* are appropriate for independent student study and exploration. The parent component is available for reproduction or adaptation in a teacher newsletter to parents.

Literature units are designed as 2-week instructional modules. The 15 units within each grade level comprise a 30-week, year-long thematic plan with additional time allowed for testing and holiday activities.

A Curriculum Cookbook for Teachers

Creative Connections is presented as a "curriculum cookbook for teachers." The pleasure will be in reading the recipes and selecting one to try or adapt for your own classroom and students from the following literature categories:

Picture books

Folktales

Fantasy and science fiction

Historical fiction

Poetry and verse

Biography

Information books

Literature, the connection, conduit, or cable, to a child's world of learning, is to be enjoyed and savored by both teacher and students.

Bon Appetit!

GRADE ONE	GRADE TWO	GRADE THREE

PEOPLE
 	
Will I Have a Friend?
Alexander and the Horrible,
  No Good, Very Bad Day
	PEOPLE
	
	Ira Sleeps Over
	Gung Hay Fat Choy
		PEOPLE
		
		Crow Boy
		The Story of Sequoyah
		Columbus
		Fool of the World and the
		  Flying Ship

IMAGINATIONS *Mother Goose Treasury* *The Sky Is Full of Song* *Little Rabbit's Loose Tooth* *Petunia* *Where the Wild Things Are*	IMAGINATIONS *Story of Babar* *Horton Hatches the Egg* *Corduroy* *Winnie-the-Pooh* *May I Bring a Friend?* *Mr. Rabbit and the Lovely* *Present*	IMAGINATIONS *Island of the Skog* *Bunnicula* *Leo the Late Bloomer* *Fables* *Inch by Inch* *Cricket Songs*
ENVIRONMENTS *Make Way for Ducklings* *Snowy Day* *Carrot Seed* *Peter Spier's Rain* *Very Hungry Caterpillar*	ENVIRONMENTS *Popcorn Book* *Song of the Swallows* *Little House* *Tale of Peter Rabbit* *Miss Rumphius* *Story of Johnny Appleseed*	ENVIRONMENTS *Bananas: From Manolo to* *Margie* *Little House in the Big Woods*
COMMUNICATIONS *Anno's Counting Book* *A, B, See!* *What Mary Jo Shared*	COMMUNICATIONS *Amos and Boris*	COMMUNICATIONS *The Post Office Book* *Jack Jouett's Ride* *Why Mosquitoes Buzz in* *People's Ears*

Correlation with
Ginn Reading Program, © 1982

GRADE ONE	GRADE TWO	GRADE THREE
Primer	Book 2	Book 3
WHAT AM I? 　*What Mary Jo Shared* ON THE MAGIC HILL 　*Where the Wild Things Are* 　*Mother Goose Treasury* IN THE CITY 　*Peter Spier's Rain* 　*Snowy Day* CARROTS, POTATOES, PEAS AND TOMATOES 　*Carrot Seed* 　*Very Hungry Caterpillar*	NEW FRIENDS 　*Winnie-the-Pooh* 　*Amos and Boris* 　*May I Bring a Friend?* ANIMALS ALL AROUND 　*Corduroy* TOOL 　——— ANIMALS AT PLAY 　*Tale of Peter Rabbit* BY THE SEA 　*Song of the Swallows* AMERICANS ALL 　*Story of Johnny Appleseed* MAGIC TALES 　*Horton Hatches the Egg*	TRY, AND TRY AGAIN 　*Leo the Late Bloomer* THE BIG TOWN 　——— MESSAGES 　*The Post Office Book* 　*Jack Jouett's Ride* ANIMAL WORLD 　*Cricket Songs* JUST FOR FUN 　*Why Mosquitoes Buzz in* 　*People's Ears* WONDERS OF THE WORLD 　*Fool of the World and the* 　*Flying Ship*
Book 1	Book 2	Book 3
SCHOOL DAYS 　*Anno's Counting Book* 　*A, B, See!* ANIMAL FUN 　*Make Way for Ducklings* 　*Petunia* NEW THINGS FROM OLD 　*Little Rabbit's Loose Tooth* NEW FRIENDS 　*Will I Have a Friend?* WORLD OF ART 　*The Sky Is Full of Song* I HAVE A HOME 　*Alexander and the Horrible,* 　*No Good, Very Bad Day*	WORLD OF GIANTS AND MONSTERS 　——— SURPRISES 　*Popcorn Book* 　*Mr. Rabbit and the Lovely* 　*Present* CAN I? I CAN 　*Ira Sleeps Over* GOING PLACES 　*Gung Hay Fat Choy* ONCE UPON A TIME 　*Story of Babar* 　*Little House* COLLECTING THINGS 　*Miss Rumphius*	TALES FROM EVERYWHERE 　*Fables* 　*Crow Boy* 　*The Story of Sequoyah* STRANGE AS IT SEEMS 　*Inch by Inch* LOOK ALL AROUND YOU 　*Little House in the Big Woods* 　*Bananas: From Manolo to* 　*Margie* EXPLORERS 　*Columbus* WORLD OF MYSTERY 　*Bunnicula* 　*Island of the Skog*

Correlation with
Harcourt Brace Jovanovich Bookmark Reading
Program: Eagle Edition, © 1983

GRADE ONE	GRADE TWO	GRADE THREE
Pre-Primer FRIENDSHIP *Will I Have a Friend?* TREASURES *Mother Goose Treasury* COLORS *Very Hungry Caterpillar* **Primer** HOMES NATURE *Anno's Counting Book* *Snowy Day* *Carrot Seed* *Peter Spier's Rain* SECRETS *What Mary Jo Shared*	**Book 2** DAY AND NIGHT *Little House* THE WAY WE USE OUR HANDS TO LEARN ABOUT THE WORLD FRIENDS, OLD AND NEW *Story of Babar* *Amos and Boris* *Winnie-the-Pooh* HUMOR *Horton Hatches the Egg* BIRDS *Song of the Swallows* "SPECIAL" THE WORD *Mr. Rabbit and the Lovely Present* *Gung Hay Fat Choy*	**Book 3** LEARNING ABOUT ME *Crow Boy* CITIES *The Post Office Book* PEOPLE WHO MAKE THEIR MARK IN AN HISTORIC WAY *The Story of Sequoyah* *Jack Jouett's Ride* *Columbus* GETTING THERE *Fool of the World and the Flying Ship* GROWING *Inch by Inch* *Bananas: From Manolo to Margie* FIGURING THINGS OUT *Fables*
Book 1 PEOPLE AND ANIMALS ON THE MOVE *Make Way for Ducklings* *Little Rabbit's Loose Tooth* USING IMAGINATION *A, B, See!* *The Sky Is Full of Song* *Where the Wild Things Are* RESPONSIBILITIES *Petunia* *Alexander and the Horrible, No Good, Very Bad Day*	**Book 2** GROWING AND CHANGING *Popcorn Book* THINGS THAT ARE SPECIAL *Corduroy* ART *May I Bring a Friend?* NEIGHBORS *Story of Johnny Appleseed* FEAR *Ira Sleeps Over* *Tale of Peter Rabbit* BEING CLEVER *Miss Rumphius*	**Book 3** FIRST EXPERIENCES *Little House in the Big Woods* GIFT OF MUSIC *Cricket Songs* PEOPLE BEING THEMSELVES *Leo the Late Bloomer* *Why Mosquitoes Buzz in People's Ears* WAYS PEOPLE HAVE FUN MYSTERIES *Bunnicula* *Island of the Skog* JOURNEYS

Correlation with
Scott Foresman Reading Program: An American Tradition, © 1987

Grade One

ADVENTURES

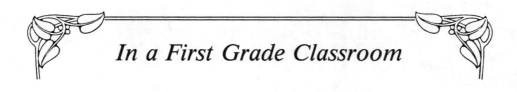

In a First Grade Classroom

ANNO'S COUNTING BOOK

Author: Mitsumasa, Anno
Illustrator: Mitsumasa, Anno
Publisher: Thomas Y. Crowell Company, 1977
Suggested Grade Level: K-2
Classification: Core Materials
Literary Form: Picture book illustrated with watercolors
Theme: Counting is an adventure with numbers.

About the Book

STUDENT OBJECTIVES:

1. Count from 1 to 12 correctly.

2. Recognize that the weather is not the same every day.

3. Identify the 4 seasons—winter, spring, summer, and fall with the assistance of picture prompts.

SYNOPSIS: *Anno's Counting Book* is a walk through numbers beginning with 1 and continuing through 12. The cardinal numbers are printed on the righthand page and the corresponding shaded number block is illustrated on the lefthand page. Anno has also illustrated a colorful walk through the 12 months and 4 seasons within this book's illustrations. *Anno's Counting Book* has been selected as an exemplary counting book because of its curriculum integration of number concepts and seasons into a single volume.

ABOUT THE AUTHOR-ILLUSTRATOR: Anno Mitsumasa, March 20, 1926- .
    Anno is a famous Japanese author-illustrator. His works may be enjoyed at many grade levels because of the level of sophistication of art. What a first grader "sees" may not reach the depth of understanding possible. His books are enchanting, but also have a deft "sleight of hand" and relate directly to mathematical concepts. Anno is a former elementary teacher with a sense of humor who constantly seeks to activate the reader's imagination. Examine his work for the unique, including hidden animals in *Anno's Animals* and both famous paintings and fairy tale characters throughout his other books.

SELECTED ADDITIONAL TITLES BY THE AUTHOR-ILLUSTRATOR:

Anno's Alphabet
Anno's Animals
Anno's Journey
Anno's USA
Anno's Counting House
The King's Flower

Note that *The King's Flower* is a folktale and is Anno's first for young students. It is a delightful tale of a king who must have everything big, bigger, and the biggest. Imagine that his tooth brush requires 2 men to carry it. He orders a candy bar so large that the men cannot carry it through the castle gates! And so goes the story until he discovers that some things can be both small and beautiful.

Using the Book

Suggested Approach to the Book

Model Lesson #1

- Introduce the author-illustrator as a person who enjoys "thinking" and finds that seeing things in different ways is a "playful" activity.

- Play a modified charades game with the class and describe a bear, whale, elephant, snake, bunny, kangaroo, and bee.

- Tell students that they are going to look very carefully at the pictures in order to "see" all the play ideas Anno has included.

- Read the story through and then share the illustrations with students.

Model Lesson #2

- Introduce counting and number relations using the back-of-the-book explanation by Anno that early cavemen used pebbles to count the number of deer, birds, men, days, and even water. Counting, according to Anno, is the replacing of pebbles with words representing numbers.

- Use pebbles to represent the number of student birthdays in each of 12 months. Transfer this information to Number Blox graphing paper. It is also possible to use ages of the students as graph coordinates.

Model Lesson #3

- Art appreciation through picture books: Compare the art of Anno and his counting concept book with

    Gretz, Suzanna, *Teddy Bears 1 to 10*
    Wildsmith, Brian, *Brian Wildsmith 1, 2, 3*

Library Media Center Connections

1. Display counting books from the library collection and include an abacus, various counting blocks including Pattern Blocks, and weights and measurement materials supplemented with audiovisual materials.

2. Ask the staff to introduce

    Fisher, Aileen, *I Like Weather*
    Provensen, Alice, *The Year at Maple Hill Farm*

3. In the library media center, encourage students to create a picture using numbered items as in *Anno's Counting Book*.

Computer Connections

Random House, *Charlie Brown's 1, 2, 3's*
Weekly Reader, *Stickybear Numbers*

Theme Reading Connections: Counting and Number Books

Berenstain, Stan, *Bears on Wheels*
Boynton, Sandra, *Hippos Go Berserk* (poetry)
Carle, Eric, *1, 2, 3, to the Zoo*
Crews, Donald, *Black Dots*
Crowther, Robert, *Most Amazing Hide and Seek Counting Book*
Hawkins, Colin, *Adding Animals* (pull tab book)
Hoban, Tana, *Count and See*
Hutchins, Pat, *I Hunter*
Martin, Bill, *Sounds of Numbers* (poetry)
Mayer, Mercer, *Little Monster's Counting Book*
Milne, A. A., *Pooh's Counting Book*
Oxenbury, Helen, *Number of Things*
Russell, Sandra, *Farmer's Dozen*
Sendak, Maurice, *One Was Johnny*
Tafuri, Nancy, *Who's Counting*
Zolotow, Charlotte, *One Step, Two ...*

Activities to Connect Literature and Curriculum

ART

Create a number representational picture using numbered items as in *Anno's Counting Book*. These make interesting number books for library media center and classroom display.

Construct "Seasons of Color" circles, divided into 4 parts to represent the color of seasons. Suggested colors are fall orange, winter white, spring green, and summer yellow. Pinwheels can be made from the color circles by cutting each colored section almost to the center, twisting the section once, and pinning each color to a handle. The handle may be constructed by tightly rolling construction paper on the diagonal slant and stapling the ends or using plastic straws and connecting the pinwheel with a loose brad.

LANGUAGE ARTS

Key vocabulary words for clustering and writing:

rain
sun
snow
fog
numbers

Introduce a calendar of months for the classroom and list school activities that are important to students in grade 1.

SCIENCE

Reproduce a monthly calendar and suggest that students keep a record of the weather. This information could be presented in graphic form on a monthly or long-term basis.

Incorporate a science lesson on weather forecasting including equipment required. Consult with your media center or science resource for additional supplies/information.

Plan to further integrate this lesson into the rainy or snow season and actually measure the amount.

Beyond the Book

Guided Reading Connections across a Curriculum Rainbow: Seasons

Clifton, Lucille, *Everett Anderson's Year*
Gregory, Sally, *Sing a Song of Seasons* (poetry)
Lobel, Arnold, *Frog and Toad All Year*
Provensen, Alice, and Martin Provensen, *Book of Seasons*
Udry, Janice, *A Tree Is Nice*
Updike, John, *A Child's Calendar*
Wildsmith, Brian, *Seasons*

Enriching Connections

FOR GIFTED STUDENTS

Design a number book using a "house" or animal theme. Collect cash register tapes and graph the number of items in each transaction. Which ones are computer generated? How do you tell?

FOR PARENTS

Explain the weather forecast presented on television to your child. Divide a paper plate in half with a horizontal pencil line. Ask your child to color a sun on the top half and raindrops on the bottom half. For a month record the date on the bottom or top that corresponds with the local weather each day.

MOTHER GOOSE TREASURY

Author: Briggs, Raymond, editor
Illustrator: Briggs, Raymond
Publisher: Coward, McCann and Geoghegan, 1966
Suggested Grade Level: K-4
Classification: Recreational and Motivational Materials
Literary Form: Mother Goose poetry
Theme: A magical world of nonsense and rhyme.

About the Book

STUDENT OBJECTIVES:

1. Memorize 5 Mother Goose poems.

2. Recite as a choral group Mother Goose poems.

3. Discover other Mother Goose poem selections.

SYNOPSIS: A historical presentation of the beginning of children's literature that is passed down by word of mouth from generation to generation. The *Treasury* is an extensive collection of both recognized and obscure Mother Goose rhymes including some very interesting selections.

ABOUT THE AUTHOR-ILLUSTRATOR: Raymond Briggs, January 18, 1934- .
Briggs remembers his childhood during World War II. He was sent to live with his aunts in a village about an hour away from London. He still remembers the sounds of London being bombed and his 2 aunts yelling to get the suitcases if they had to evacuate the house. The enemy only came near his sanctuary once—the bombs caused the glass to fall out of the family grandfather clock! Briggs hated school; it was too traditional. He wanted to do other things than what was expected of him.

Quentin Blake had an influence on him in that Briggs liked his cartoons. When he decided to be a cartoonist, he made a startling discovery—the best jobs were in cartooning or illustrating for children's books. He spent 2 years working on the *Mother Goose Treasury*. Almost 900 individual finished illustrations were prepared for this volume. He worked in pen and ink, alternating black-and-white double-paged spreads with 2-page color presentations. This is possibly the most extensive presentation of Mother Goose materials in print. As editor, Briggs selected 400 rhymes for the 200-page book.

Briggs is not overly fond of children—he likes to observe them, but is not interested in cleaning up after them. In fact, "I would not want children around the house; they're too much work, they make noise, they smell, they cause dirt, and you're always cleaning up after them."

In 1967 the Kate Greenaway award for the best illustrated English book was presented to Raymond Briggs. This award is equivalent to the United States award for the best illustrated book of the year—the Caldecott. When asked if receiving the award had changed his life any, he quipped that he now wore a hat 2 sizes larger.

SELECTED ADDITIONAL TITLES BY THE ILLUSTRATOR:

Elephant and the Bad Baby
Father Christmas
Fee Fi Fo Fum
Jim and the Beanstalk
Ring-a-Ring O' Roses
Snowman
White Land

Using the Book

Suggested Approach to the Book

Model Lesson #1

- Share the biographical materials of Raymond Briggs with students. It is interesting to add a few comments on the history of the Mother Goose rhymes and rhythms during this introduction. The earliest Mother Goose rhymes were published during the 1600s and 1700s in England. Replica prints of some of these books are available to supplement the lesson. The zenith was probably reached during the 1800s in England, when Kate Greenaway published her illustrated *Mother Goose: Or, the Old Nursery Rhymes* in 1881. Mother Goose stories and rhymes are an important part of the children's literature heritage and many excellent, well-researched editions are available today.

Model Lesson #2

- Choose, read, and enjoy various selection with the class. Explain that there are both good and bad children in the stories and that the pictures add to the story.

- The pictures may be old-fashioned, but they provide good helps to what is going on in the selection. Example—Hector Protector wears green and goes to see the queen. He was not liked and sent away. You might ask the class to tell why. This is an excellent opportunity for collaborative learning in first grade. Assign small groups to figure out an answer. Select a spokesperson to give possible reasons. Brainstorm the replies on the board.

- An original Maurice Sendak illustration shows Hector thrusting a sword with a snake wrapped around it at the queen. Do you like Hector Protector? Who is he protecting? Give your answer.

Model Lesson #3

- Continue to share these old stories and rhymes. Begin to memorize several for choral reading in class. Allow opportunities for language development through the use of alliteration, rhythm, and rhymes. Also point out the use of exaggeration. Nursery rhymes are examples of fantasy also.

Model Lesson #4

- Food experience: Pretend you are on your way to Banberry Cross in England and need to buy some hot cross buns for a morning snack. Purchase cinnamon rolls from the deli case at the grocery store and bake as a class snack.

Model Lesson #5

- Art appreciation through picture books: Compare

     Blake, Quentin, *Quentin Blake's Nursery Rhyme Book*
     Scarry, Richard, *Richard Scarry's Animal Nursery Tales*

Library Media Center Connections

1. Collect and present a display of a large number of Mother Goose books.

2. Special library media center activity for students: Paperclip markers at appropriate pages to visually compare the following Mother Goose rhymes as illustrated in different volumes:

     Three Men in a Tub
     Little Boy Blue
     Jack and Jill
     Little Miss Muffet

Theme Reading Connections: Mother Goose

Atkinson, Allen, *Old King Cole & Other Favorites*
De Paola, Tomie, *Mother Goose Story*
Greenaway, Kate, *Mother Goose: Or, the Old Nursery Rhymes*
Marshall, James, *James Marshall's Mother Goose*
Scarry, Richard, *Best Mother Goose Ever*
Wildsmith, Brian, *Mother Goose*

Activities to Connect Literature and Curriculum

ART

Create a booklet of Mother Goose nursery rhymes.
Using scrap material, dress a potato puppet like Mother Goose and use to role play and recite nursery rhymes.

Make Mother Goose character placards and attach yarn so students may wear them for language arts recitations.

CITIZENSHIP

How would you behave if you lived with the Old Woman in the Shoe?

LANGUAGE ARTS

Pair students to recite and act out a favorite Mother Goose selection. The teacher will make suggestions to avoid duplication of presentations.

MUSIC

After the language arts presentation, play Mother Goose rhyme music and encourage participation in a classroom parade. This is a good opportunity to use rhythm instruments. Children may wear name card placards to identify their Mother Goose characters.

SOCIAL STUDIES

Look at Mother Goose facsimile books and discuss why the pictures used in these early prints were so very different in color and style from the Raymond Briggs book of 1966. Compare a 1980s Mother Goose book.

Beyond the Book

Guided Reading Connections across a Curriculum Rainbow: Jack and the Beanstalk

Briggs, Raymond, *Jim and the Beanstalk*
Cauley, Lorinda, *Jack and the Beanstalk*
De Regniers, Beatrice, *Jack and the Beanstalk*
Galdone, Paul, *Jack and the Beanstalk*
Haley, Gail, *Jack and the Bean Tree*

Enriching Connections

FOR GIFTED STUDENTS

Write a modern-day tale of *Jack and the Beanstalk*. The giant now lives in a floating satellite and Jack must travel by rocket ship. Create a new villain for this space version.

FOR PARENTS

Listen to your child retell a version of *Jack and the Beanstalk*.
Share your favorite childhood nursery rhyme book with your child.

WILL I HAVE A FRIEND?

Author: Cohen, Miriam
Illustrator: Hoban, Lillian
Publisher: Macmillan Co., 1967
Suggested Grade Level: K-1
Classification: Recreational and Motivational Materials
Literary Form: Picture book
Theme: It is important to meet a new friend on the first day of school.

About the Book

STUDENT OBJECTIVES:

1. Label 5 activities that are happening on the first day of school in Jimmy's class.

2. Describe the class's own first day of school activities.

3. Name 2 friends' names inside and outside of school.

SYNOPSIS: Jimmy's dad takes him to school on the first day and Jimmy worries about finding a new friend there. He observes all the activities in the school room and is invited to share a toy. Thus a new friendship begins with Paul.

ABOUT THE AUTHOR AND ILLUSTRATOR: Miriam Cohen, October 14, 1926- .
Lillian Hoban, May 18, 1925- .
Miriam Cohen and Lillian Hoban have teamed together a number of times in producing a series of titles that include Jimmy, Paul, and Anna Maria as students in the same class. Lillian Hoban began illustrating children's books in 1961 when her husband, Russell Hoban, an illustrator, began to write children's books. One of her most popular illustrated books is *Bread and Jam for Francis*, which uses the pencil technique.

SELECTED ADDITIONAL TITLES BY THE AUTHOR:

First Grade Takes a Test (*Note:* Ideal to introduce test taking)
No Good in Art
Starring First Grade
When Will I Read?

SELECTED ADDITIONAL TITLES BY THE ILLUSTRATOR:

Arthur's Christmas Cookies
Baby Sister for Francis
Day the Teacher Went Bananas
Mole Family Christmas

Using the Book

Suggested Approach to the Book

Model Lesson #1

- The teacher will read *Will I Have a Friend?* aloud to the class after explaining that this is the story of a little boy's very first day at school and he is worried about making a new friend.

    1. What are the children in the story doing in the class?
    2. Which of those things named have we done in our class?
    3. Are there some activities that the class members would like to do?
    4. List those activities on easel paper for future use.

Model Lesson #2

- Art appreciation through picture books: Compare the art of Lillian Hoban to that in the following 2 picture books

    Cohen, Miriam, *Starring First Grade*
    Hoban, Russell, *Bread and Jam for Francis*

    Note the time difference of 18 years between the publishing of these 2 titles and their illustrations of the same children in first grade. Also compare *Will I Have a Friend?* illustrations of the same children with those in *Starring First Grade*. How are they alike? What differences can be observed in art technique, printing, color, and paper quality?

Library Media Center Connections

1. Arrange for a story hour about school/friends.

    Lobel, Arnold, *Frog and Toad Are Friends*

2. Request that a special picture book corner be set up to introduce media center services.

3. Special library media center activity for students: Toad is sick—he has the measles. Please send him a get well card and pretend his friend, Frog, sent it. Make sure to include Frog's signature.

Instructional Materials Connections

National Geographic Wonders of Learning Kit, *Amphibians and How They Grow*

Theme Reading Connections: Friends and School

Aliki, *We Are Best Friends*
Berenstain, Stan, *Berenstain Bears Go to School*
Carle, Eric, *Do You Want to Be My Best Friend?*

Charmatz, Bill, *Troy St. Bus*
Cohen, Miriam, *Best Friends*
Crews, Donald, *School Bus*
Ets, Marie Hall, *Come Play with Me*
Hill, Eric, *Spot Goes to School*
Hoban, Russell, *Best Friends for Francis*
Hopkins, Lee, *Best Friends* (poetry)
Howe, James, *Day the Teacher Went Bananas*
Lobel, Arnold, *Frog and Toad Are Friends*
Marshall, James, *George and Martha*
Mayer, Mercer, *Little Monster at School*
Winthrop, Elizabeth, *Tough Eddie*
Zion, Gene, *Meanest Squirrel I Ever Met*
Zolotow, Charlotte, *Quarreling Book*

Activities to Connect Literature and Curriculum

ART

Make a "Garden of Friends." Using butcher paper as the backdrop, create a blue sky, green grass mural and attach student-produced, cutout flowers. The center of the flowers are student Polaroid prints or self-portraits and the petals are the names of their home and school friends. Attach Velcro to the back of the photographs, as they can be used in other ways during the year (e.g., on an attribute chart). *See also* Mary Jo unit.

Student art may include drawings of favorite class activities.

Include a clay activity to correlate with the story. Does the clay "feel wet, cold, and heavy" as in *Will I Have a Friend?*

CITIZENSHIP

Discuss the behavior of Danny, who jumped up and acted like a monkey. That way of acting is not acceptable behavior in the classroom.

Assign rotating classroom duties to student helpers.

Bring an inexpensive toy or book to share. This might best be done on a designated day and at a certain time for a specified length of time.

Introduce cooperative learning by letting students share within groups simultaneously. Call time to complete the project.

LANGUAGE ARTS

Key vocabulary words for clustering and writing:

> school
> milk
> juice
> cookies
> friend

A class rule chart could be generated from student responses about the characteristics that make you like a friend.

MATH

Set up an interest center of blocks and display the *Will I Have a Friend?* book cover showing Jimmy doing a block activity. This is also an ideal introduction to block number activities including Pattern Blocks and Tangrams.

Using number squares, introduce counting by graphing to the class. Possible number problems might include

How many walk to school and how many ride the bus?
How many moms go to work and how many stay at home?
How many students have brothers? Sisters?

SOCIAL STUDIES

Examine the art work in *Will I Have a Friend?* and explain that the story was not written recently, but in 1967. Point out that the store price of apples was then 10 cents a pound. Note also that fish were stored in a barrel outside the store. How do markets store fish today?

Explain that during the year the class will be looking at the places where stories take place and that this story is in the city and will be similar to another story — *Make Way for Ducklings.*

Beyond the Book

Guided Reading Connections across a Curriculum Rainbow: Frogs

Hogan, Paula, *Frog* (cassette and book)
Howe, Judy, *What I Like about Frogs*
Kent, Jack, *Caterpillar and Polliwog*
Langstaff, John, *Frog Went A-Courtin'* (Caldecott Award — 1956)
Mayer, Mercer, *Boy, a Dog, a Frog, and a Friend*
Petty, Kate, *Frogs and Toads*
Potter, Beatrix, *Tale of Mr. Jeremy Fisher*
Schultz, Ellen, *I Can Read about Frogs and Toads*
Zemach, Harve, *Princess and the Froggie*

Enriching Connections

FOR GIFTED STUDENTS

Sort through a jar of buttons and choose one that toad might like to replace his lost button.

Toad is embarrassed about his swim suit. What kind do you think he would like? Can you design and color a new one for him?

What kind of birthday present would Toad give to Frog? Draw it and place a package wrapping over top of your art so it's a surprise package.

FOR PARENTS

Encourage the child to use blocks creatively for a home project and to explain the project's design to an adult. Send the teacher a follow-up note stating that this activity was completed and what was constructed.

Allow the child to invite a friend over to play, but stress the family rules, including a parent talking to the friend's parent to finalize arrangements including time of visit and transportation. If a note is required for the teacher to allow a child to go to another child's home after school, please send the appropriate note.

Share your remembrance of your first grade teacher and class. What are some differences in technology available today and then? What kind of school library did you have?

Read a *Frog and Toad* story to your child.

A, B, SEE!

Author: Hoban, Tana
Illustrator: Hoban, Tana
Publisher: Greenwillow, 1982
Suggested Grade Level: K-1
Classification: Extended Materials
Literary Form: Picture book in photoessay form
Theme: Look and see the alphabet in picture form.

About the Book

STUDENT OBJECTIVES:

1. Recite the alphabet from A to Z.

2. Distinguish between letters of the alphabet using letter prompts.

3. Match letters of the alphabet with objects that begin with the same letter.

SYNOPSIS: Alphabet letters are representational and perfect photograms are integrated to illustrate the letters and are correlated with corresponding objects.

ABOUT THE AUTHOR-ILLUSTRATOR: Tana Hoban, birthdate not available.

Tana Hoban grew up in a country house in Lansdale, Pennsylvania. Her early memories were of sleeping on a porch until it became quite cold, and of her family garden and chickens. She received training in art and has been drawing since she was the youngest in her sketch and life classes as a little girl. A camera was given to Tana by her husband-to-be. After her daughter was born, she began to take pictures of children. She had photographs on the covers of 16 magazines in 1 year.

"My books are about everday things that are so ordinary that one tends to overlook them. I try to rediscover these things and share them with children."*

---

*Doris de Montreville and Elizabeth D. Crawford, eds. *Fourth Book of Junior Authors and Illustrators* (New York: H. W. Wilson, 1978).

Her books should be classified as photoessays as she is a master photographer as well as a creator of realistic photograms. To see Tana Hoban's books is to rediscover life's beauty.

SELECTED ADDITIONAL TITLES BY THE AUTHOR-ILLUSTRATOR:

Big Ones, Little Ones
Circles, Triangles, and Squares
Count and See
Dig, Drill, Dump, Fill
I Read Signs
I Read Symbols
I Walk and Read
Is It Larger? Is It Smaller?
Is It Red? Is It Yellow? Is It Blue?
Is It Rough? Is It Smooth? Is It Shiny?
Look Again
More Than One
One Little Kitten
1 2 3
Push-Pull, Empty-Full
Round and Round and Round
Shapes and Things
Shapes, Shapes, Shapes
Take Another Look
What Is It?
Where Is It?

Using the Book

Suggested Approach to the Book

Model Lesson #1

- Introduce Tana Hoban as a lady whose work is taking pictures of children and for children's picture books. Explain that the class will look at pictures that represent alphabet letters and alphabet-first-letter objects—for example, *a* is for apple, airplane, arrow, and acorn. All these items are shown on the first page. Share a page or two each day and involve the class in discovering what the photogram objects pictured are.

Model Lesson #2

- Choose another Tana Hoban book to read and share with the class.

Model Lesson #3

- Create photograms with small groups. Have available large punch-out alphabet letters. Encourage students to use letters of their initials. Using construction paper for practice, direct students to place their chosen letters on the pages and add a few other items such as leaves, scissors, pencils, flowers, and paper clips.

- Photograms can be exposed in the sun or using strong classroom light, depending upon type of paper used.

- After approving the students' designs, expose and develop according to paper directions.

Model Lesson #4

- Art appreciation through picture books: Compare the art form and different approach to zoo animals in

  Carle, Eric, *1, 2, 3, to the Zoo*
  Hoban, Tana, *Children's Zoo*

Model Lesson #5

- Bake ABC cookies as a classroom project. Short cut idea—roll out grocery store cookie dough and cut with alphabet cookie cutters.

Library Media Center Connections

1. Set up a display of a large variety of alphabet books. When small groups visit the library media center, have a selection of alphabet books on the tables for viewing.

2. Special media center activity for students: Choose an alphabet letter. Draw it on construction paper and add an object that begins with the same letter. Cutting and pasting pictures from magazines is appropriate.

Computer Connections

Weekly Reader, *Stickybear ABC*
Weekly Reader, *Stickybear Opposites*

Theme Reading Connections: Alphabets

Baskin, Leonard, *Hosie's Alphabet*
Burningham, John, *John Burningham's ABC*
Crews, Donald, *We Read A to Z*
Crowther, Robert, *Most Amazing Hide-&-Seek Alphabet* (pull tab book)
De Brunhoff, Laurent, *Babar's ABC*
Duvoisin, Roger, *A for the Ark*
Eichenberg, Fritz, *Ape in a Cape*
Emberley, Ed, *Ed Emberley's A.B.C.*
Floyd, Lucy, *Agatha's Alphabet with Her Very Own Dictionary*
Gretz, Suzanna, *Teddy Bear ABC*
Hague, Kathleen, *Alphabears*
Hoguet, Susan, *I Unpacked My Grandmother's Trunk*
Johnson, Crockett, *Harold's ABC*
Lobel, Arnold, *On Market Street*
MacDonald, Suse, *Alphabatics*

Milne, A. A., *Pooh's Alphabet Book*
Munari, Bruno, *ABC*
Oxenbury, Helen, *Helen Oxenbury's ABC of Things*
Pienkowski, Jan, *ABC*
Rey, R. A., *Curious George Learns the Alphabet*
Scarry, Richard, *Richard Scarry's ABC Word Book*
Sendak, Maurice, *Alligators All Around*
Stevenson, James, *Grandpa's Great City Tour*
Waber, Bernard, *Anteater Named Arthur*
Wildsmith, Brian, *Brian Wildsmith's ABC*
Yolen, Jane, *All in the Woodland Early*

Activities to Connect Literature and Curriculum

ART

Supply giant alphabet letters for tracing. Use the traced, construction paper letter form as the base for cut-and-paste pictures of objects that begin with that letter. Let each student select a letter to trace and decorate. Use as a bulletin board alphabet and connect the letters with yarn.

Use large alphabet letters as patterns for spatter paint art.

CITIZENSHIP

Suspend alphabet letters representing the first names of students in the class from the ceiling. Construct them like kites, with a tail. Attach the names of students to each letter as they are recognized as good classroom citizens.

LANGUAGE ARTS

Practice printing the student's first name and room number in preparation for media center book check-out.

Design an ABC board game for the class using a commercial blank game board. Mix up the ABCs on the board. Use older student tutors to supervise game playing.

SCIENCE

Produce a zoo animal ABC book.

Beyond the Book

Guided Reading Connections across a Curriculum Rainbow: Single Concepts

Boynton, Sandra, *Opposites*
Burningham, John, *John Burningham's Opposites*
Emberley, Ed, *Picture Pie*

Fisher, Leonard Everett, *Look Around!*
Kightley, Rosalind, *Opposites*; *Shapes*
Lionni, Leo, *Little Blue and Little Yellow*
Peet, Bill, *Huge Harold*
Seuss, Dr., *Shape of Me and Other Stuff*
Wildsmith, Brian, *Animal Shapes*

Enriching Connections

FOR GIFTED STUDENTS

Make an ABC placemat and laminate it for a special home place setting.
Select a special ABC book and share it with the class. This is an excellent oral language activity.

FOR PARENTS

Play a game of "I unpacked my grandmother's trunk" with your child.
Reinforce classroom learning by asking the child to identify the letter sound with which the names of various objects begin.

*   *   *   *   *   *   *   *   *   *   *

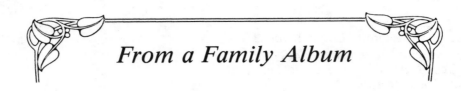

From a Family Album

MAKE WAY FOR DUCKLINGS

Author: McCloskey, Robert
Illustrator: McCloskey, Robert
Publisher: Viking, 1941
Suggested Grade Level: K-6
Classification: Core Materials
Literary Form: Picture book illustrated in monochromatic color—sepia
Theme: A family is a unit and has rules established for its well being.

About the Book

STUDENT OBJECTIVES:

1. Discriminate between fact and fantasy.

2. Identify the main idea of a picture.

3. Select a literal title for a picture in the story.

4. Learn to print his or her own name, address, and telephone number.

SYNOPSIS: *Make Way for Ducklings* is an example of the picture book format at its best. The style is narrative with a specific setting, characters reflecting the personification of a duck family, problem, action, and resolution. The theme of family unity is easily determined. This award-winning picture book, set in Boston, is about a mallard duck family. Mr. and Mrs. Mallard exhibit all the good traits of raising their young ducklings as a family unit. The viewpoint is a microscopic view of the life and times of the pre-World War II period, complete with a local policeman on the "beat" who has time to stop traffic for a delightful family of ducks seeking a new home. The art work is proof that a picture book can be enhanced by a single-color ink printing.

ABOUT THE AUTHOR-ILLUSTRATOR: Robert McCloskey, September 15, 1914- .
Robert McCloskey creates his art from real life and frequently uses his family as art subjects. His idea for *Make Way for Ducklings* came from an actual event he observed while in

Boston working on a mural for the Lever Bros. Building. The working policeman held up traffic for the street crossing of a family of ducks. The same type of event took place in Japan recently, where the police held traffic for a family of ducks who needed to cross a busy street to find a new home.

The author-illustrator lived in New York City, but returned to Boston to create sketches of the city's architecture and other scenes for the book. McCloskey purchased 4 mallard ducks and kept them in his New York City apartment in order to draw pictures of how the ducks lived. He felt good about the ducks enjoying his bathtub!

Caldecott Awards are presented annually for the best illustrated United States children's picture books. McCloskey's editions of *Make Way for Ducklings* in 1942 and *A Time of Wonder*, 1958, received these prestigious awards. He was the first illustrator to receive 2 Caldecott Medals.

SELECTED ADDITIONAL TITLES BY THE AUTHOR-ILLUSTRATOR:

Blueberries for Sal
Lentil
One Morning in Maine
Time of Wonder

Using the Book

Suggested Approach to the Book

Model Lesson #1

- Introduce the author-illustrator Robert McCloskey through the attached biographical materials.

Model Lesson #2

- Prior to reading the story aloud, the teacher may explain that the class will be sharing a picture book about a duck family. These particular ducks are not farmyard ducks, but wild ducks that do not rely on human care to meet their needs. Consequently, they—not someone else—are in charge of their own food, shelter, and other needs. Compare the care of farmyard ducks and the mallard ducks. Explain personification. (Ducks here have assumed the characteristics of a human family.)

Model Lesson #3

- Use cluster technique to describe ducks. Write on the board all the student responses. Be nonjudgmental about student's oral responses. Encourage participation by all students in this introduction. Choose several of the cluster words to use for spelling and writing.

- Assemble supplementary materials for the unit including books about ducks, both fiction and nonfiction; books about families; chamber of commerce and travel agency brochures about Boston and your community, if available; and any other materials that would complement this unit, including a duck's nest.

Model Lesson #4

- Read *Make Way for Ducklings* straight through for the pleasure of the story and the enjoyment of the pictures. Explain that you will be returning to the book during the next lesson and at that time you will talk more about the story and ask questions about things that happened in it. Also, be thinking about what is different about the pictures from other books that have been read in class this year.

Model Lesson #5

- Discuss the following material with the class.

  Setting: The ducks live on the Boston Commons. How is that park like a park in your community?

  Characters: Who are the characters we meet in the story? Do they all have names? One character is a community helper. Name him and describe his work.

  Problem: The Mallard family has a problem. Where is the best place to build a nest and await the arrival of new ducklings? What makes a good nesting place? Would your city park provide such a spot?

  Action: Where do Mr. and Mrs. Mallard look to find a nest? Are there other possibilities?

  Resolution: The nest spot and the future home are different places. How might this be explained? Is the final home selection a good one? Why or why not?

  Theme: Why do you think Mr. McCloskey wrote about a family of ducks? What kind of rules do you think are necessary for a family?

Model Lesson #6

- Return to the book and discuss the setting, characters, problem, action, and resolution of the problem with the class. Sample questions to elicit responses follow.

  1. Why did Mrs. Mallard worry about "foxes in the wood or turtles in the water?"
  2. What is a public garden? Are there any similar places in your community? Name them and locate them on a city map.
  3. Describe the breakfast activities of Mr. and Mrs. Mallard.
  4. What was the swan boat? How was it used?
  5. Draw a pond boat of your own design.
  6. What reasons did Mrs. Mallard give for choosing this place to build a nest and raise ducklings?
  7. What activities are people doing in the park?
  8. What "horrible thing" rushed passed Mrs. Mallard?
  9. What city did Mr. McCloskey choose for the story?
  10. Locate 2 famous landmarks in Boston that a tourist might want to visit on a sightseeing tour.
  11. What places in Boston would you choose to visit? Why?
  12. What are some special places to visit in your county and state?
  13. Draw a picture of a place you have visited nearby.

Model Lesson #7

- Continue discussing the community and family.

1. What is the capital of your state? What happens there?
2. Locate the state capital on a map.
3. Show pictures of the state capital and describe the workings of government.
4. Your city has places that provide community services. Name some of these services.
5. Tell what the homes in Louisburg Square are like. Do you know of any like them in your community? Does your community have any condominiums? Are any of them as old as the homes in Louisburg Square? Why or why not?
6. When was Boston founded? When was your community settled?
7. How did your community get its name?
8. Has anyone written a history of your community? If so, write the author a class thank-you note for searching out so much important information.
9. Tell what the Charles River looks like from the air. What would your city look like from the air? Does it have a large river? What would stand out in your community if we took a picture from an airplane?
10. Why did the Mallards have to hurry and find a home quickly? Look up the word *molt* in a dictionary.
11. The Mallards swam over to the park every day. They made friends with Mike, who fed them peanuts. What was Mike's job? Why do you think he wore a uniform? Does it look like a uniform worn by a policeman today? To reach a decision, study the pictures of Mike carefully.
12. Draw a policeman's uniform worn today. Does a policeman wear the same uniform in different towns and cities? Why or why not? Does your community have policewomen? How many? Invite a police officer to visit your class.
13. How many eggs did Mrs. Mallard lay? Is this the usual number?
14. What reason did Mrs. Mallard have to leave her nest?
15. Using name cards, act out the calling of duckling names with students in the class. Each may stand up when the correct duckling's name is called. Different students may take turns role-playing the different characters.
16. Name the 8 ducklings. Did you notice something special about the sound of their names?
17. If you could have selected 8 names, what would they have been?
18. Can your class write a poem together about ducks in a park? Your teacher will write it on the board for you to copy and illustrate.
19. Mr. Mallard decided to take a trip. When and where will he meet Mrs. Mallard? How important is it to follow directions when you plan to meet someone?
20. Mrs. Mallard taught her ducklings to swim and dive. What else did she teach them? Was it an important lesson for ducklings?

Model Lesson #8

- Continue the discussion with the following questions:

1. There is 1 thing that Mrs. Mallard taught the ducklings that is the same as something you are learning in first grade. What is it? Do you line up quietly at the door when the bell rings?
2. Mrs. Mallard was satisfied with her ducklings' behavior and took them for a special trip. Did they follow her in a straight line?

3. Look at the cars in the picture. Are they old or new? What does a car look like in the 1980s? Draw a black-and-white police car. Cut it out and paste it on paper with a black-and-white striped background as a special art project. Why are police cars painted black-and-white, school buses, yellow, and fire engines, red?

4. Who came running when he heard the quacking? What did he do to help? What noise did Mike make? What did he do to help Mrs. Mallard and her family? Do you know that the same thing happened in Japan in 1986? The police stood by and watched for several days while a duck family prepared to cross the street. When the ducks were ready, the police stopped the traffic in Tokyo and the ducks crossed the busy street. Do you think that this event will ever be repeated?

5. Notice that Mike ran to a police telephone booth to get help. Do we have police call booths today? Ask a police officer to let your class listen in on a radio call.

6. Look at the picture of the ducks turning the corner. Notice the sign in the window—"BOOKS—LENDING LIBRARY"—What do you think that means? Where do you go to check out books? How many libraries does your city have? Tell about the children's room in the library. What do children do there?

7. Do you have a library card? If not, ask your teacher to help you to acquire one.

8. Name some of your favorite books. What makes a book special?

9. In *Make Way for Ducklings* a man is identified as a street sweeper. How are the streets swept today?

10. How many policemen arrived to hold traffic back for Mrs. Mallard's crossing on Beacon Street? How would this be done today?

11. Where did Mrs. Mallard lead her ducklings?

12. Did the ducklings remember their manners? How?

13. Tell about their homecoming.

14. What do the Mallards do all day long in the park?

Model Lesson #9

- Art appreciation through picture books: Compare the following picture books as related to art form, setting, story, and conclusion. Compare the copyright dates also.

    Leaf, Munro, *The Story of Ferdinand*
    McCloskey, Robert, *Make Way for Ducklings*

Library Media Center Connections

1. To use study/research skills students will locate the title page of a book and locate an entry in a picture dictionary.

2. Special media center activity for students: Choose an animal study print from a group of pictures and give reasons for the choice. Grouping should illustrate the diverse styles of art.

Theme Reading Connections: Ducks

Andersen, Hans Christian, *Ugly Duckling*
Ellis, Anne Leo, *Dabble Duck*
Flack, Marjorie, *Angus and the Ducks*; *Story about Ping*
Isenbart, Hans Heinrich, *Duckling Is Born*

Potter, Beatrix, *Tale of Jemima Puddle-Duck*
Tafuri, Nancy, *Have You Seen My Duckling?*
Wildsmith, Brian, *Little Wood Duck*
Wright, Edith, *Edith and the Duckling*

Activities to Connect Literature and Curriculum

ART

Make a simple classroom map using cutout symbols of objects.

Plan to make a family cartoon mural and ask children to make pictures of themselves and their family. Cut out and attach them to the mural. Using the cartoon balloon technique, include information about where students live, what they do together as a family, and any other aspect of family life they would like to share. Pictures of their homes and pets may be added.

HEALTH

Create a chart showing the proper care of pets, including the 4 basic needs of all animals—food, water, air, and shelter.

Care for a classroom pet for a brief period. Ask parents during back-to-school orientation to share a pet later in the year.

Arrange for a classroom visit of a guest speaker such as an animal control officer.

LANGUAGE ARTS

Key vocabulary words for clustering and writing:

foxes	nest
peanuts	quacked
waddles	street sweeper
squawked	mallard
policeman	breakfast
turtles	duckling
proud	molt

Help students make a personal dictionary to store spelling and writing cluster words during the unit. This dictionary will also be used for other first grade literature units.

Write class thank-you notes to guest speakers.

SOCIAL STUDIES

Invite a guest speaker to class to tell about his or her work in a park or garden.

Compare the duties of a policeman, animal control officer, and public gardener.

Beyond the Book

Guided Reading Connections across a Curriculum Rainbow: Boston and Police Officers

Broekel, Ray, *Police*
Chwast, Seymour, *Tall City, Wide City*
Farber, Norma, *As I Was Crossing Boston Common* (poetry)
Florian, Douglas, *City*
Goodall, John S., *Paddy's New Hat*
Hannum, Dottie, *Visit to the Police Station*
Isadora, Rachel, *City Seen from A to Z* (alphabet)
Keats, Ezra Jack, *My Dog Is Lost!*
Lenski, Lois, *Policeman Small*; *Sing a Song of People* (swan boat cover) (poetry)
McGinley, Phyllis, *All around the Town* (alphabet)

Enriching Connections

FOR GIFTED STUDENTS

Draw a picture relating to the story, *Make Way for Ducklings*, mount it on a light card stock, laminate it, and cut it into large puzzle pieces. For fun, exchange puzzles with other students.

Write a class poem about ducks. Learn the poem and share it with parents.

Compose a list of possible rules for the Mallard family. Which rules could apply to your own family?

Choose a name and draw a label for a new, packaged duck food.

Look at a nonfiction animal book and share pictures with the class of kinds of ducks other than mallards.

FOR PARENTS

Enjoy a family outing to a park or lake that has duck residents. Encourage your child to observe and relate his or her observations of ducks.

Read aloud a duck picture book.

Draw a placemat featuring ducks and use it for the child's own special setting.

WHAT MARY JO SHARED

Author: Udry, Janice
Illustrator: Mill, Eleanor
Publisher: Albert Whitman, 1966
Suggested Grade Level: K-1
Classification: Extended Materials
Literary Form: Picture book
Theme: Everyone has something to share.

About the Book

STUDENT OBJECTIVES:

1. Develop positive self-images through sharing experiences.

2. Participate in class through speaking experiences.

3. Choose an object or experience to share in class.

4. Model listening behavior while other students are speaking.

SYNOPSIS: Mary Jo does not think she has anything important to share with her class. She waits and worries. She worries and waits. Mary Jo finally makes a decision and her sharing is first rate. Like Ezra Jack Keat's main characters, Mary Jo is a black child at a time when black children were not usually the subjects of a picture book. The soft illustrations beautifully portray the story of Mary Jo and her home and school environments.

ABOUT THE AUTHOR AND ILLUSTRATOR: Janice Udry, June 14, 1928- .
Eleanor Mill, birthdate not available.
　　　　Janice Udry grew up in middle America, and as she relates, lived in the only town in the world known for manufacturing ferris wheels—Jacksonville, Illinois. Her town had large front porches, wooden swings, and old oak trees. Perhaps that environment accounts for her love of trees. She and her husband, a sociologist, had moved to California and sadly observed the loss of the orange groves as they were cleared to make room for houses for an expanding population. She wrote *A Tree Is Nice* in response to these feelings. This lovely book, illustrated by Marc Simont, was awarded the 1957 Caldecott Award. Her Mary Jo book series is still popular 20 years after its initial publication.
　　　　Eleanor Mill was born in Detroit.

SELECTED ADDITIONAL TITLES BY THE AUTHOR:

Mary Jo's Grandmother
Moon Jumpers
What Mary Jo Wanted

Using the Book

Suggested Approach to the Book

Model Lesson #1

- Explain to students that they are going to hear about a very special student in the first grade—Mary Jo. Her class is very similar to theirs. They have a sharing time each day and this is a story about *What Mary Jo Shared*.

- Sometimes it is very hard to decide on something to share with the class. You reach a decision and then someone else uses the same idea before your turn comes to share. Now what?

- Read the story aloud and share the illustrations.

Model Lesson #2

- Ask the children the following questions:
    1. What kinds of sharing experiences have taken place in this class?
    2. What does the writer mean when she describes Mary Jo as "shy"?
    3. What can we do in class to help someone who is shy?
    4. Why didn't Mary Jo want to share her new pink umbrella?
    5. Does the picture give a clue?
    6. What did Mary Jo share in her imagination?
    7. What happened in class when she began to share?
    8. Was her sharing choice a good one? Why or why not?

Model Lesson #3

- Art appreciation through picture books: Compare the art style and use of color in these titles written by Udry.

    A Tree Is Nice, illustrated by Marc Simont
    What Mary Jo Shared, illustrated by Eleanor Mill

Library Media Center Connections

1. Request that the library media center storytime selection be a Mary Jo book.

2. Special library media center activity for students: Invite the class members to share an item for several days and display it in the library media center. Label each item with the student's name.

Theme Reading Connections: Family

Hines, Anna G., *Daddy Makes the Best Spaghetti*
Lenski, Lois, *Papa Small*

Minarik, Else, *Papa Bear Comes Home*
Watanabe, Shigeo, *Where's My Daddy?*

Activities to Connect Literature and Curriculum

ART

Pretend that it is a rainy day. Design an umbrella you would like to carry to school. Use a master copy of a black outlined umbrella for all students.

As a class activity create a cut-and-paste mural using student portraits of their parents.

Fold a piece of paper in half. Assign 1 student to draw one-half of Mary Jo's picture. Unfold and pass the picture to another student to complete. Display all the completed art work.

Using 4-foot strips of brown butcher paper, draw each child's body outline while he or she is lying on the floor on top of the butcher paper strip. Cut out the body outlines. Ask the students to do their own body-sized self-portraits with tempera paints. Let dry and reverse the body outlines and ask students to draw a picture of their mothers or fathers. Let students place these "kids" in their own desks as identification markers for back-to-school night or open house. These happy "kids" have been known to become family treasures.

LANGUAGE ARTS

Key vocabulary words for clustering and writing:

share	kitten
umbrella	elephant
grasshopper	father
turtle	mother
rabbit	brother
mice	teacher

Write a letter to a grandparent and tell what you shared in class. The letter form could be provided by the teacher.

MATH

Design an attribute chart. Include physical characteristics of height, color of hair and eyes, number of brothers and sisters, and favorite television shows, pets, and ice cream flavors.

Use a flannel board to showcase 1 attribute each month. Children's Polaroid™ photographs with a Velcro square on the back side may be grouped under the attribute. Example—ice cream flavors listed are chocolate, vanilla, and strawberry. Place the child's picture under his or her choice.

Polling techniques may be used. Ask the custodian what his or her favorite ice cream treat is and add his or her picture to the flannel board.

NUTRITION

Plan a "snack sharing." Ask each student to bring a washed piece of fruit or a package of raisins or crackers to share during a specified snack time. One-half of the class could share one day and the other half could bring the snack the following day. (Have additional snacks available.) Include this information in a newsletter for parents.

Beyond the Book

Guided Reading Connections across a Curriculum Rainbow: Sharing

> Keats, Ezra Jack, *Peter's Chair*
> Parrish, Peggy, *Mind Your Manners*
> Sherman, Ivan, *I Do Not Like It When My Friend Comes to Visit*
> Winthrop, Elizabeth, *That's Mine*
> Zolotow, Charlotte, *New Friend*

Enriching Connections

FOR GIFTED STUDENTS

Make a list of activities involving good manners. Divide the activities into 2 columns with headings (e.g., Home, School).

Select a library book that Mary Jo would have liked to share with the class. Give reasons for the selection.

FOR PARENTS

If possible, volunteer to help in your child's classroom for a specific time.

If you are unable to visit the classroom, volunteer to do 1 activity at home that will assist the teacher.

* * * * * * * * * * *

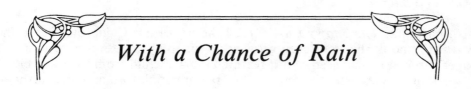

With a Chance of Rain

THE SNOWY DAY

Author: Keats, Ezra Jack
Illustrator: Keats, Ezra Jack
Publisher: Viking, 1962
Suggested Grade Level: K-1
Classification: Core Materials
Literary Form: Picture book using collage technique
Theme: Enjoy the magic of a snowy day.

About the Book

STUDENT OBJECTIVES:

1. Choose a title for selected page illustrations.

2. Locate the title page of a book.

3. Classify clothing types worn in summer and winter.

4. Identify 3 occupations by the clothing worn by workers.

SYNOPSIS: The text is sparse in words, but powerful in presentation of the snowy day activities of Peter, the child. This selection is both innovative and charming. At the time of publication, black children were not main characters in picture books. There is no reference to this in the text, but it is integrated into a winning picture book.

ABOUT THE AUTHOR-ILLUSTRATOR: Ezra Jack Keats, March 11, 1916-1983.
Ezra Jack Keats was like many students—he had few financial resources. His life was a difficult one growing up in a tough Brooklyn neighborhood. His love of art was evident early. One day a gang was going to beat him up, but discovered that he was carrying his art under his arm. Its quality saved the day and the gang opted to forgo the beating. Because he didn't have enough money, he was unable to accept the art scholarship he won at high school graduation. Keats did not become a commercial artist until he returned from World War II.

His first book, *The Snowy Day*, earned the important Caldecott Award in 1963. Not only was it the book that had been growing in his mind for several years as a result of a newspaper clipping he had seen, but it featured a black child from the inner city. Like all of Keats's work, it is an excellent example of the picture book format and a further example of sparse prose. He believed that the pictures could provide the stage setting for his inner city characters.

Some of the enduring characters included in his work are Peter of *The Snowy Day*, Archie, and Louie. His characters grow up and move from the home into the community. His books are reflective of a certain time frame in American culture and provide a kaleidoscopic view of a city's neighborhood children.

Primary media forms used in Jack Ezra Keats's books are collage, his personal stamp as an illustrator, and acrylic. His choice of materials is varied and has included newspaper, fabric, and wallpaper. His last books reflected a different art style—shadow art.

SELECTED ADDITIONAL TITLES BY THE AUTHOR-ILLUSTRATOR:

Apartment 3
Goggles
Hi, Cat!
Jennie's Hat
A Letter to Amy
Louie
Louie's Search
My Dog Is Lost!
Pet Shop
Peter's Chair
The Trip
Whistle for Willie

Using the Book

Suggested Approach to the Book

Model Lesson #1

- Introduce the author-illustrator Ezra Jack Keats through the attached biographical material.

Model Lesson #2

- Read *The Snowy Day* through while sharing the content and illustrations with the class. Explain that the class will be doing many activities with this book and that they should pay close attention to the reading. As a preview question ask students to look carefully at the pictures and explain how the artist created them.

Model Lesson #3

- As an introduction to the class explain that *The Snowy Day* will be used to begin a study of weather and clothing and that many activities will be assigned.

Setting: A city apartment

Character: Peter, a young child

Problem: Enjoying activities in the snow

Action: All the different views of a snowy day

Resolution: Inviting a friend from across the hall to play outside the next day

Theme: Enjoy the world of a snowy day

Model Lesson #4

- Ask the children the following questions:

1. Look at the 2 pages before the title page. What season is shown?
2. Who is the boy in *The Snowy Day*?
3. What does he see when he looks out the window?
4. What happened during the night?
5. What kind of clothes does he put on to go outside?
6. Do you ever wear snowsuits? Where?
7. Why was the snow piled alongside of the street?
8. What sound might you hear if you went walking in the snow?
9. Look at Peter's tracks in the snow. Why are they different?
10. What does he find in the snow that can make a different track?
11. What does he do with the stick?
12. Why doesn't Peter join the big boys in the snowball fight?
13. What does he make?
14. He pretended he was an _____.
15. How do you make a snowball? Is there any way to create one without using real snow? Think about it.
16. Where did he put his snowball?
17. Why did it disappear?
18. What did Peter dream that night?
19. Did the dream come true?
20. What do you dream about?
21. Who did Peter invite to play with him?
22. Who would you invite?
23. Where is Peter's home?
24. Do Peter and his friend live in a home like yours?
25. Why or why not?
26. Ask a guest speaker to demonstrate weaving. Have students use a small cardboard loom to make a fabric sample.
27. Bring in or make hats for various occupations.

Model Lesson #5

- Food experience: Bake a snowman cake. Emphasize math measurements including oven temperature, baking time, and proper testing for doneness. Discuss clean hands and proper food handling and storage. Demonstrate cooking safety, use of knives, oven mitt, and oven. Design a class wall chart to show proper measurements and ingredient quantities.

Snowman Cake

> Mixing bowl, utensils, and baking pans — 2 round or 1 snowman form
> 1 box white cake mix
> 1 package white frosting
> 1 can shredded coconut to be used on top of frosting
> 1 package gumdrops, jellybeans, or M&Ms for decoration of snowman cake
> 1 twig to be placed in hand
> 1 black construction paper hat to complete figure

> Send recipe home in a booklet shaped like a snowman and correlated as an art project.

Model Lesson #6

- Art appreciation through picture books: Compare the following picture books in relation to illustrations and the treatment of snow as well as literary form

  > Frost, Robert, *Stopping by the Woods on a Snowy Evening*, illustrated by Susan Jeffers
  > Keats, Ezra Jack, *The Snowy Day*

Library Media Center Connections

1. Assemble supplementary materials including books about weather and books written and illustrated by Ezra Jack Keats.

2. Special media center activity for students: Compile a display board of snowman art grouped into a snowman figure, using the collage art technique.

Computer Connections

Developmental Learning Materials, *Comparison Kitchen*
Learning Well, *Body Awareness*

Theme Reading Connections: Homes and Snow

Baker, Jeannie, *Home in the Sky*
Briggs, Raymond, *Snowman*
Burton, Virginia Lee, *Katy and the Big Snow*
Flack, Marjorie, *Angus Lost*
Frost, Robert, *Stopping by the Woods on a Snowy Evening*
Hader, Berta, and Elmer Hader, *Big Snow*
Moncure, Jane, *Winter*
Sauer, Julia, *Mike's House*
Tresselt, Alvin, *Big Snow*
Wood, Lucille, *Winter Days*
Zion, Gene, *Summer Snowman*

Activities to Connect Literature and Curriculum

ART

Spatter paint using geometrical-cut, construction paper snowflakes.

Using black construction paper, construct a class-sized mural using cutout winter scenes and characters. To achieve a very dramatic effect, sponge with white tempera paint, allow to dry and then proceed with green fir trees and other winter objects. Invite students to add numerous geometrical snowflakes.

As a boy Ezra Jack Keats used his mother's porcelain kitchen table as an art drawing surface because paper was too scarce. Try a dry erasable board for the same effect.

CITIZENSHIP

Design a snowflake stamp using a Dr. Scholl's foam shoe insert. Stamp student work and reward good classroom citizenship with stamps on a snowflake chart.

LANGUAGE ARTS

Key vocabulary words for clustering and writing:

Peter	stick
crunch	night
morning	tracks

Clustering: Use words generated from boardwork to dictate a story. First grade students like to dictate their writing assignment to older student tutors after illustrating the paper. Story writing topic: Peter's fun.

Compare *Frosty the Snowman* and *The Gingerbread Man*. Make up an adventure that they might share. Dictate it to an older student tutor and illustrate the story also.

Write a class snowman poem.

SCIENCE

What is weather? Give examples of weather.

Name several holidays and describe the weather that usually accompanies each.

Keep a classroom weather calendar for a month prior to beginning the unit.

Tell what kinds of clothes are appropriate for different kinds of weather.

Use an ice crusher to crush ice cubes. Scoop into a snow cone cup. Add fruit juice. Save some crushed ice to provide a tactile experience and explain that ice is like fresh snow.

SOCIAL STUDIES

Locate on a map areas that are very cold and very hot.

Beyond the Book

Guided Reading Connections across a Curriculum Rainbow: Clothing

Andersen, Hans Christian, *The Emperor's New Clothes*
Barrett, Judi, *Animals Should Definitely Not Wear Clothing*
Beskow, Elsa, *Pelle's New Suit*
Bruna, Dick, *I Can Dress Myself*
Fisher, Aileen, *Where Does Everybody Go?*
Freeman, Don, *Corduroy*
Mitgutsch, Ali, *From Sheep to Scarf*
Politi, Leo, *Little Leo*
Seuss, Dr., *The 500 Hats of Bartholomew Cubbins*
Slobodkina, Esphyr, *Caps for Sale*

Enriching Connections

FOR GIFTED STUDENTS

What is the difference between rain and snow? When do we have rain? Graph the rain in your community for a limited time period.

Why do some people want to take a vacation away from cold and snow? What would happen if it snowed in Hawaii on Christmas Eve?

FOR PARENTS

Visit one of the "local snow" areas with your child. Explore winter recreation activities.
Visit a recreation facility with your child when snow is "imported."
Read an Ezra Jack Keats book or another weather picture book together.
Cut out geometrical snowflakes together and use them for home decorating.
Observe together the way animals act in the rain.

THE CARROT SEED

Author: Krauss, Ruth
Illustrator: Johnson, Crockett
Publisher: Harper & Row, 1945
Suggested Grade Level: K-2
Classification: Core Materials
Literary Form: Picture book
Theme: Believing can result in seeing.

About the Book

STUDENT OBJECTIVES:

1. Identify various fruits and vegetables including carrots, tomatoes, cucumbers, apples, bananas, grapes, and oranges.

2. Categorize fruits and vegetables into groups that grow above ground and groups that grow below the ground.

3. Distinguish between root and nonroot vegetables.

4. Recognize that many fruits grow on trees and bushes.

SYNOPSIS: A very young boy plants a seed and is told by his mother, father, and brother that it "wouldn't come up." It did, and with a delightful ending. An easy reader that children can relate to because of simple language patterns.

ABOUT THE AUTHOR AND ILLUSTRATOR: Ruth Krauss, July 25, 1911- .
Crockett Johnson, October 20, 1906-1976.
Ruth Krauss and Crockett Johnson (real name David Johnson Leisk), a married couple, shared the credits for *The Carrot Seed*. Ruth Krauss has had no formal training in writing for children, but relates that much of her writing is tied in with her early education in the fine arts—art and music. Crockett Johnson was a syndicated newspaper cartoonist of *Barnaby*, which in the 1940s was printed in 52 United States newspapers and read by over 5,600,000 cartoon lovers.

SELECTED ADDITIONAL TITLES BY THE AUTHOR:

Charlotte and the White Horse
Hole Is to Dig
I'll Be You and You Be Me
Somebody Else's Nut Tree, and Other Tales from Children

SELECTED ADDITIONAL TITLES BY THE ILLUSTRATOR:

Harold and the Purple Crayon
A Picture for Harold

Using the Book

Suggested Approach to the Book

Model Lesson #1

- Show students a packet of carrot seeds. Open the package and pour the seeds onto a plate. Show how tiny a seed is. Let students examine the seeds. Show a bunch of carrots and explain that 1 small seed produced each carrot and that the story you are going to read begins with just 1 carrot seed. Read the story and share the illustrations.

Model Lesson #2

- Plant several seeds in a terrarium and watch for growth each day with the class. Use a class calendar and record data about the seeds daily.

Model Lesson #3

- Art appreciation through picture books: Read and share the illustrations of *Growing Vegetable Soup* by Lois Ehlert. Note that the supergraphic illustrations show both the vegetable seed and the actual plant shape. Make vegetable soup and serve a small portion for snack time. A recipe is included on the back book flap. Integrate this food experience into the math program by teaching measurement of food products.

Library Media Center Connections

1. Display a selection of fruit and vegetable books. Arrange a basket of fruits and vegetables as a display centerpiece. Include some unusual produce. (Unusual to a first grader might be green peppers, eggplant, mushrooms, and cilantro.) Provide a snack sample, if possible.

2. Special media center activity for students: Cut out fruit and vegetable pictures from magazines and create a "Horn of Plenty" collage.

Instructional Materials Connections

National Geographic Wonders of Learning Kit, *What Is a Seed?*

Theme Reading Connections: Gardening and Food

Appelmann, Karl-Heinz, *Dandelions*
Brown, Marc, *Your First Gardening Book*
Carle, Eric, *Tiny Seed*
Fujikawa, Gyo, *Let's Grow a Garden* (poetry)
Johnson, Hannah Lyons, *From Seeds to Jack-O-Lantern*
Kessler, Leonard, *Do You Have Any Carrots?*
Lobel, Arnold, and Anita Lobel, *Rose in My Garden*
Magill, David, *I Can Grow Vegetables*
Moncure, Jane, *See My Garden Grow*
Overbeck, Cynthia, *Vegetable Book*
Poulet, Virginia, *Blue Bug's Vegetable Garden*
Rockwell, Anne, *How My Garden Grew*
Rylant, Cynthia, *This Year's Garden*

Activities to Connect Literature and Curriculum

ART

Use carrots to print special wrapping paper. Give each student a piece of absorbent construction paper, various precut carrot stamps, and orange paint to create random pattern carrot prints.

The teacher will need to cut the carrots in pieces and cut designs (like woodblocks) prior to the art project. Supply green paint for stems and leaves.

LANGUAGE ARTS

Imagine that you are a little carrot pushing up the ground. Write a class story using words clustered on the board about carrots. Writing theme—a carrot pops up.

NUTRITION

Tell students that carrots can be used to create a great dessert. Bake a carrot cake.
Cut whole carrots in half lengthwise. Spread peanut butter on the top, add raisins, and enjoy "Ants on a Hill" for snack time.

SCIENCE

Plant carrot tops in a shallow dish garden with small pebbles and 1 inch of water. They should sprout in a week and last about a month. Use carrot tops that are about 1½ inches tall including trimmed foliage.

Beyond the Book

Guided Reading Connections across a Curriculum Rainbow: Farms

Azarian, Mary, *Farmer's Alphabet* (alphabet)
Dunn, Judy, *Animals of Buttercup Farm*
Maris, Ron, *Is Anyone Home?*
Miller, Jane, *Seasons on the Farm*
Tafuri, Nancy, *Early Morning in the Barn*

Enriching Connections

FOR GIFTED STUDENTS

Plan a menu with a favorite vegetable and a favorite fruit. Ask permission to help prepare the food for your family.
Draw and color pictures of growing vegetables and fruits.
Grow a root vegetable at home. Care for it as outlined in *The Carrot Seed*—water and weed as necessary.

FOR PARENTS

Visit a farmer's market with your child. Observe the variety of fruits and vegetables available in the market. Purchase 1 item to take home and eat.
Allow your child to help make a favorite food dish. Model good safety habits and food storage rules.

PETER SPIER'S RAIN

Author: Spier, Peter
Illustrator: Spier, Peter
Publisher: Doubleday, 1982
Suggested Grade Level: K-3
Classification: Recreational and Motivational Materials
Literary Form: Picture book illustrated with pen drawings
Theme: Rain is part of nature's cycle.

About the Book

STUDENT OBJECTIVES:

1. Describe different kinds of weather including rain.

2. Choose play activities that are appropriate for a rainy day.

3. Explain changes in the environmental surroundings that are brought about by rain.

SYNOPSIS: Two children are playing in their backyard when the rain comes. Various rainy day activities are illustrated. When the storm passes, the children return to play the next day in a wet backyard. A wordless presentation of the multiple effects of rain on the environment of 2 children.

ABOUT THE AUTHOR-ILLUSTRATOR: Peter Spier, June 26, 1927- .
　　Peter Spier was born in Amsterdam, Holland. He later lived and went to school in a fairy tale village, Broek in Waterland. His village's claim to fame is Hans Brinker and his Silver Skates. He relates that Americans come to visit the village and want to know more about this story. The villagers, when asked about Hans Brinker, always say that they do not know a Brinker family, but they will be glad to ask their neighbor if he knows the family. This is a very subtle joke about an imaginary boy, Hans Brinker. Peter Spier tells about his daily trips to school on a very old, swaying train with fishermen in wooden shoes who stowed their smelly catch of herring and smoked eels in baskets stacked in the train aisles. After getting off the train in Amsterdam, he took a boat ride, walked some, and finally caught the streetcar to school.
　　Perhaps all these childhood experiences contributed to his colorful art. His pictures are lovely, very busy and even chaotic. Spier uses hundreds of pictures in a book. He explains that he does research on the area and then visits the place with his sketchbook, draws pictures of what he sees, labels them with the colors he observes, and then returns home to begin illustrating the story.
　　Peter Spier is a prolific illustrator and has to his credit over 100 books. He prefers to write and illustrate his own stories. Notable books include *Noah's Ark*, 1977 Caldecott Medal Winner, and *Fox Went out on a Chilly Night*, 1961 Caldecott Honor Winner.

SELECTED ADDITIONAL TITLES BY THE AUTHOR-ILLUSTRATOR:

And So My Garden Grows
Bored—Nothing to Do
Crash! Bang! Boom!
Erie Canal
Fast-Slow, High-Low
Gobble, Growl, Grunt!
Hurrah, We're Outward Bound
Legend of New Amsterdam
London Bridge Is Falling Down
Of Dikes and Windmills
Oh, Were They Ever Happy!
People
Star Spangled Banner
To Market! To Market!

Using the Book

Suggested Approach to the Book

Model Lesson #1

- Introduce the author-illustrator as a person who presents a many-sided view of rain. Include the attached autobiographical sketch including the fact that Spier's hometown was Hans Brinker's also. Tell the story of the *Silver Skates* to the class and explain that it was written over 100 years ago in 1865 and was the kind of story that kids liked then, and that it is still a good story even today.

Model Lesson #2

- The teacher will read *Peter Spier's Rain* aloud to the class after explaining that this picture book presents many different ways that rain affects our environment and homes.
    1. Ask students to identify 10 items that are pictured on the title page. Do all these items belong in the backyard? Could any be placed in the frontyard of a home?
    2. What kind of clothing is needed for a rainy day outing? How do these clothes differ from clothing worn for a day in the snow? What kind of clothing would we wear for a day at the beach?
    3. Look at the blue shadow art picture with 2 children silhouetted under the umbrella. Would any other pictures in the book look good using the same art technique? Why?
    4. List on the board 20 different ways that things are different because it is raining.
    5. List some of the places the children visit on their walk.
    6. Name some indoor fun things the children can do when it rains.
    7. What happened to the rain during the night after the boy and girl fell asleep?
    8. Is the backyard different after the rain? How?

Model Lesson #3

- Art appreciation through picture books: Compare the art of *Peter Spier's Rain* to Ezra Jack Keats, *Letter to Amy*

- Pay particular attention to the differences in the rain and the storm.

- Note that 1 title is a wordless book. Should it have text? Let students supply words for some of Peter Spier's book. This can be effectively done by using an opaque projector.

Library Media Center Connections

1. Select another book about rain for storytime.

    Kalan, Robert, *Rain*, illustrated by Donald Crews

    Notice still another approach to the subject of rain—the word *rain* used to depict raindrops.

2. Special media center activity for students: View the very special film, *Rain*, which has no words, but only a musical background. Compare the similarities of the film to Spier's wordless book.

3. Divide the class into 4 or 5 small groups that will come to the media center for group work.

4. Create a class rain mural on a large 10-foot piece of blue butcher paper.
    Group 1—divides the paper into sky and grass sections. Draws soft curving hills on the bottom half of the paper. Colors the hills green.
    Group 2—glues on white cotton clouds and draws raindrops where needed.
    Group 3—draws or cuts and pastes buildings and adds them to the mural.
    Group 4—adds streets, traffic lights, benches, flowers, and vehicles.
    Group 5—adds the sun and people.

Computer Connections

Grolier, *Exploring Your World: All about You and the Weather*

Instructional Materials Connections

National Geographic World of Learning Kit, *Why Does It Rain?*

Theme Reading Connections: Rain

Bauer, Caroline Feller, *Rainy Days: Stories and Poems* (professional reading)
Bonnici, Peter, *First Rains*
Branley, Franklyn M., *Flash! Crash, Rumble, and Roll*
Bright, Robert, *My Red Umbrella*

De Paola, Tomie, *Cloud Book*
Ernst, Lisa Campbell, *Up to Ten and Down Again* (counting)
Freeman, Don, *Rainbow of My Own*
Hines, Anna G., *Taste the Raindrops*
Hurd, Elizabeth Thacher, *Johnny Lion's Rubber Boots*
Keller, Holly G., *Will It Rain?*
Palmer, Michelle, *Rainy Day Rhymes: Collection of Chants, Forecasts & Tales*
Scheer, Julian, *Rain Makes Applesauce* (poetry)
Zolotow, Charlotte, *Storm Book*

Activities to Connect Literature and Curriculum

ART

Create a silhouette of a rainy day picture. Color with bright blue crayon the silhouette on a light blue paper background. Add raindrops to create a storm.
Paint a picture of rain in a zoo or park with watercolors.

LANGUAGE ARTS

Design an alphabet book integrated with a weather theme. Have students contribute individual pages. Display the *Weather ABC Book* in the media center.

SCIENCE

Record the temperature on a calendar each time it rains. What is the temperature trend? Can it be graphed on a Number Blox paper chart?

SOCIAL STUDIES

What jobs do people do that must stop when it rains? Explain.
What food crops, if flooded, will die?

Beyond the Book

Guided Reading Connections across a Curriculum Rainbow: Weather

Arvetis, Chris, *Why Does It Thunder and Lightning?*
Breiter, Herta, *Weather*
Hefter, Richard, *Stickybear Book of Weather*
Moncure, Jane, *What Causes It?*
Pienkowski, Jan, *Weather*
Supraner, Robyn, *I Can Read about Weather*

Enriching Connections

FOR GIFTED STUDENTS

Keep a weather log for 30 days. Listen to a weather or marine forecast to learn the next day's forecast. Is the forecasted weather a problem?

With help, cut and paste clothing pictures representing different weather onto blank bingo game cards. Use as a small group interest center.

FOR PARENTS

Listen to a weather or marine forecast with your child. If a marine forecast is available, explain about the Coast Guard forecast warnings for small boats. Tell how the Coast Guard serves as a water police force. They give tickets and clear accident traffic as well as giving assistance to boats in trouble.

* * * * * * * * * * *

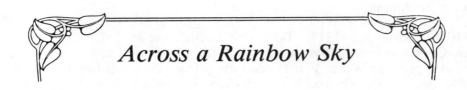

THE VERY HUNGRY CATERPILLAR

Author: Carle, Eric
Illustrator: Carle, Eric
Publisher: Collins-World, 1969
Suggested Grade Level: K-2
Classification: Core Materials
Literary Form: Picture book using collage technique
Theme: Food is a basic need for all living things.

About the Book

STUDENT OBJECTIVES:

1. Locate answers to questions containing clue words (who, what, where, why, when, how).

2. Select outcomes for a given paragraph.

3. Observe and describe the life cycle of a butterfly.

4. Experiment with various textures and patterns using collage, painting, glueing, or printing and create art with texture or pattern.

5. Compare the natural forms of leaves in nature and spatter paint leaves to show texture.

6. Identify variations of primary color in *The Very Hungry Caterpillar*. Identify bright-dull and light-dark.

SYNOPSIS: *The Very Hungry Caterpillar* is an excellent multifaceted picture book. A caterpillar is born on Sunday, becomes hungry on Monday, and chews his way through the week until he becomes satiated. He makes a cocoon around himself, sleeps, and through metamorphosis becomes a beautiful butterfly. Concepts introduced include days of the week, counting, nutrition, and metamorphosis, and all in a wonderful graphic style. This is an excellent example of the picture book style. The material is presented in a sequential manner and correlates well with first grade curriculum.

ABOUT THE AUTHOR-ILLUSTRATOR: Eric Carle, June 25, 1929- .

Eric Carle was born in Syracuse, New York, and moved to Germany in 1935 with his parents. He spent the World War II years away from the United States and did not return until 1952, when he worked as a graphics designer for the *New York Times*. His first 2 books, *1, 2, 3, to the Zoo* (1968) and *The Very Hungry Caterpillar* (1969), were instant successes. *The Very Hungry Caterpillar* has been translated into 14 languages and has sold 4 million copies.

One of Carle's earliest memories is of his kindergarten education in the United States and his move to Germany, where he did not have the art supplies he had enjoyed so much before. This is one of the reasons he attributes to his creation of picture books: "When I first began to think about children's books, it reawakened in me struggles of my own childhood, touching an area of my own growing up. A child spends five years basically at home—a place of warmth, play, and protection. Then school begins, and all of a sudden it is a world of schedule, abstraction, and organized learning. Very simply put, I decided I wanted to create books that make this transition easier."*

Eric Carle is a master of the art of picture books. His use of media in books includes paper collage, woodcut, linocut, oil, tempera, and pastel. He is also a master of the single-concept picture book.

SELECTED ADDITIONAL TITLES BY THE AUTHOR-ILLUSTRATOR:

Brown Bear, Brown Bear, What Do You See?
Do You Want to Be My Friend?
The Greedy Python
The Grouchy Ladybug
The Mixed-Up Chameleon
1, 2, 3, to the Zoo
The Rooster Who Set out to See the World
The Secret Birthday Message
The Very Busy Spider

Note: The Very Hungry Caterpillar is dedicated to Eric Carle's sister, Christa. Eric Carle enjoys drawing in the zoo and observed a "crystal-eyed chameleon." The book, *The Mixed-Up Chameleon*, evolved from his work with children and was dedicated to all the children of the world who had worked with him. It is interesting to note that *The Secret Birthday Message* is dedicated to Bill Martin, and that Eric Carle illustrated Martin's popular book, *Brown Bear, Brown Bear, What Do You See? The Grouchy Ladybug* features the concept of passing time and presents examples of Ladybug's good and bad manners. Enjoy and share the texture of the spider's web in *The Very Busy Spider*.

Using the Book

Suggested Approach to the Book

Model Lesson #1

- Introduce the author-illustrator Eric Carle through the attached biographical material.

---

*Richard Buckley and Eric Carle, *The Greedy Python* (Natick, Mass.: Picture Book Studio, 1985), dust cover.

Model Lesson #2

- Prior to reading the story aloud, the teacher may want to explain to the class that this is a book about an insect and its ferocious appetite. Most of the action will take place in a week and then the caterpillar will rest. At the end something exciting and unexpected will occur when the caterpillar wakes up from its nap.

  Setting: A plant leaf

  Character: A very hungry caterpillar

  Problem: What to do about a hungry tummy

  Action: Consumption of many food varieties

  Resolution: A surprise ending

  Theme: All living things eat and grow

Model Lesson #3

- Read *The Very Hungry Caterpillar* through while sharing the content and illustrations with the class. Explain that the class will be doing many activities with this book and that they should pay very careful attention to the reading. As a preview question ask students to look carefully at the pictures and explain how they think the artist created the holes in the leaves.

Model Lesson #4

- Fill in the blanks orally while reading these lines from *The Very Hungry Caterpillar*.

  On Monday the very hungry caterpillar ate through _____ and was still very hungry.

  On Tuesday the very hungry caterpillar ate through _____ and was still very hungry.

  On Wednesday the very hungry caterpillar ate through _____ and was still very hungry.

  On Thursday the very hungry caterpillar ate through _____ and was still very hungry.

  On Friday the very hungry caterpillar ate through _____ and was still very hungry.

  On Saturday the very hungry caterpillar ate through _____ and was still very hungry. List today's food.

  Which foods might be considered
  dessert?
  meat?
  fruit?
  vegetables?

  1. What did the very hungry caterpillar have that night after eating so much?
  2. How many different foods did he eat on Saturday?
  3. Name them.

    4. What is your favorite food? Make a 1-10 number book and include your food preferences.

    5. Plan a good breakfast to eat before coming to school. Collect pictures and use them for a breakfast collage. Label the food.

Model Lesson #5

- Introduce the 4 food groups. Analyze a school lunch to see if the nutrition requirements are met.

- Plan a well-balanced Thanksgiving dinner. Use a paper plate for each food group. Place the plates on a bulletin board surface and encourage students to sort the Thanksgiving food into the basic food groups by attaching their pictures to the appropriate paper plate.

Model Lesson #6

- Ask the children the following questions:

    1. Why did caterpillar feel better after eating a nice, green leaf?

    2. How do you feel after eating a large amount of Halloween candy?

    3. Why did the very hungry caterpillar become so fat?

    4. Describe his house. What does it look like? How long did he stay in it?

    5. Have you ever seen plant leaves with holes in them? What kind of animal other than a caterpillar could have nibbled on them?

    6. What did the very hungry caterpillar become when he had shed his cocoon?

    7. What parts of the very hungry caterpillar's body stayed as he became a butterfly? Look at a butterfly picture to get help.

    8. Look at the end pages in the front and back of the book. Why do you think they look like holes have been punched out of the paper?

    9. Punch holes out of several different pieces of colored construction paper. Make a collage of the colored papers that represent the very hungry caterpillar's food. Use the dots to add to your stamped finger prints to form animal designs. Use a pencil to add additional parts to the art assignment.

Model Lesson #7

- Food experience: Arrange a special "very hungry caterpillar" school lunch and ask food services to serve it to the class. Use this as a social opportunity to model good manners and health habits.

Model Lesson #8

- Art appreciation through picture books: Compare the following picture books for art illustration, style, color, story plot, and surprise ending.

    Carle, Eric, *The Greedy Python*
    Wildsmith, Brian, *Python's Party*

Library Media Center Connections

1. What is an insect? Describe his special body features, including 3 body parts, 4 wings, 2 feelers, and 6 legs.

2. Introduce a calendar and the days of the week.

3. Introduce sequencing activities including the day's schedule.

4. Practice counting 1-10.

5. Use individual student number lines for counting activities throughout the year. For example, bisect the number of eating days and label *Very Hungry Caterpillar*. Repeat the activity when the class reads *Make Way for Ducklings*. Break the number line at the number 8 and label it with the book title. Repeat with other literature selections that involve number concepts.

6. Assemble supplementary materials for the unit including books about insects, books illustrated by Eric Carle, and science experiments highlighting cocoons.

7. Special media center activity for students: Create butterflies from plastic egg cartons, construction paper, tissue paper, pipe cleaners, and any other available art supplies.

Computer Connections

Learning Well, *Grown up and Small*

Instructional Materials Connections

National Geographic Wonders of Learning Kit, *Butterflies*

Theme Reading Connections: Caterpillars and Butterflies

Brown, Marcia, *All Butterflies* (alphabet)
Fisher, Aileen, *You Don't Look Like Your Mother*
Fitzsimons, Cecilia, *My First Butterflies* (pop up field guide)
Garelick, May, *Where Does the Butterfly Go When It Rains?*
Hogan, Paula, *Butterfly* (cassette and book)
McClung, Robert, *Sphinx: The Story of a Caterpillar*
Overbeck, Cynthia, *Butterfly Book*
Politi, Leo, *The Butterflies Come*
Selsam, Millicent, *Terry and the Caterpillar*
Zim, H. S., *Insects*

Activities to Connect Literature and Curriculum

ART

Ask students to bring to class an empty cereal box. Redecorate it so that it is the same cereal container, but with a new label.

HEALTH

Write to Kellogg Co. for a class breakfast game kit:

> Kellogg Co.
> Home Economics Service
> Department T 975
> Battle Creek, MI 49016

What do people in other countries eat for breakfast?

> Japan-raw fish
> Holland-meat, cheese, and hard rolls
> France-croissants and hard rolls
> England-kippers

Chart for 1 week the foods eaten for breakfast by students.
Note that September is "Better Breakfast Month."

LANGUAGE ARTS

Key vocabulary words for clustering and writing:

moon	egg	leaf
hungry	caterpillar	sun
food	Sunday	Monday
Tuesday	Wednesday	Thursday
Friday	Saturday	calendar
metamorphosis	insect	nutrition
menu		

Clustering: Use words generated from boardwork to dictate a story. First grade students like to dictate their writing assignment to older student tutors after illustrating the paper.

SCIENCE

Hatch silkworms as a class project. Are they similar to the very hungry caterpillar? Keep a science experiment chart and show the daily body change. Available from:

> Carolina Biological Supply Company
> P.O. Box 187
> Gladstone, OR 97027

Match food to original source. Example, egg to chicken, milk to cow.

Beyond the Book

Guided Reading Connections across a Curriculum Rainbow: Food

De Paola, Tomie, *Pancakes for Breakfast*
Greene, Phyllis, *Bagdad Ate It*
Hoban, Lillian, *Arthur's Christmas Cookies*

McCloskey, Robert, *Blueberries for Sal*
Numeroff, Laura, *If You Give a Mouse a Cookie*
Ross, Wilda, *What Did the Dinosaurs Eat?*
Seixas, Judith, *Junk Food—What It Is, What It Does*
Seuss, Dr., *Green Eggs and Ham*
Spier, Peter, *Food Market*
Ziefert, Harriet, *Munchety Munch! A Book about Eating*

Enriching Connections

FOR GIFTED STUDENTS

Go to the library and ask the librarian to help you select a nonfiction book about butterflies. How many different kinds of butterflies can you count?

Using number blocks count and graph the number of different colored butterflies in the book. Group by yellow, red, orange, yellow, blue, brown, and dark colors.

Observe how many butterflies you see in a day. What were they doing?

Does the outside weather make a difference in the number of butterflies you spotted?

FOR PARENTS

Encourage your child to participate in home menu planning.

Model good nutrition habits. Be aware of the sugar content in foods.

Discourage the high consumption of "junk foods."

Discuss the role of good food and its relationship to good health.

THE SKY IS FULL OF SONG

Author: Hopkins, Lee Bennett
Illustrator: Zimmer, Dirk
Publisher: Harper & Row, 1983
Suggested Grade Level: 1-3
Classification: Extended Materials
Literary Form: Poetry
Theme: A celebration of seasons through poetry

About the Book

STUDENT OBJECTIVES:

1. Recognize that some works are poetry.

2. Paraphrase the meaning of selected poetry.

3. Know that all poetry does not rhyme.

SYNOPSIS: A thematic approach to poetry through 38 selections, and a comfortable introduction of the lovely sounds of poetry.

ABOUT THE AUTHOR AND ILLUSTRATOR: Lee Bennett Hopkins, April 13, 1938- .
Dirk Zimmer, birthdate not available.

Lee Hopkins was a poor child who as the oldest child did not have time for reading and books; he had to help earn a family living. His goal was to become a teacher and he reached that goal. As an elementary teacher he discovered how important books were to children. He also learned the joy of poetry as a teacher and believes "that poetry should flow freely in our children's lives; it should come as naturally as breathing."*

He primarily writes and edits poetry anthologies. Hopkins establishes a theme, chooses from several hundred selections, and carefully maintains a balance among poets by publishing 20 or 30 poems.

Dirk Zimmer is known for his woodcuts.

SELECTED ADDITIONAL TITLES BY THE AUTHOR:

Beat the Drum: Independence Day Has Come
Best Friends
By Myself
Circus! Circus!
Creatures
Elves, Fairies, Gnomes
Go to Bed! A Book of Bedtime Poems
Good Morning to You, Valentine
Heh-How for Halloween
How Do You Make an Elephant Float and Other Delicious Riddles
Merrily Comes Our Harvest In: Poems for Thanksgiving
Rainbows Are Made: Poems by Carl Sandburg
Sing Heh for Christmas Day!
Surprises
To Look at Anything

Using the Book

Suggested Approach to the Book

Model Lesson #1

- Explain to the class that this selection will be different from the other stories that they have heard. This book contains many short, pleasant sounding selections. Listen to a selection and describe how it is different from a picture book that has been read previously in class.

- Relate to the class that many of the poems chosen describe a season (e.g., Autumn).

Model Lesson #2

- Continue to read and enjoy various chosen selections.

---

*Sally Holmes Hotze, ed., *Fifth Book of Junior Authors and Illustrators* (New York: H. W. Wilson, 1983).

Model Lesson #3

- Art appreciation through picture books: Look carefully at the woodcuts included in *The Sky Is Full of Song*. Explain how woodcuts are produced. Use a teacher-supplied woodcut to illustrate a poetry writing assignment.

Library Media Center Connections

1. Arrange a display of poetry books and select a title for story hour.

   Martin, Bill, *Brown Bear, Brown Bear, What Do You See?*

2. Special media center activity for students: Color and assemble the pages of a foreshadowing workbook such as *Brown Bear, Brown Bear, What Do You See?*

Computer Connections

Grolier, *Rhyming to Read*

Theme Reading Connections: Poetry

Atwood, Ann, *Little Circle*
Brown, Marc, *Finger Rhymes*
Fisher, Aileen, *Skip around the Year*
Gregory, Sally, *Sing a Song of Seasons*
Hoban, Russell, *Good Night*
Sendak, Maurice, *Seven Little Monsters*
Seuss, Dr., *One Fish, Two Fish, Red Fish, Blue Fish*
Stevenson, Robert L., *Child's Garden of Verse*

Activities to Connect Literature and Curriculum

ART

Bulletin board idea: Twist brown butcher paper into a trunk. Attach to an appropriate bulletin board background. Begin the year with orange leaves drawn by students. Remove the leaves and add snow in the winter. Let the tree sprout spring buds and flowers and conclude the year with student-made fruit. Use the tree during the year as a science resource focal point. Include the life cycle of butterflies. Add a stream and include frogs and toads. Integrate with literature selections including *Make Way for Ducklings*, *The Very Hungry Caterpillar*, and *Frog and Toad Are Friends*.

LANGUAGE ARTS

In class, write a rhyming poem. Direct students to copy the poem from the board and illustrate it with individual art.

Keep copies of the class poems and individual student art. Assemble each child's work into an anthology booklet to display at open house at the end of the school year.

MUSIC

Compose a class poem, use appropriate music as a background introduction, and have the class record the poem. Keep the recording tape as a master copy and add other choral selections throughout the year. Make several copies and check them out to students to take home and share with their parents.

Beyond the Book

Guided Reading Connections across a Curriculum Rainbow: Trees

Arnold, Caroline, *Biggest Living Thing*
Brandt, Keith, *Discovering Trees*
Dickinson, Jane, *All about Trees*
Florian, Douglas, *Discovering Trees*
Podendorf, Illa, *Trees*
Warren, Elizabeth, *I Can Read about Trees and Plants*

Enriching Connections

FOR GIFTED STUDENTS

Imagine that you are publishing a book about trees. Draw a book cover for your book. Add some colorful end pages to your book.

FOR PARENTS

If possible, visit a producing fruit orchard. Observe the size of the trees and the care given. Purchase a small amount of fruit to eat at home.
When you visit the grocery store, show your child the various kinds of fruits available.
Bake a fruit dessert and encourage your child to help you.
Introduce dried fruit as a food in your home.

* * * * * * * * * * *

Through the Eye of Imagination

LITTLE RABBIT'S LOOSE TOOTH

Author: Bate, Lucy
Illustrator: De Groat, Diane
Publisher: Crown, 1975
Suggested Grade Level: K-2
Classification: Extended Materials
Literary Form: Picture book illustrated with pencil, charcoal, and watercolor pictures.
Theme: Losing a first tooth has many aspects, including a visit from the Tooth Fairy.

About the Book

STUDENT OBJECTIVES:

1. Explain and demonstrate proper care of teeth.

2. Choose good eating habits to support good health and body growth.

3. Understand that the dentist is a good health helper.

SYNOPSIS: Lucy Bate provides a peek into the warm family life of a rabbit family. The view is enhanced many times by the lovely art work of Diane De Groat. A warm family portrait of a rabbit family and its youngest member — a little girl who wonders what she should do with her loose tooth when it appears in the chocolate ice cream.

ABOUT THE AUTHOR AND ILLUSTRATOR: Lucy Bate, March 19, 1939- .
Diane De Groat, May 24, 1947- .
Lucy Bate is a playwright whose works have been presented in Boston, Denver, and Yugoslavia. Diane De Groat grew up in New Jersey and was taught art by the same instructor who conducted art lessons for her grandmother. An early job after art school was designing and selecting art for a textbook publisher of readers. She also produced some of the art herself. One of her art techniques for children's books is the use of charcoal, pencil, and watercolors. In 1978 she was awarded the California Young Reader Medal for *Little Rabbit's Loose Tooth.*

SELECTED ADDITIONAL TITLES BY THE ILLUSTRATOR:

Alligator's Toothache
Animal Fact—Animal Fable
Badger on His Own
Ewoks Join the Fight
Running Bear's Exercise Book
Twins Strike Back

Using the Book

Suggested Approach to the Book

Model Lesson #1

- The teacher will share the brief biographical sketch available and ask students to look carefully at the pictures as the story is read. Students will need to know that they will be sharing their feelings about the pictures when the story is finished. How do you think the artist colored the pictures? Do we have any art materials in our classroom like those the artist might have used? Are the colors bright or soft?

Model Lesson #2

- Ask the children the following questions:

    1. Tell something about the rabbit family from the pictures.
    2. Remind the class that this is another example of animals acting and dressing like human beings. It is called personification. Relate personification to other stories, including *Make Way for Ducklings*.
    3. Notice the dedication—could it be a special book in honor of her husband and children, Gabrielle and Rebecca?
    4. What foods were too hard for Little Rabbit?
    5. What food in the refrigerator did she think was soft enough?
    6. Name the foods pictured that were on the week's menu.
    7. Have you ever lost a tooth in chocolate ice cream?
    8. What "window" was Little Rabbit talking about?
    9. Name 3 things Little Rabbit thought about doing with the tooth?
    10. Name 3 additional things you might do with a tooth.
    11. Did Little Rabbit let the Tooth Fairy have the tooth?
    12. What gift did the Tooth Fairy leave?
    13. From the pictures, describe Little Rabbit's home.
    14. What things are like your home?

Model Lesson #3

- Art appreciation through picture books: Compare the tooth theme of these 2 books.

    Bate, Lucy, *Little Rabbit's Loose Tooth*, illustrated by Diane De Groat
    Williams, Barbara, *Albert's Toothache*, illustrated by Kay Chorao

Library Media Center Connections

1. For story hour, read

    McCloskey, Robert, *One Morning in Maine*

2. Special media center activity for students: Make "tooth treasure chests" from 35mm film cans with lids. Decorate as desired. Empty film cans are usually available without charge from film processors.

Instructional Materials Connections

National Geographic Wonders of Learning Kit, *Your Teeth*

Theme Reading Connections: Tooth Fairy and Teeth

Cooney, Nancy, *Wobbly Tooth*
De Groat, Diane, *Alligator's Toothache*
Duvoisin, Roger, *Crocus*
Feagle, Anita, *Tooth Fairy*
Gunther, Louise, *Tooth for the Tooth Fairy*
Krementz, Jill, *Taryn Goes to the Dentist*
McPhail, David, *Bear's Toothache*
Seuss, Dr., *Tooth Book*

Activities to Connect Literature and Curriculum

ART

Design and make a Tooth Fairy envelope from felt. Extra details may be given to the project by lacing three sides together and attaching a Velcro dot closing.
Draw the family portrait and include Little Rabbit in a special dress.
Draw a woodsy scene and include Little Rabbit's house in a tree.

CITIZENSHIP

Award *Little Rabbit* buttons for special classroom citizenship.

LANGUAGE ARTS

Write notes to Little Rabbit and tell her about your home and family. These may be stapled in booklets with rabbit-shaped covers.

MATH

Display a Little Rabbit chart with all the student names listed and the dates on which they lost a tooth. The chart could be bordered by a window to symbolize Little Rabbit's special window.

NUTRITION

Plan a menu using carrots. Why are carrots "good for you?"

SCIENCE

What job does the dentist do? When should we visit the dentist?

Beyond the Book

Guided Reading Connections across a Curriculum Rainbow: Rabbits

Adams, Adrienne, *Easter Egg Artists*
Fatio, Louise, *Happy Lion's Rabbits*
Fisher, Aileen, *Listen, Rabbit* (poetry)
Gag, Wanda, *ABC Bunny* (alphabet)
Hoban, Tana, *Where Is It?*
Hogrogian, Nonny, *Carrot Cake*
Kraus, Robert, *Big Brother*
Parrish, Peggy, *Too Many Rabbits*
Spier, Peter, *Little Rabbits*
Wells, Rosemary, *Max's New Suit*

Enriching Connections

FOR GIFTED STUDENTS

Write a new rabbit adventure story.
Cut out a set of paper doll rabbits by the paper fold technique.
Think up a plan to pull a loose tooth. What painless ways are possible?

FOR PARENTS

Look in a cookbook for a new carrot recipe. Invite your child to help make this new dish.
Help your child learn correct teeth-brushing strokes.
Visit a children's petting zoo and play with the rabbits.
Read a special rabbit story to your child and talk about the book's illustrations.

PETUNIA

Author: Duvoisin, Roger
Illustrator: Duvoisin, Roger
Publisher: Knopf, 1950
Suggested Grade Level: K-2
Classification: Extended Materials
Literary Form: Picture book illustrated with pen and ink
Theme: Education is studying, not carrying a book.

About the Book

STUDENT OBJECTIVES:

1. Dramatize *Petunia.*

2. Sequence the positioning of the animals in the pyramid who tried to render aid to the kitten.

3. Evaluate the value of advice given to the animals by Petunia.

SYNOPSIS: Petunia finds a book and believes she is educated. She proceeds to give advice to the barnyard animals. Because Petunia thinks she can read but cannot, problems arise. This is an opportunity to observe Buttercup Farmyard in action.

ABOUT THE AUTHOR-ILLUSTRATOR: Roger Duvoisin, August 28, 1904-1980.
Roger Duvoisin was married to another noted children's author, Louise Fatio. He was born in Geneva, Switzerland, and grew up liking to draw. He states that the love of his life was drawing, but he could not get the hooves of his horses in perspective. His uncle could draw dancing horses whose hooves did not look like overshoes, and this made Duvoisin happy. Trees were also difficult subjects for him and so Duvoisin asked his artist aunt to help him. She gave him instructions and his tree art got worse! He worked in France as a textile artist and eventually had an opportunity to work in the United States. The firm went bankrupt after a few years. It was then the Great Depression and Duvoisin did not wish to sail home. Instead he was able to publish a book—the beginning of an auspicious career in children's literature.
The Caldecott Award was given to him in 1948 for his illustrations in *White Snow, Bright Snow.* The use of large expanses of white with a small touch of color for emphasis was reflected in this book. *Petunia* also illustrates this art technique. Note—today the *Petunia* series has been reprinted into 1 volume, *Petunia the Silly Goose Stories.* The original printing format used black-and-white double-paged spreads alternating with color work. Today's book has the addition of color on every page.
Duvoisin's most popular works were the *Petunia* books of the 1950s and the *Veronica* series of the 1960s. Children love the books, but librarians are particularly pleased with Petunia because she knows that knowledge is to be found in books!
Observe how the barnyard is a microcosm of our world. The members have conflict, resolve the problem, and continue living within the community system in friendship and with respect for each other.

In an interview before his death, Duvoisin said "It is too bad that making illustrations also requires telling about yourself. I am sorry that nothing dramatic like hunting lions in Africa or exploring the North Pole has taken place in my life, but you can make it up if you wish."

SELECTED ADDITIONAL TITLES BY THE AUTHOR-ILLUSTRATOR:

Crocus
Donkey-Donkey
Happy Lion Series (Illustrated for Louise Fatio)
Mother Goose
Periwinkle
Petunia Series
Veronica Series

Using the Book

Suggested Approach to the Book

Model Lesson #1

- Share the author-illustrator biographical information attached. Ask students if they have ever noticed children's bed linens in the department stores featuring trains, bears, autos, and animals? Tell them that a person called a textile artist created the design and that the illustrator Duvoisin used to do designs for materials before he became a children's writer and illustrator.

Model Lesson #2

- Read *Petunia* to the class and share the illustrations.
    1. How do we know that Petunia lives on Pumpkin Farm?
    2. Before we even begin reading, we learn that she is a silly goose. Why do you think that statement is made?
    3. What did she see that she had not seen in the meadow before?
    4. How does Petunia decide that if "he who owns Books and loves them is wise," she can become wise?
    5. Why did her neck stretch out several inches?
    6. Who is King? Is that a good name for the animal? Why?
    7. What advice was given to King, the rooster? Ida, the hen? Noisy, the dog? Straw, the horse?
    8. What happened when the animals followed Petunia's advice and ate the "candies?"
    9. What must Petunia do now to become truly wise? Do you want to be wise, also?

Model Lesson #3

- Art appreciation through picture books: Compare for art colors and technique

    Duvoisin, Roger, *Veronica*
    Marshall, James, *George and Martha*

Library Media Center Connections

1. Choose a *Veronica* story for story hour. Another appropriate selection is Peggy Parrish's *Amelia Bedelia*, because Amelia and Petunia are similar—they take everything at its literal meaning.

2. Special media center activity for students: Make stick puppets of Petunia, King, Ida, Noisy, and Straw. Role-play their parts in the barnyard adventure.

Computer Connections

Developmental Learning Materials, *Number Farm*

Instructional Materials Connections

National Geographic Wonders of Learning Kit, *Farm Animals*

Theme Reading Connections: Books and Libraries

Aliki, *How a Book Is Made*
Bauer, Caroline Feller, *Too Many Books*
Bonsall, Crosby, *Tell Me Some More*
Cohen, Miriam, *When Will I Read?*
Felt, Sue, *Rosa Too Little*
Fujimoto, Patricia, *True Book of Libraries*
Hoban, Lillian, *Arthur's Prize Reader*
Tester, Sylvia, *Visit to the Library*

Activities to Connect Literature and Curriculum

ART

Using a roll of shelf paper, recreate the story of Petunia. Lightly mark the shelf paper into 3-foot sections and assign student group work. Tell the story in sequence with drawings. Load the roll onto an opaque projector roller and roll the story through the projector like a film. Record the student retellings on cassette tape. Include a musical beginning and ending.

Design a farmyard map and position the animals in their places.

CITIZENSHIP

When should we give advice to friends?

LANGUAGE ARTS

Key vocabulary words for clustering and writing:

meadow	boom	kitten
pig	book	friends

dog	horse	rooster
goose	comb	chicken
cow	proud	happy

Write an ABC book for Petunia.

MATH

Name the 3 most important animals in the barnyard. Chart the responses using Number Blox chart paper.

MUSIC

Sing "The Farmer in the Dell" and act out the round during class.

SOCIAL STUDIES

Talk about the changing number of farms today. Explain that some farms are getting larger through consolidation and the use of technical equipment to increase production.
List a number of farm products.
Would you rather live in the city or on a farm? Why?

Beyond the Book

Guided Reading Connections across a Curriculum Rainbow: Farming

Barrett, Judi, *Old MacDonald Had an Apartment House*
Bunting, Eve, *Big Red Barn*
Child, Lydia, *Over the River and through the Woods*
De Paola, Tomie, *Country Farm*
Hutchins, Pat, *Rosie's Walk*
Jacobson, Karen, *Farm Animals*
Lenski, Lois, *Little Farm*
McDonald, Betty, *Hello, Mrs. Piggle-Wiggle*
Scarry, Richard, *On the Farm*
Williams, Garth, *Chicken Book*
Zuromskis, Diane, *Farmer in the Dell*

Enriching Connections

FOR GIFTED STUDENTS

Petunia's book does not have a picture on the cover. What would be a good cover design? Fold an 11-by-14-inch piece of construction paper to book cover size and illustrate her book.

Think very carefully about the contents of the book, as the cover makes us want to read the book.

We talked earlier about textile designers and their work. Design a set of bedsheets and a bedspread for your room.

FOR PARENTS

Read a book illustrated by Duvoisin to your child.
Have some fun spotlighting animal silhouettes on the wall using a flashlight.

WHERE THE WILD THINGS ARE

Author: Sendak, Maurice
Illustrator: Sendak, Maurice
Publisher: Harper & Row, 1963
Suggested Grade Level: K-3
Classification: Core Materials
Literary Form: Picture book
Theme: Enter the wonderful world of imagination and be king of the realm.

About the Book

STUDENT OBJECTIVES:

1. Locate detail in given picture to respond to critical thinking questions.

2. Recognize feelings as depicted in pictures.

3. Discriminate between fact and fantasy.

SYNOPSIS: The style of *Where the Wild Things Are* is one of space expanding from Max's bedroom and into a world of fantasy complete with large, lovable figures. The prose adds resonance to a magnificent art portfolio. This picture book is one of the all-time classics of children's literature and a great favorite of young readers. To miss it is to miss a signpost in reading. Note the lyrical language as Max moves in and out a year and a day. It is both fantasy and magic for children who move into another time.

ABOUT THE AUTHOR-ILLUSTRATOR: Maurice Sendak, June 10, 1928- .
Maurice Sendak is a contrast to another Caldecott Award winner, Ezra Jack Keats, also born in Brooklyn, New York, 12 years earlier. Their family economic situations were different. Keats grew up in a black inner city environment and was the target of gangs and economic struggles. Sendak was the product of an immigrant Jewish family. He is one of the most famous children's book illustrators of today. Several years ago he shared the podium at a conference in San Diego with another illustrious artist—Dr. Seuss. His books have been

named Caldecott award winners 7 times—*Where the Wild Things Are* and *In the Night Kitchen* in 1964 and 1965. Sendak has also received the important international Hans Christian Andersen Illustrator's Medal for the body of his work and has possibly been the greatest influence on children's illustrators of all time.

Books by Maurice Sendak release children from their everyday world to that of fantasy. He is a master at putting the reader in another place and another time. "Maurice Sendak's work, disguised in fantasy, springs from his earliest self, from the vagrant child that lurks in the heart of all of us" (Brian O'Doherly, *New York Times Book Review*, May 12, 1963).

Meet Max, the ageless little boy, who stirs up trouble with his mother. For punishment he is sent to bed without supper. Max, in his wolf suit, sails away into a land of imagination and Wild Things. At the time of the book's publication, critics said it would scare children. They were proved wrong as Max became the popular hero of young children, who related to him instantly.

SELECTED ADDITIONAL TITLES BY THE AUTHOR-ILLUSTRATOR:

Alligators All Around: An Alphabet
Chicken Soup with Rice
Hector Protector, and As I Went over the Water: Two Nursery Rhymes
In the Night Kitchen
Maurice Sendak's Really Rosie: Starring the Nutshell Kids
Nutcracker
One Was Johnny, a Counting Book
Outside over There
Seven Little Monsters
Sign on Rosie's Door
Very Far Away
Where the Wild Things Are

ADDITIONAL TITLES BY THE ILLUSTRATOR:

Krauss, Ruth, *A Very Special House*
Minarik, Else, *Little Bear* Series
Zolotow, Charlotte, *Mr. Rabbit and the Lovely Present*

A special note is made of a comprehensive source of information about Sendak

Lane, Selma, *Art of Maurice Sendak*

Using the Book

Suggested Approach to the Book

Model Lesson #1

- Introduce the author-illustrator Maurice Sendak through the attached biographical material. Mention to students that Sendak has become famous through his art and that he does not plan to illustrate many more children's books. He has become actively involved in designing stage sets for the Seattle Opera group. Sets have included *The Nutcracker* for holiday presentations and a special version of *Where the Wild Things Are* complete with 9-foot-high Wild Things that sing and dance over the stage with their king, Max.

Model Lesson #2

- What is imagination? Where does it live? Who is in charge of it?

  Note: The main character of Kodak's exhibit, The World of Imagination, at Epcot Center in Florida, is Figgy. He is a vibrant pink and purple character with the tail of a seal, the body of a dragon, and yellow eyes capped by the horns of a ram. His outfit is completed with a gold, red-trimmed T-shirt bearing his name. He is made up of many parts and becomes a believable symbol for the imagination, complete with music. He has the wings of an angel.

- Discuss the fact that many of the books that have been read aloud in class this year were fiction (imaginary). Let the class name some of them as part of the discussion.

Model Lesson #3

- Read *Where the Wild Things Are* through while sharing the content and illustrations with the class. Explain that the class will be doing many activities with this book and that they should pay very careful attention to the reading.

- As a preview question ask students to look carefully at the pictures and predict how the story will end for Max. This is a nice opportunity to introduce brainstorming and the fact that all answers are good ones and all students' responses should be respected. Consensus of the class may be reached on the possible outcomes of the story. Conclude the story quickly so as not to disrupt the unity of illustrations and prose.

Model Lesson #4

- Students need to know that this literature unit is an introduction to fantasy or make believe. *Where the Wild Things Are* will be a good unit to discriminate between real and "not real."

  Setting: Max's bedroom and the far-away land of the Wild Things

  Character: Max, a little boy who has made mischief

  Problem: Max is in trouble!

  Resolution: Taking an imaginary dream trip to a far-away place

  Theme: Entering the world of imagination and becoming the king of the realm

Model Lesson #5

- Ask the students these questions:
  1. What is the name of the little boy who wore his wolf suit and was naughty?
  2. What kinds of things is Max doing?
  3. What does his mother call him?
  4. What happens to Max when he talks back to his mother?
  5. What occurs at your house when this happens?
  6. Tell what Max's room looks like when he is sent to bed.
  7. How does it change on the next page? On the next?
  8. What happens to the room ceiling?
  9. Could all these things happen in your bedroom? Why or why not?

10. Describe Max's boat ride.
11. What's the name of his boat?
12. What would you name your boat?
13. What is the first Wild Thing he meets?
14. Do we still have sea monsters today?
15. What kind of greeting did the Wild Things give Max?
16. What command did Max issue to quiet the Wild Things?
17. What were the eyes of the Wild Things like?
18. Max became _____ of the Wild Things.
19. What kind of fun did Max and the Wild Things have together?
20. Max did the same thing to the Wild Things that his mother had done to him. What was it?
21. What made Max give up being the king of the Wild Things?
22. Name some good food smells. Where would these smells most likely be found?
23. How did the Wild Things behave when Max boarded the boat?
24. How long did it take Max to reach home and his room?
25. What was waiting for Max when he arrived home?
26. Did Max really leave his room to visit the Wild Things?
27. How could you visit the Wild Things?
28. Which Wild Thing would you invite to dinner? Why?

Model Lesson #6

• Food experience: Plan an afternoon "Wild Thing" snack party. What would be good food for Wild Things, who use tremendous energy and need to stay healthy? Draw a Wild Thing placemat and ask food services to visit and discuss good snack foods. Plan to include a snack and drink. If available, show a video production of *Where the Wild Things Are*.

Model Lesson #7

• Art appreciation through picture books: Compare the following picture books for content, art work, and surprise endings.

    Kellogg, Steven, *The Mysterious Tadpole*
    Sendak, Maurice, *Where the Wild Things Are*

Library Media Center Connections

1. Assemble supplementary materials about imagination, Wild Things—real and unreal— and books illustrated by Maurice Sendak.

2. Select one of the following Sendak illustrated works for story hour:

    Krauss, Ruth, *A Very Special House*
    Minarik, Else, *Little Bear* Series
    Zolotow, Charlotte, *Mr. Rabbit and the Lovely Present*

3. Special media center student activity: Make stick puppets of Max and the Wild Things. Create some new Wild Things.

4. Students may cut out animal pictures from magazines, paste them on construction paper, and turn them into favorite Wild Things by drawing additional details on the animals.

Theme Reading Connections: Night and the Moon

Asch, Frank, *Happy Birthday, Moon; Moon Bear*
Berger, Barbara, *Grandfather Twilight*
Bonsall, Crosby, *Who's Afraid of the Dark?*
Branley, Franklyn M., *What the Moon Is Like*
Brown, Margaret Wise, *Goodnight Moon*
Carle, Eric, *Papa, Please Get the Moon for Me*
Keats, Ezra Jack, *Dreams*
Larrick, Nancy, *When the Dark Comes Dancing* (poetry)
Martin, Bill, *Barn Dance!*
Marzollo, Jean, *Close Your Eyes*
Seuss, Dr., *Dr. Seuss's Sleep Book*
Simon, Seymour, *Moon*
Slobodkina, Esphyr, *Many Moons*

Activities to Connect Literature and Curriculum

ART

Ask students to draw and color a sample of the imagination that lives within them.
Using a mirror, create a self-portrait or have students create portraits of each other.
Create student "Wild Things" in various art media. Plan an art exhibit to display them.

CITIZENSHIP

Identify a "special person" of the week.

LANGUAGE ARTS

Explain to the class that you are going to a new, unopened recreation park similar to Disneyland and you will be packing a trunk for the vacation and will need some special items. Begin packing with an example of a letter A object such as an alphabet book, a B object such as a banana, and so on. Call on students to add additional items. Repeat each new alphabet addition beginning with the letter A object.

Give a prize for the best "imagination" contribution of the week. Supply an Imagination Box for the entries.

Record a class production of *Where the Wild Things Are.*

Write a letter inviting Max to visit your class. (P.S.: He can bring the Wild Things.)

What do you think Max would be like? What would he want to do at recess? What would his favorite book be? Can you guess what his favorite dinner would be?

Key vocabulary words for clustering and writing:

Max	private
ocean	vines
gnashed	roared
forest	king
boat	

Clustering: Use these words and others to enter into a literature log. Use 3 words to brainstorm and write a paragraph on the blackboard about Max's adventure in imagination. The class should copy the paragraph generated through brainstorming and illustrate it with individual art. Make a new version of Max's trip and place it in the year 2000 in a spacecraft. Some students might like to place their stories in the days of dinosaurs. Dictate these stories to an adult helper.

MATH

Use the discussion questions listed in "Language Arts" for a survey. Graph the answers on a classroom chart using number blocks.

Beyond the Book

Guided Reading Connections across a Curriculum Rainbow: Sleep and Monsters

Burningham, John, *Would You Rather ...*
Cohen, Miriam, *Jim Meets the Thing*
Collington, Peter, *Angel and the Soldier Boy*
Gackenback, Dick, *Harry and the Terrible Whatzit*
Hazen, Barbara, *Gorilla Did It*
Hoff, Syd, *Danny and the Dinosaur*
Mayer, Mercer, *There's a Nightmare in My Closet*; *There's an Alligator under My Bed*
Most, Bernard, *If the Dinosaurs Came Back*
Stevenson, James, *What's under My Bed?*
Wood, Audrey, *The Napping House*
Zion, Gene, *Harry by the Sea*

Enriching Connections

FOR GIFTED STUDENTS

Draw and color on muslin cloth Wild Thing pillow designs that will be assembled by classroom aides or volunteers.
Draw a map of your bedroom at home.

FOR PARENTS

Make up a bedtime story for your child. Encourage him or her to supply some of the facts and "help" you.

Make a simple cookie dough and cut out Wild Thing cookies together.
Ask that your child retell *Where the Wild Things Are* to you.
Read a Maurice Sendak story together and enjoy his art.

ALEXANDER AND THE HORRIBLE, NO GOOD, VERY BAD DAY

Author: Viorst, Judith
Illustrator: Cruz, Ray
Publisher: Halliday Lithograph Corp., 1972
Suggested Grade Level: 1-6
Classification: Core Materials
Literary Form: Picture book illustrated in black ink
Theme: Not everything in life is perfect.

About the Book

STUDENT OBJECTIVES:

1. Recall pleasant events that have happened in the past.

2. Select an event and describe why it was a happy occasion.

3. Role-play a "Horrible, No Good, Very Bad Day."

SYNOPSIS: Alexander is involved in a chain of events that are unpleasant and no one takes the time to "listen" to him that day. This is a unique portrayal through ink sketches of a boy's awful day. It did last the whole day, too.

ABOUT THE AUTHOR AND ILLUSTRATOR: Judith Viorst, birthdate not available. Ray Cruz, June 30, 1933- .
    Judith Viorst is a very popular children's literature writer. Her humor is understated and she possesses a dry, charming wit. She also has been a columnist for *Redbook* magazine. The needs of her 3 sons have provided the subjects for her children's books. Her feeling is that even though her sons are getting older, her main characters will be suspended in present time.
    Ray Cruz started his drawing career at age 5 in Spanish Harlem, New York. He also, like Roger Duvoisin, worked as a textile artist. His background also includes wallpaper and package design as well as advertising.

SELECTED ADDITIONAL TITLES BY THE AUTHOR:

Alexander Who Used to Be Rich Last Sunday
I'll Fix Anthony

My Mama Says There Aren't Any Zombies, Ghosts, Vampires, Creatures, Demons, Monsters, Fiends, Goblins or Things
Rosie and Michael
Sunday Morning
Tenth Good Thing about Barney
Try It Again, Sam: Safety When You Walk

Using the Book

Suggested Approach to the Book

Model Lesson #1

- Talk about the author and illustrator. Read the story and discuss the unique ink sketches that are the illustrations. Is there another book that has been read to the class that has one-color ink sketches? What about the monochromatic colors of Robert McCloskey's *Make Way for Ducklings* or *Blueberries for Sal?*

Model Lesson #2

- Ask the children the following questions:

    1. Describe Alexander's room as illustrated on the opening page.
    2. Can you tell anything about Alexander by examining his facial expression?
    3. What did his fortunate 2 brothers find in their cereal boxes?
    4. Find Australia on a map.
    5. Where did Alexander ride in the Volkswagen? Was he happy?
    6. Explain his art work—an invisible castle.
    7. How do you feel when a friend chooses another friend instead of you?
    8. How did Alexander feel about not having a tasty dessert in his lunch?
    9. What is a cavity? What is the dentist going to do about it?
    10. Tell about his trip to buy tennis shoes.
    11. If you were Alexander's Dad, would you let him come to the office? Why?
    12. How did Alexander feel when he went to bed?

Model Lesson #3

- Art appreciation through picture books: Compare

    Sendak, Maurice, *Where the Wild Things Are*
    Viorst, Judith, *My Mama Says There Aren't Any Zombies, Ghosts, Vampires, Creatures, Demons, Monsters, Fiends, Goblins or Things*

Library Media Center Connections

1. Share a map and a simple social studies picture book about life in Australia.

2. Special media center activity for students: Create monster art. Make a flap book with each student contributing a page. Divide a sheet of paper into 3 horizontal sections with

dotted lines. Draw a monster head, body, and feet. Cut into 3 sections. Staple into a decorated cover. Flip the book pages to show combinations of different heads, bodies, and feet.

Theme Reading Connections: Bad Day

Andrews, F., *Nobody Comes to Dinner*
Berenstain, Stan, *Berenstain Bears Get in a Fight*
Fujikawa, Gyo, *Sam's All-Wrong Day*
Giff, Patricia, *Today Was a Terrible Day*
Hoban, Russell, *Sorely Trying Day*
Lexau, Joan, *I Should Have Stayed in Bed*
Oxenbury, Helen, *Car Trip*
Wells, Rosemary, *Unfortunately Harriet*

Activities to Connect Literature and Curriculum

ART

Paint monster pictures and hold a contest to determine the happiest and nicest monster in the group.

CITIZENSHIP

Discuss monster behavior at home and in school.

LANGUAGE ARTS

Key vocabulary words for clustering and writing:

sleep
good
bad
breakfast
mom

Design a large, blank bulletin board scroll. Entitle it "The Best Day Ever." Use it to record all the good things that happen in the classroom each day. Curl the top and bottom page so that it looks like an official document.

MATH

Count and record all the things that happened to Alexander that awful day.

SOCIAL STUDIES

Invite a native of Australia or a knowledgeable visitor to class to talk about Australia. Show an appropriate first grade film or sound filmstrip about Australia to the class.

Beyond the Book

Guided Reading Connections across a Curriculum Rainbow: Play

Alexander, Martha, *I'll Be the Horse, If You Play with Me*
Ets, Marie Hall, *Play with Me*
Lenski, Lois, *Let's Play House*

Enriching Connections

FOR GIFTED STUDENTS

Pantomine in sequence the Marie Hall Ets story, *Play with Me*. Add other class members to play the part of additional animals for another performance.
Teach a new game to the class.

FOR PARENTS

Enjoy playing a game with your child. It is an enriching experience.
Check out a library book on pantomine and shadow puppetry. One with pictures of Marcel Marceau would be a nice choice.

*   *   *   *   *   *   *   *   *   *   *

Grade Two

INTRODUCTIONS

Through Giants of Sea and Land

STORY OF BABAR

Author: De Brunhoff, Jean
Illustrator: De Brunhoff, Jean
Publisher: Random House, 1933
Suggested Grade Level: 1-3
Classification: Recreational and Motivational Materials
Literary Form: Picture book
Theme: Life is a series of sequential events.

About the Book

STUDENT OBJECTIVES:

1. Dramatize the *Story of Babar*. (There should be enough roles for the entire class.)

2. Explain the selection of old-fashioned clothes worn by Babar.

3. Evaluate Babar's decision to leave the city and the Old Woman to return to the jungle.

SYNOPSIS: Babar's mother is slain by a hunter and Babar escapes. Babar finds refuge in the city and is befriended by the Old Woman. She provides for all of the elephant's needs, but Babar eventually returns home to the jungle. He is chosen king and marries Celeste. If we could meet a live, well-dressed elephant, Babar would fit the image of that elephant.

ABOUT THE AUTHOR-ILLUSTRATOR: Jean De Brunhoff, 1899-1937.
Babar was created by Jean De Brunhoff as a picture book character to enhance the bedtime stories told by his wife to their young sons. His original illustrations were first hand-colored and made into a book for his sons. The homemade book was later printed in 1931 as a large format picture book, *The Story of Babar, the Little Elephant*. It was a bestseller, with over 50,000 sold. Today there are 34 titles printed in 17 languages. Until 1960, when the cost of printing reached an all time high, all the Babar books were in the large format size.

Jean De Brunhoff died of the disease tuberculosis at the age of 38, leaving his son Laurent as a 12-year-old and 2 other sons. Laurent De Brunhoff published a new Babar book, the first in what was to become a series of 6, after the death of his father. It was surprising how identical his Babar's Cousin was to other books illustrated by his father and already in-print. He has since continued the story of the little elephant, Babar. "If there is a moral in the Babar books," says Laurent De Brunhoff, "it is 'Pas de panique.' Don't panic."* Many differing opinions have been given about what the city of Babar's life is. Some say it is a utopia while others feel that the city reflected the political attitudes of Jean De Brunhoff.

SELECTED ADDITIONAL TITLES BY THE AUTHOR-ILLUSTRATOR:

Babar and Father Christmas
Babar and His Children
Babar and the Zephir
Babar the King
Babar's Anniversary Album

SELECTED TITLES BY LAURENT DE BRUNHOFF:

Babar Comes to America
Babar Learns to Cook
Babar Visits Another Planet
Babar's ABC (alphabet)
Babar's Visit to Bird Island
Serafina the Giraffe

Using the Book

Suggested Approach to the Book

Model Lesson #1

- Present the attached biographical material on Jean and Laurent De Brunhoff and explain that you are going to observe the adventures of an elephant who will become king.

- Read the *Story of Babar* aloud and share the illustrations.

Model Lesson #2

- Some questions for class discussion.
    1. Do we have any forests where elephants might live in the United States?
    2. Examine the picture of elephants at play on pages 4-5. Name 5 activities that are happening in the picture.
    3. What sad thing happens to Babar's mother?
    4. What does Babar do then?

---

*Robert Wernick, "A Lovable Elephant That Youngsters Never Ever Forget," *Smithsonian Magazine* (July 1984): 90-96.

5. What does the town look like to Babar?
6. Can you tell which man in the picture on page 10 is a policeman? How?
7. How do you know that the lady pictured on page 11 is the very rich Old Lady?
8. Retell Babar's visit to the big store.
9. Describe Babar's choice of clothing.
10. Do fathers dress that way today?
11. Do you think the Old Lady spoiled Babar? Why?
12. Name the 2 elephants who came racing out of the jungle.
13. Why does Babar choose to return to the jungle?
14. How do you think the Old Lady feels about Babar's departure?
15. What happens when Babar arrives back home?
16. Do you think that having lived in the city and wearing fine clothes are the necessary qualifications for being named king?
17. Who is the usual king of the jungle? Why?
18. How did the animals celebrate the wedding?
19. Can you count the wedding guests on page 45?
20. When you read the ending of the book, do you think any more adventures have been planned? Why?

Model Lesson #3

- Art appreciation through picture books: Compare the lives of these 2 main characters and the way they each found a home:

De Brunhoff, Jean, *Babar the King*
Ungerer, Tomi, *Crictor*

Library Media Center Connections

1. Share a Babar book for storytime.

2. Learn about elephants through research. Describe an elephant. What kind of food does an elephant eat? Where do elephants live? How long do elephants live? How many calves does an elephant have?

Theme Reading Connections: Elephants

Aliki, *Wild and Woolly Mammoths*
Dolch, Edward, *Elephant Stories*
Ets, Marie Hall, *Elephant in a Well*
Foulds, Elfrida Vipont, *Elephant and the Bad Baby*
Hoff, Syd, *Oliver*
Hoffman, Mary, *Animals in the Wild: Elephants*
Hogan, Paula, *Elephant*
Johnson, Sylvia, *Elephants around the World*
Kipling, Rudyard, *Elephant's Child*
Kraus, Robert, *Mrs. Elmo of Elephant House*
Mayer, Mercer, *Ah-Choo*
Naden, C., *I Can Read about Elephants*
Peet, Bill, *Ella*

Petersham, Maud, *Circus Baby*
Posell, Elsa, *Elephants*
Quigley, Lillian, *Blind Men and the Elephant*
Ylla, *Little Elephant*

Activities to Connect Literature and Curriculum

ART

Divide the class into 5 groups. Let each group be responsible for the background panel for a part of the *Story of Babar*. Tape all 5 completed panels together to form a screen. Mold and fire elephant clay figures. Place them in front of the screen panels. Include the following:

1. Jungle scene—include Babar and mother
2. Trip to big store
3. Living at the Old Woman's house
4. Visit of cousins
5. Return to jungle

Using washable paints, make "handables." Paint a hand to look like an elephant or other jungle animal. Role-play what each would say to King Babar.

LANGUAGE ARTS

Key vocabulary words for clustering and writing:

Babar	king	Arthur
elevator	elephant	dromedary
mushroom	photograph	hunter
digging	queen	Celeste
floorwalker	monkey	ceremony

Pretend you are the dromedary. Make up a wedding list of animals. Write a note that you will deliver telling the guests about the wedding ceremony. Don't forget to design and use royal stationery for the invitation.

MATH

Through research, can you learn how many African and Asiatic elephants are in the world? Next graph the information on a bar or pie graph.

MUSIC

Form a rhythm instrument band. Plan to present a special music program for the coronation tea party.

NUTRITION

Plan a coronation tea party for Babar and Celeste. Serve punch and cookies. Use this as an opportunity to practice social behaviors.

SOCIAL STUDIES

Locate on a map the 2 main habitats in the world for elephants.

What if it were necessary to find a new home for elephants because a fire had destroyed their jungle home? Where would you suggest? Why? Think through the problem carefully because we would be moving a large number of animals with special needs because of their size and food requirements.

Beyond the Book

Guided Reading Connections across a Curriculum Rainbow: Weddings

Goodall, John, *Naughty Nancy*
Grimm, Jacob, *Mrs. Fox's Wedding*
Lear, Edward, *Owl and the Pussy-Cat* (poetry)
Williams, Garth, *Rabbit's Wedding*

Enriching Connections

FOR GIFTED STUDENTS

Design a set of crowns for King Babar and Queen Celeste.

Find out about royal garments. What is the material like? What do the costumes look like? Make a Babar and Celeste paper doll set with clothing.

FOR PARENTS

Pose the following questions to your child. What would it be like if we were to move to a jungle home like Babar's? What kind of safety precautions would be needed? What kind of foods would be available in contrast to foods we eat at home? What would our home be like? Can you imagine going to school in a new environment? What would we do for fun and recreation? Would newspapers and magazines be available? What things would be better than things at home?

Enjoy a trip to the zoo and visit the elephant enclosure.

HORTON HATCHES THE EGG

Author: Seuss, Dr.
Illustrator: Seuss, Dr.
Publisher: Random House, 1940
Suggested Grade Level: 2-4
Classification: Recreational and Motivational Materials
Literary Form: Picture book written in original Dr. Seuss language style
Theme: We all love our children.

About the Book

STUDENT OBJECTIVES:

1. Paraphrase *Horton Hatches the Egg.*

2. Predict the story's ending.

3. Consider the decision of Horton to keep the elephant bird.

SYNOPSIS: Horton, the elephant, is asked to nest-sit for a lazy bird, Mayzie. He does sit through the days and nights, through 51 weeks in all. Mayzie abandons her egg, but lays claim to the hatched elephant bird. The book contains many zany word plays with supposedly no meaning—but truth is in the eyes of the reader.

ABOUT THE AUTHOR-ILLUSTRATOR: Dr. Seuss, March 2, 1904- .
It is hard to believe that the famous Dr. Seuss had an unspectacular childhood, but his early life seems rather uneventful and without any strange beasts and exciting verse. Dr. Seuss's real name is Theodor Seuss Geisel. After having a normal childhood and adolescence, he became student editor of the Dartmouth College humor magazine. After graduation from college, he sold a cartoon to the *Saturday Evening Post* magazine and signed it "Dr. Seuss" because he considered it fitting that his real name only be used for serious business. He became associated with the Standard Oil Company through a clever turn of words in advertising, when he coined the phrase "Quick, Henry, get the Flit." Flit was a pesticide in use at the time.
Dr. Seuss was very active during World War II and worked intensely for the United States government, writing and directing educational films. He also became a Lieutenant Colonel in the Signal Corps. He was given the Legion of Merit award for his war efforts. Part of his many professional credits include an Academy Award movie, *Design for Death*, in 1947 and another Academy Award in 1950 for a best motion picture cartoon (Gerald McBoing-Boing). His first book for children was published in 1937 under the title *And to Think That I Saw It on Mulberry Street.* This story was conceived while crossing the Atlantic Ocean. He composed the words to the rhythm of the ship's engines. The illustrations were drawn after he landed in the United States. According to Dr. Seuss, this book was rejected by 29 publishers. His second book was the *500 Hats of Bartholomew Cubbins.*

Dr. Seuss launched a new career with the publication of his third book, *Cat and the Hat*. His educational philosophy was that children need to become instant readers and that his books could accomplish that task. "All of a sudden reading becomes wonderful, a marvelous thing to do!" Dr. Seuss explains that to draft a book 11 times was not unusual, and he has done as many as 20 rewrites. At a University of California, San Diego, conference, Dr. Seuss mentioned that his early advertising contracts expressly forbade his writing or drawing unless the work was for children's books. He said that he decided to use the opportunity offered and try his skills with children's books. What happened is now children's literature history. *Horton Hatches the Egg* is the author's favorite book because he had so much fun writing and illustrating it. A piece of transparent paper with an elephant drawn on it fell over a sheet of paper with a tree picture on it. That became Horton sitting on his now famous, funny egg. He explains his lack of art school training thus: "My animals look that way because I never learned to draw." Dr. Seuss has never had any children, but promises to amuse them for you.

SELECTED ADDITIONAL TITLES BY THE AUTHOR-ILLUSTRATOR:

Butter Battle Book
Cat and the Hat Beginner Dictionary
Dr. Seuss's ABC (alphabet)
Foot Book
Fox in Sox
Green Eggs and Ham
Happy Birthday to You
Hop on Pop
How the Grinch Stole Christmas
Hunches of Bunches
I Can Lick 30 Tigers Today and Other Stories
I Can Read with My Eyes Shut
I Had Trouble Getting to Solla Sollew
If I Ran the Circus
If I Ran the Zoo
King's Stilts
Lorax
Marvin K. Mooney, Will You Please Go Now!
McElligot's Pool
Mr. Brown Can Moo! Can You?
Oh Say Can You Say?
Oh, the Thinks You Can Think
On Beyond Zebra
One Fish, Two Fish, Red Fish, Blue Fish
Please Try to Remember the First of October!
Scrambled Eggs Supper!
Shape of Me and Other Stuff
Sneetches and Other Stories
There's a Wocket in My Pocket
Thidwick, the Big-Hearted Moose

Using the Book

Suggested Approach to the Book

Model Lesson #1

- No literature study would be complete without the introduction of the unique writer and illustrator, Dr. Seuss. Enjoy sharing the biographical information about him with your students. They will probably be acquainted with him already.

- Tell the students the story that Dr. Seuss relates about his last presentation to school students. He was drawing for a large group in the school auditorium. The audience became restless and he asked them why. In true children's fashion, the group said that someone in the school could draw better. He asked the student to come forward and draw for him. With the famous Seuss aplomb, he agreed that the child was a better artist, and henceforth Dr. Seuss would not be drawing in public!

Model Lesson #2

- Read and enjoy *Horton Hatches the Egg*.

- Pause when Horton's egg begins to hatch. Ask the critical thinking question—whom does the baby belong to and why? Allow enough time for students to discuss and work through the problem. Finish reading the story when the discussion is completed.

Model Lesson #3

- Read and enjoy another book written and illustrated by Dr. Seuss.

Model Lesson #4

- Art appreciation through picture books: Compare the art, colors, and story in the following:

      Petersham, Maud, *Circus Baby*
      Seuss, Dr., *Horton Hatches the Egg*

Library Media Center Connections

1. Read a Dr. Seuss book for story hour.

2. Using an elephant pattern, make outrageous elephant bookmarks. Cut into the outline of the elephant trunk slightly with scissors to allow the bookmark to curl over the page. Select bright colors.

3. Research the difference between African and Indian or oriental elephants. Draw and color a picture of each elephant. Label on the picture the differences between the 2 elephants as observed in your research.

Theme Reading Connections: Perseverance

Aesop, *Miller, His Son, and the Donkey*
Aliki, *Weed Is a Flower*
Keats, Ezra Jack, *John Henry*
Piper, Watty, *Little Engine That Could*

Activities to Connect Literature and Curriculum

ART

Assign half of the class as artists and the other half as helpers. The helpers sit back-to-back with the artists. Each helper chooses 3 statements to describe a wild animal. He or she presents these ideas to the artist, who in turn draws a picture on an artist pad of that animal. The artist then takes the place of the helper and repeats the process with a different assigned animal. This is an excellent assignment to explain the need for stating directions carefully.

Special Note: Another class lesson could be how to write step-by-step instructions giving directions for how to tie a shoe lace correctly.

Read David Elmer McKee's *Patchwork Elephant* to the class and design colored patchwork elephants to illustrate the story. Mount on black construction paper and display all art products.

CITIZENSHIP

Give Horton Elephant awards to students who finish difficult assignments.

LANGUAGE ARTS

Rewrite as a collaborative learning assignment in poetry form a short version of *Horton Hatches the Egg*. Assign different segments to different learning groups.

Write a Mother's Day poem from the viewpoint of the elephant bird child.

From the elephant theme books presented in class, choose 1 story that you have enjoyed and share it in an assigned collaborative learning group. Select 1 report from each group to be presented aloud to the class.

Compose an elephant tale—a tall tale about an elephant. Record the stories on cassette tape as an oral language exercise.

MATH

List all the books about elephants that students have read. Record the number of students who have read each title. Graph the results.

NUTRITION

Bake elephant-shaped peanut butter cookies for snack time. Use measurement concepts learned in math class.

SCIENCE

Incubate and hatch chicken eggs. Record the daily observation information on a chart.

Beyond the Book

Guided Reading Connections across a Curriculum
Rainbow: Hatching Eggs

Andersen, Hans C., *Ugly Duckling*
Butterworth, Oliver, *Enormous Egg*
Heller, Ruth, *Chickens Aren't the Only Ones*
Henley, Karyn, *Hatch!*
Lauber, Patricia, *What's Hatching out of That Egg?*
Milhous, Katherine, *Egg Tree*
Peet, Bill, *Pinkish, Purplish, Bluish Egg*
Potter, Beatrix, *Tale of Jemima Puddle-Duck*
Rockwell, Anne, *Gollywhopper Egg*
Selsam, Millicent, *Egg to Chick*

Enriching Connections

FOR GIFTED STUDENTS

Draw and decorate 2 very large construction paper eggs. Cut out the 2 egg shapes and use for writing paper folder covers. Staple the 2 egg shapes over several half sheets of writing paper. Write a make-believe story beginning with the story starter, *The Biggest Egg I Ever Saw*.

Use a library book to learn how long it takes to hatch chicken, duck, swan, and other bird eggs. Design a chart to record this information.

FOR PARENTS

Horton, an elephant, sat on the egg of a bird until it hatched. Talk to your child about the way different animals are born. Turtles lay eggs in the sand and leave them to hatch. Birds lay eggs and sit on them to keep them warm during incubation. Mammals like dogs and cats have live animal births. Go to the library and select a book about animals. Read the book together and find out how the different animals are hatched or born. Relate to your child the story of how he or she was born.

AMOS AND BORIS

Author: Steig, William
Illustrator: Steig, William
Publisher: Farrar, Straus, and Giroux, 1971
Suggested Grade Level: K-2
Classification: Recreational and Motivational Materials
Literary Form: Picture book illustrated with watercolors
Theme: A good turn done is sometimes repaid at a future time.

About the Book

STUDENT OBJECTIVES:

1. Identify the largest sea and land animals.

2. Paraphrase and retell part of a story taken from this unit.

3. Plan a new adventure for Amos and Boris.

SYNOPSIS: This is a fable-related adventure of Amos, the mouse, who finds himself adrift on the sea and is befriended by Boris, the whale. Beautiful watercolor washes and ink drawings illustrate the sea adventures of a mouse and a whale.

ABOUT THE AUTHOR-ILLUSTRATOR: William Steig, November 14, 1907- .
William Steig was surrounded by art and artists when he was growing up. His mother and father, as well as his 3 brothers, were painters, and all the family members were involved in the field of fine arts. His career has been illustrating for *The New Yorker* magazine for 30 years. He is a prolific illustrator who can draw left-handed at an incredible speed.

Robert Kraus, author and publishing associate of Windmill Books, introduced Steig to the writing and illustrating of children's books. At age 61, Steig published his first children's book, *Roland, the Minstrel Pig*.

Steig's books are finely crafted and illustrated. He says that it is difficult to be consistently precise in illustrating characters so that they are still wearing the same clothing and look the same from page to page. Steig feels that he finds freedom through the body movements and motions of his characters. They can be different from page to page. His books carry a message through the animal main characters. The animals dress, act, and have the same kinds of problems as humans. The anatomy of the animal bodies is correct and their facial expressions show real emotion. His use of animal characters is an example of personification.

Many of Steig's stories remind us of other classical works. *Amos and Boris* is a story of friendship akin to that of Aesop's *Lion and Mouse*. Abel, the marooned mouse on an island in *Abel's Island*, is reminiscent of *Treasure Island*, and Pinocchio is pictured in Steig's *Sylvester and the Magic Pebble*. In accepting the Caldecott Award for *Sylvester and the Magic Pebble* in 1970, Steig related that "it is very likely that Sylvester became a rock and then again a live donkey because I had once been so deeply impressed with Pinocchio's longing to have his spirit encased in flesh instead of wood."

Note the continual use of mice in his writing. We have an opportunity to meet Derek in the *Real Thief*, Abel through *Abel's Island*, and Amos in *Amos and Boris*.

Another interesting aspect of William Steig's art career, possibly relating to the influence of Carlo Collodi's *Pinocchio*, is his wood carving. He has enjoyed working in the medium of wood as a sculptor and has exhibited his work in art galleries.

SELECTED ADDITIONAL TITLES BY THE AUTHOR:

Bad Speller
Caleb and Kate
Doctor De Soto
Eye for Elephants
Gorky Rises
Rotten Island
Yellow and Pink

Using the Book

Suggested Approach to the Book

Model Lesson #1

- Present biographical material on William Steig to the class. Tell students that the story is a fantasy adventure. The story could not have happened, but this adventure story is a very good one because the animals have become like people through personification. It is a good example of a caring friendship between 2 characters. Read the story aloud and share the softly illustrated pages.

- Examine the end pages. They set the stage for the book. Ask students if they can imagine the sounds of the waves. The waves on the pages look like a pattern of rhythm. Play a tape recording of ocean sounds as you read the story.

- Stop reading the story when Boris is washed onto the sand. Brainstorm with the class solutions to the problem. What are the things that Amos, a small mouse, might do to help his old friend? Use this as an activity to support critical thinking skills. Complete the story after the class discussion.

Model Lesson #2

- Examine the pictures of Amos building his boat. Are there any other ways to build a boat? Brainstorm the technology of boat building today. Go to the media center and research ways to build boats.

Model Lesson #3

- Ask the following questions:

   1. Amos worked on his boat by day and studied navigation at night. Why did he need to study navigation?

2. What supplies did he pack on the boat? Why did Amos choose each item? Give reasons.
3. Why on the 6th of September, when Amos launched his boat, did he have to wait for high tide? Explain high and low tides in terms of science and the position of the moon in relation to the earth.
4. Can you think of reasons for attaching a small flag to the ship's mast?
5. Why did Amos name his boat the *Rodent*? Look up the meaning of the word in a classroom dictionary. Is the name appropriate? What are some other possible names for his boat? Explain your reasons for selecting the name.
6. What do you think it would be like to sail on a boat by yourself?
7. Look at the double-page pictures of the phosphorescent sea. How does the picture make you feel? Explain.
8. Describe how Amos fell into the water.
9. What happened to the *Rodent*?
10. Can mice swim?
11. What is a mammal? Name some mammals.
12. "Holy clam and cuddlefish!" said the whale. Explain this quote.
13. Why do some mammals live on land and others in the sea?
14. What is a whale sounding? What happened to Amos when Boris forgot about his passenger and sounded?
15. What did the 2 new friends do during the week it took to take Amos home?
16. What kinds of things did the 2 friends share?
17. What kinds of things could you talk about with a new friend?
18. Name the food from the sea that Amos ate. If you can secure some from a science materials supply house, put a sample of plankton into a jar and show it to the class.
19. What kind of food do we eat that is found in the ocean?
20. Reread the farewell scene. Is it possible that a mouse could help a whale or a lion? Think about the possibilities.
21. On a map find the Ivory Coast of Africa. That is where Boris swam after dropping Amos off at home.
22. Describe Hurricane Yetta and what happened to Boris.
23. How did the old friends feel in meeting again in a desperate situation?
24. How did Amos, the mouse, save the life of Boris, the whale?
25. Did they expect to meet again?

Model Lesson #4

- Art appreciation through picture books: Compare the art styles, color, and story text in

  McCloskey, Robert, *Bert Dow, Deep-Water Man*
  Steig, William, *Amos and Boris*

Library Media Center Connections

1. Plan a display on oceanography including study prints, books, sound filmstrips, and available specimens of sea life.

2. Use a microscope to examine sea life specimens.

3. If possible, examine a growing piece of seaweed or ocean kelp. Touch it, smell it, feel it, and imagine its place in the sea. Research the food potential of seaweed for human consumption.

4. Taste Japanese rice crackers flavored with seaweed. These are available in the food specialty or oriental sections of many grocery stores.

Instructional Materials Connections

National Geographic Wonders of Learning Kit, *Whales*

Theme Reading Connections: Whales

Anderson, J. I., *I Can Read about Whales*
Behrens, June, *Whalewatch!*; *Whales of the World*
Bunting, Eve, *Sea World Book of Whales*
Duvoisin, Roger, *Christmas Whale*
Hogan, Paula, *Whale*
King, Patricia, *Mable the Whale*
Lauber, Patricia, *Great Whales*
McGovern, Ann, *Little Whales*
Patent, Dorothy, *All about Whales*
Posell, Elsa, *Whales and Other Sea Mammals*
Ricciuti, Edward, *Catch a Whale by the Tale*
Roy, Ronald, *Thousand Pails of Water*
Sabin, Francene, *Whales and Dolphins*
Selsam, Millicent, *First Look at Whales*
Stein, R. C., *Story of the New England Whalers*
Watanabe, Yuichi, *Wally the Whale Who Loved Balloons*
Whale Museum, *Gentle Giants of the Sea*

Activities to Connect Literature and Curriculum

ART

Create an oceanography mural. Cut and paste various fish forms onto a blue butcher paper background. Using rainbow paint colors, complete the mural with the addition of rocks, coral, and sea plants. Place a whale on the ocean and add Amos to the scene.

Design sea-going vessels and add them to the mural. Stress design and the ocean-going fitness of the vessel.

HEALTH

Amos exercised on the whale's back. What is the value of exercise? Design an exercise program for Amos.

LANGUAGE ARTS

Examine the list of things that Amos took with him on his trip. What other objects might he have added? Write a list of necessary food, equipment, and supplies that you think are important.

Revise the list and select materials that you think would be necessary if the trip were going to be made in a 1-man atomic energy powered vessel in the year 2000.
Pretend you are Amos and write a thank-you note to Boris for delivering you home.
As a class, write another short adventure tale for Amos and Boris.

MUSIC

Rewrite the words to the song "Row, Row, Row Your Boat" to include words about Amos and Boris.
Listen to recorded whale sounds.

SOCIAL STUDIES

Find out about work activities that elephants can perform. List them on a chart. Remember some of the activities that elephants did when you read the *Story of Babar*.

Beyond the Book

Guided Reading Connections across a Curriculum Rainbow: Oceanography

Amery, H., *Seaside*
Asch, Frank, *Sand Cake*
Blance, Ellen, *Monster Goes to the Beach*
Bond, Michael, *Paddington at the Seaside*
Bowden, Joan, *Why the Tides Ebb and Flow*
Burningham, Shirley, *Come Away from the Water, Shirley*
Davidson, Amanda, *Teddy at the Seashore*
Field, Eugene, *Wynken, Blynken and Nod*
Haas, Irene, *Maggie B*
Kimura, Yasuko, *Fergus and the Sea Monster*
Kraus, Robert, *Herman the Helper*
Mitgutsch, Ali, *From Sea to Salt*
Oxenbury, Helen, *Beach Day*
Peet, Bill, *Kermit the Hermit*
Schulz, Charles, *Snoopy's Fact and Fun Book about Seashores*
Sea World, *Sea World Alphabet Book* (alphabet)
Selsam, Millicent, *First Look at Sea Shells*
Sipiera, Paul, *I Can Be an Oceanographer*
Thompson, Brenda, *Under the Sea*

Enriching Connections

FOR GIFTED STUDENTS

Design a flag for Amos's boat.

Research the international flags flown on vessels. Make a colored chart of them and explain what each flag's message is to seamen.

When is it important to quarantine a vessel and its passengers?

FOR PARENTS

Discuss with your child some of the values of friendship.

Add an aquarium to your home. Learn about the care and feeding of its residents.

Visit the ocean or a sea aquarium, if possible.

* * * * * * * * * * *

Of Bear Friends

CORDUROY

Author: Freeman, Don
Illustrator: Freeman, Don
Publisher: Viking, 1968
Suggested Grade Level: K-2
Classification: Core Materials
Literary Form: Picture book
Theme: Love at first sight—even when a button is missing.

About the Book

STUDENT OBJECTIVES:

1. Describe a special toy.

2. Compare the plots of several bear theme stories.

3. Choose a favorite story from several selections.

SYNOPSIS: A delightful little bear waits in the department store toy section for just the right owner to come and take him home. A warm story of the love of a child for a department store bear. The theme of friendship is woven into the story.

ABOUT THE AUTHOR-ILLUSTRATOR: Don Freeman, August 11, 1908-1978.
　　Don Freeman was interested in music and spent his early years playing one-night stands across the country from California to New York. In New York he fell in love with the theater and began to sketch scenes from plays for *The New Yorker* and the *New York Herald* newspaper. Art became a serious pursuit—he was sketching someone on the subway and left the train without his instrument! He had to sell his art to live on from then on, as he never found his instrument. He loved New York City and always found a perfect living place in the city. As he related, he and his wife and child once lived on Columbus Circle. His apartment was removed from under him and what had been the apartment address is now the New York Coliseum. This experience provided the story line for *Fly High, Fly Low*, the story of 2 pigeons who have their lamp post home removed.

SELECTED ADDITIONAL TITLES BY THE ILLUSTRATOR:

Beady Bear
Bearymore
Come Again, Pelican
Dandelion
Guard Mouse
Inspector Peckit
Mop Top
Pocket for Corduroy
Rainbow of My Own
Space Witch
Tilly Witch

Using the Book

Suggested Approach to the Book

Model Lesson #1

- Introduce Don Freeman and *Corduroy*. Tell students that they are going to be reading a series of bear stories and that this is a special one about love and friendship.

- Read the story and share the delightful illustrations with the class. Ask if any of their favorite toys are missing parts or are damaged.

- Explain why Corduroy had such a hard time pulling the mattress button off. Ask if they remember any other stories in which the main character tries to find his missing button— Frog from the *Frog and Toad* series lost a jacket button.

- Do department stores have night watchmen today? How has modern technology changed that occupation?

Model Lesson #2

- Art appreciation through picture books: Compare art media, bear body forms, and story text in

    Freeman, Don, *Beady Bear* (illustrations are in black ink)
    Freeman, Don, *Corduroy*

- Black ink illustrations are also found in Judith Viorst's *Alexander and the Horrible, No Good, Very Bad Day.*

Library Media Center Connections

1. Read a Don Freeman story selection for story hour.

2. Invite students to bring their bears for a "Teddy Bear Day" in the media center.

3. Research the 7 varieties of bears in the world, including big brown bears, American black bears, Asiatic black bears, polar bears, sun bears, sloth bears, and spectacled bears. As a class project, assign the drawing of 1 bear species to each student. Cut the pictures out and use them to form a bear collage.

4. Bears may also be classified by size, and pictures cut out of black paper and displayed as silhouette art.

Special note: A beginning research book, *How Many Bones in a Bear*, by Suzanne Horn, is available from Book Lures.

Theme Reading Connections: Bears

Barrett, John, *Bear Who Slept through Christmas*
Bucknall, Carolyn, *One Bear All Alone* (counting)
Bunting, Eve, *Valentine Bears*
Carle, Eric, *Robber and Honeybee* (pop-up book)
Cauley, Lorinda, *Goldilocks and the Three Bears*
Dalgliesh, Alice, *Bears on Hemlock Mountain*
Fatio, Louise, *Happy Lion and the Bear*
Galdone, Paul, *Three Bears*
Gantschev, Ivan, *Rump Rump*
Hoff, Syd, *Grizzwold*
Kraus, Robert, *Milton the Early Riser*
Peet, Bill, *Big Bad Bruce*
Steiner, George, *Bear Who Wanted to Be a Bear*
Ward, Lynd, *Biggest Bear*
Wildsmith, Brian, *Bear's Adventure*

Activities to Connect Literature and Curriculum

ART

Make paper bag puppets. Attach bear's face and mouth to bottom section of bag.
Create a new flag for the state of California using the bear as the state symbol.

CITIZENSHIP

Give "Beary Good Citizenship" ribbons for good classroom behavior.

LANGUAGE ARTS

Construct an "ABC Book of Bears."
Write a new bear story about Corduroy. Have him go to the New York Coliseum to visit the location of his creator's former home.
Write a letter asking Corduroy and his Lisa to come to a bear snack party. Illustrate it with a rainbow.

NUTRITION

Plan a bear snack party. Use math measurement skills to mix the dough for roll-out cookies. Use a bear cutout mold. Plan this activity to coincide with the media center display of bears. Invite the bears to the party.

SCIENCE

As a class, identify and label on a world map the homes of the 7 varieties of bears.

SOCIAL STUDIES

Explain that the symbol of the United States is the eagle. The Soviet Union has the bear as its symbol. Can you find out why?

Beyond the Book

Guided Reading Connections across a Curriculum Rainbow: Toys

Gackenback, Dick, *Poppy the Panda*
Hoban, Lillian, *Arthur's Honey Bear*
Lerner, Mark, *Careers in Toy Making*
Matthiesen, Thomas, *Child's Book of Everyday Things*
Politi, Leo, *Mr. Fong's Toy Shop*
Spier, Peter, *Toy Shop*

Enriching Connections

FOR GIFTED STUDENTS

Design a new teddy bear sewing pattern. Use permanent crayon markers on muslin fabric to outline the form and complete the features and clothing. Saddle stitch the 2 outline pieces together after filling with soft washable polyfill. Use as a special bed pillow.

FOR PARENTS

Make up a bedtime story together centered around your child's favorite toy. To encourage oral language development, ask your child to retell the story later in the week at bedtime.

WINNIE-THE-POOH

Author: Milne, A. A.
Illustrator: Shepard, Ernest H.
Publisher: Dutton, 1926
Suggested Grade Level: K-4
Classification: Core Materials
Literary Form: Picture book illustrated with ink drawings
Theme: The adventures of a British bear named Winnie-the-Pooh are fun and many.

About the Book

STUDENT OBJECTIVES:

1. Compare *Winnie-the-Pooh* and *Corduroy* bear stories.

2. Develop a new adventure when Winnie-the-Pooh hears a news report about the bear napping of Corduroy from owner, Lisa, while she is visiting England.

3. Make a list of other theme bear stories and the main characters of each.

SYNOPSIS: A collection of bear stories starring Pooh and his friend, Christopher Robin. This is a book from a habit-forming series about a poetic bear of "little brain" who is delightful.

ABOUT THE AUTHOR AND ILLUSTRATOR: A. A. Milne, January 18, 1882-1956.
Ernest H. Shepard, December 10, 1879-1976.
A. A. Milne was an assistant editor of the British humor magazine, *Punch*, when he began to write children's books. The main characters were named for his own son, Christopher Robin, and the bear he received on his first birthday—Pooh. Milne stresses that the child Christopher Robin is a study of his own childhood joys and those other joys that he believes should be a part of childhood, not a composite portrait of his son. In fact, he quit writing the Christopher Robin series because people were coming to view his child as if he were the imaginary Christopher Robin. Milne vowed not to write any more of those stories until he was a grandfather in order to protect the privacy of his child.

Story characters include that darling bear, Pooh, "the one of little brain"; Piglet, who is petite and wants to be important; Eeyore, the donkey, who doesn't believe he is very popular; and Rabbit, who wants to be a leader. Unifying the whole group is that young adult figure, Christopher Robin, who always seems to arrive at the right time to make matters right. "The author considered himself their biographer rather than creator. 'I described them rather than invented them. Only Rabbit and Owl were my own unaided work.' The boy and his friends lived in the woods which closely resembled the area around Cotchford Farm, Surrey, to which the Milnes had moved in 1925."*

Ernest Shepard also worked for *Punch* as an illustrator. Shepard's illustrations reflect the beauty of English villages and countrysides, and the words of Milne's own poetic talent

---

*John C. Stott, *Children's Literature from A to Z* (New York: McGraw-Hill, 1984).

are in perfect balance with these. The text and pictures are inseparable. Shepard also did the well-known illustrations for Kenneth Grahame's *Wind in the Willows* in 1931. When shown the original sketches for the book, Grahame said, "I'm glad you've made them real." Milne also wrote a play, *Toad at Toad Hall*, based on Grahame's *Wind in the Willows*.

SELECTED ADDITIONAL TITLES BY THE AUTHOR AND ILLUSTRATOR:

Christopher Robin Book of Verse
Christopher Robin Story Book
House at Pooh Corner
Now We Are Six
Pooh Song Book
Pooh Story Book
Pooh's Birthday Book
When We Were Very Young
World of Christopher Robin
World of Pooh

BOOKS BY VIRGINIA H. ELLISON INSPIRED BY THE POOH BOOKS:

Pooh Cook Book
Pooh Get Well Book
Pooh Party Book

Using the Book

Suggested Approach to the Book

Model Lesson #1

- Relate the background of the author, A. A. Milne, and explain that the Pooh and Christopher Robin books have remained popular. The original versions were illustrated in black ink, and today several new versions have been published that have been enhanced by the addition of color, probably by a computer. Also explain that several new books have been published about Pooh and that the illustrations are "after the style of Ernest H. Shepard." The art is not the original work of E. H. Shepard, but drawn by another artist to look like his illustrations.

- Share copies of the following books with the class:

    House at Pooh Corner
    Winnie-the-Pooh (pop-up books)

Model Lesson #2

- Read selections from *Winnie-the-Pooh*.

- Explain that Pooh was the name of a favorite swan of Christopher Robin and that Winnie was a special polar bear in the London Zoo.

Model Lesson #3

- Secure a copy of *Pooh Sketchbook* and show students copies of the Shepard drawings that have been given to the Victoria and Albert Museum in London. The drawings were created between 1924 and 1928 and showcase the genius of Shepard. Accompanying quotes are included with the sketches.

Model Lesson #4

- Art appreciation through picture books: Compare the 2 distinct styles of illustrators of bear books in the United States and in England.

  Freeman, Don, *Pocket for Corduroy*
  Milne, A. A., *Pooh Story Book*

Library Media Center Connections

1. Read a Milne book for story hour.

2. Draw very large, simple teddy bears, color them, mount them on construction paper, and display.

3. Using the web/cluster technique, list all the bear books that are in the card catalog. Classify the book titles into imaginary and information book categories through webbing. Add films, study prints, and other materials to the web. When the lesson is complete, send the web and materials back to the classroom for a student interest center.

Theme Reading Connections: Other English Teddy Bears

Bestall, Alfred, *Rupert* Series
Bond, Michael, *Bear Called Paddington*; *Paddington at the Circus*

Activities to Connect Literature and Curriculum

ART

Draw large teddy bear shapes on construction paper, using 1 bright-colored ABC object and the corresponding alphabet letter to complement the bear design. Mount the illustration on construction paper, laminate, cut like a puzzle, place in an envelope, and exchange puzzles among students.

Make teddy bear place mats for a teddy bear picnic. Laminate and save for home use after the picnic.

CITIZENSHIP

Drop marbles into a classroom honey jar as a reward for positive classroom behavior. Promise a teddy bear picnic when the honey jar is full of marbles.

LANGUAGE ARTS

Key vocabulary words for clustering and writing:

Pooh	grandfather
buzz	Christopher Robin
Piglet	North Pole
forest	bees
Eeyore	good-bye

For a writing exercise use the story starter, "On the Day I First Met Pooh...."

Design and write an invitation to parents to join you at school for a special teddy bear picnic on the lawn. Suggest that they bring blankets to sit on. Younger brothers and sisters should be invited to school that day also. This type of program presents a positive image of the teacher and the school.

Plan a special program presentation. Poetry selections from *Winnie-the-Pooh* may be recited. Encourage students to write and present original poetry selections. Role-play a special selection from 1 of the bear theme stories read in class.

March in a class parade to the picnic site, singing the "Teddy Bear Picnic" song. A record of the music accompanies some editions of the book.

NUTRITION

Ask food services in your school district to plan with you and prepare a special picnic basket lunch that day. A sample menu would include

Piglet in bun
Kanga and Roo fruit salad
Rabbit carrot sticks
Eeyore milk
Pooh and Owl cookies

SOCIAL STUDIES

As a class project, draw a map of the planned teddy bear picnic route and post it on a large bulletin board. This is an introduction to pictorial graphic maps. Include a legend. Relate the lesson to the map on the end pages of *Winnie-the-Pooh*.

Beyond the Book

Guided Reading Connections across a Curriculum Rainbow: Living Bears

Graham, Ada, *Bears in the Wild*
Johnston, Jenny, *Polar Cub Grows up in the Zoo*
May, Julian, *Glacier Grizzly*
Patent, Dorothy, *Bears of the World*
Rosenthal, Mark, *Bears*
Wildlife Education, *Polar Bears*

Enriching Connections

FOR GIFTED STUDENTS

Practice reading aloud a short adventure of Pooh and his friends. Show excitement for the story with your voice. Practice until the story sounds good. If you are comfortable with your presentation, try telling the story to someone.

Pretend that Pooh is your classroom partner. What kind of help would he need in school? Could you help him? Prepare an illustrated booklet to help Pooh learn about your school through pictures and words.

Help color a computer-printed banner for the teddy bear picnic.

FOR PARENTS

Ask your child to retell a story that has been read in class this week. Explain that you are the listener and he or she is the storyteller. Encourage the child to tell the story in a clear voice and with body movement.

IRA SLEEPS OVER

Author: Waber, Bernard
Illustrator: Waber, Bernard
Publisher: Houghton Mifflin, 1972
Suggested Grade Level: 1-3
Classification: Core Materials
Literary Form: Picture book drawn with felt-tipped markers
Theme: Sometimes it is hard to be grownup and give up childhood's comforting toys.

About the Book

STUDENT OBJECTIVES:

1. Predict if Ira will take his teddy bear with him when he spends the night with a friend.

2. Recommend a solution to the problem.

3. Justify the solution.

SYNOPSIS: Ira is invited to a friend's home for the night. Should he or shouldn't he take his teddy bear? A delightful story line and one that lends itself very well to critical thinking questions—Should he? Why? Will he? Why not?

ABOUT THE AUTHOR-ILLUSTRATOR: Bernard Waber, September 27, 1924- .

Bernard Waber is another example of the theory that you don't have to be rich to be an illustrator. He remembers growing up in Philadelphia during the depression and worrying about the inevitable moves when another business failure would confront his family. He always worried that the new neighborhood would not have a public library and a movie house!

Waber started out early copying movie star photographs. He later discovered in art school that if he drew a comic twist or two to his work, he received compliments. He worked in New York as a graphic artist for both *Life* and *Seventeen* magazines. His decision to be a children's illustrator was reached through the enjoyment of reading books aloud to his children. In fact, his children asked him "Daddy, why don't you look at the grown-ups' books?" It wasn't easy to explain a father squeezed into a junior-sized chair, happily absorbed in a picture book.

Waber favors felt-tipped pens and Magic Markers™ for his work because of their instant drying characteristics. He likes to work at his art while riding the Manhattan train to work every day. Waber has absorbed the spirit of New York, and uses it to spread a creative art color wash of city scenes over his books. Special areas of the city that he has included are the East Side, in *House on East 88th Street* and the Fulton Fish Market area in *Rich Cat, Poor Cat*.

SELECTED ADDITIONAL TITLES BY THE AUTHOR-ILLUSTRATOR:

Anteater Named Arthur
Bernard
How to Go about Laying an Egg
I Was All Thumbs
Just Like Abraham Lincoln
Lorenzo
Lovable Lyle
Lyle and the Birthday Party
Lyle Finds His Mother
Lyle, Lyle Crocodile
Mice on My Mind
Nobody Is Perfick
Rich Cat, Poor Cat
Snake
You're a Little Kid with a Big Heart

Using the Book

Suggested Approach to the Book

Model Lesson #1

- Talk about the author-illustrator, Bernard Waber. Why do you suppose he wanted to be near a library and a movie house in his new neighborhood? Why did he spend his time copying movie star photographs? Ask how many students' parents read aloud to them. How many like to hear stories? How many would rather watch television? Play? Record these answers on a chart and graph the results on Number Blox chart paper.

Model Lesson #2

- Read *Ira Sleeps Over* aloud to the class. As the story progresses, let them respond to the questions below. Allow time in class to role-play Ira and his family's roles as well as his friend Reggie's role.

- Some critical thinking questions.
    1. Should he take his teddy bear? Why? Why not?
    2. Would you take your teddy bear? Why? Why not?
    3. Why are teddy bears important to children?
    4. Describe your favorite toy.

Model Lesson #3

- Art appreciation through picture books: Compare the art technique, colors, and story of the following:

    Waber, Bernard, *Ira Sleeps Over*
    Winthrop, Elizabeth, *Tough Eddie*

Library Media Center Connections

1. For story hour read a Lyle series book.

2. Imagine that the publisher has requested sample end pages for *Ira Sleeps Over*. Create the artwork and hold an art gallery showing of the end papers. Use felt-tipped markers, which Bernard Waber uses.

3. Award prize ribbons for the best end papers. Using glue, tip-in the end papers to the actual book copies of *Ira Sleeps Over*. An extension of this activity is to ask students to design end papers for a favorite book title and glue their examples into the media center book that they selected to illustrate. All art should be signed and dated by the student.

Instructional Materials Connections

National Geographic Wonders of Learning Kit, *Reptiles and How They Grow*

Theme Reading Connections: Alligators and Crocodiles

Aliki, *Keep Your Mouth Closed, Dear*; *Use Your Head, Dear*
Aruego, Jose, *Crocodile's Tale*
Dahl, Roald, *Enormous Crocodile*
De Groat, Diane, *Alligator's Toothache*
Duvoisin, Roger, *Crocodile in the Tree*
Gross, Ruth, *Alligators and Other Crocodilians*
Hurd, Elizabeth Thacher, *Mama Don't Allow*
Knight, David, *I Can Read about Alligators and Crocodiles*

Lauber, Patricia, *Who Needs Alligators?*
Lexau, Joan, *Crocodile and Hen*
Lionni, Leo, *Cornelius*
Matthews, Louise, *Gator Pie*
Mayer, Marianna, *Alley Oop!*
Mayer, Mercer, *There's an Alligator under My Bed*
Minarick, Else, *No Fighting! No Biting!*
Schubert, Ingrid, *There's a Crocodile under My Bed*
Sendak, Maurice, *Alligators All Around*
Stevenson, James, *Monty*

Activities to Connect Literature and Curriculum

ART

Using the paper folding and cutting technique, make gator paper dolls.

As a class project, make a giant alligator using papier-mâché and make it the class mascot. Don't forget to select an appropriate name for it.

Make felt alligator bookmarks.

LANGUAGE ARTS

Emphasize the reading program. Make a construction paper copy of the alligator mascot. Attach it to the wall as an interest center. As students finish the book reading assignment, add colored-paper alligator eggs for each book read.

Write gator theme stories in booklets with alligator-shaped covers.

As a special writing assignment topic, write from the viewpoint of the alligator under the bed and use the story starter, "From under the Bed I Can See...."

Using the same starter, "From under the Bed I Can See ... ," create an ABC book using examples like "Alligator Tails."

MATH

Introduce basic fractions through alligator pies. Make large green cardboard circles and divide them like puzzle pieces into halves, thirds, and fourths for alligator dessert.

NUTRITION

Make alligator pies. Use the lemon pie recipe on the Eagle Brand™ condensed milk can. Add a few drops of green food coloring. It is easier to make the pie recipe doubled in a rectangular baking dish. Cut the pie into small squares, as it is very rich. Also, it is easier to slice if made in the morning, cooled to room temperature after baking, refrigerated, and served at recess snack time.

Integrate math measurements into the cooking lesson.

SOCIAL STUDIES

Research the differences between alligators and crocodiles. Write a 1-page report and illustrate it with pictures of both reptiles.

Beyond the Book

Guided Reading Connections across a Curriculum Rainbow: Sleep

Andersen, Hans C., *Princess and the Pea*
Boynton, Sandra, *Good Night, Good Night*
Bright, Robert, *Me and the Bears*
Brown, Margaret Wise, *Sleepy ABC* (alphabet)
Carrick, Carol, *Sleep Out*
Hazen, Barbara, *Where Do Bears Sleep?*
Lucas, Barbara, *Sleeping Over*
Murphy, Jill, *Peace at Last*
Peterson, Jeanne, *When the Moon Shines Bright: A Bedtime Chant*
Selsam, Millicent, *How Animals Sleep*
Zolotow, Charlotte, *Sleepy Book*

Enriching Connections

FOR GIFTED STUDENTS

Write a short story about a bear who is captain of the good ship, *Sleepy Time*.
Design a ship and a ship's flag for *Sleepy Time*. Attach your adventure story to this cutout artwork.

FOR PARENTS

Talk about your favorite childhood toy. Tell when, from whom, and how you received it. Do you still have it to share with your child? Tell your child about the construction and design of toys when you were young.

Go to the library, if possible, and find a book that you remember being read to you. Check it out and take it home to read aloud. Ask your child's opinion of it compared to the stories of today. Define a classic as a book which is enjoyed by many generations of children. For example, the *Velveteen Rabbit* was first published in 1922 and is still enjoyed today. Ask your child to name some books likely to become classics.

*   *   *   *   *   *   *   *   *   *   *

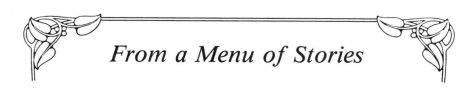

From a Menu of Stories

STORY OF JOHNNY APPLESEED

Author: Aliki
Illustrator: Aliki
Publisher: Prentice-Hall, 1963
Suggested Grade Level: 2-4
Classification: Core Materials
Literary Form: Picture book
Theme: A legendary man, Johnny Appleseed, left his imprint on the countryside as he planted apple seeds.

About the Book

STUDENT OBJECTIVES:

1. Recognize the necessity to plant seeds so that trees will grow and produce fruit to eat in the future.

2. Classify fruit variety produced by mother tree.

3. Develop a plan to plant future apple orchards.

SYNOPSIS: Johnny Appleseed was an American naturalist who planted numerous apple trees across the United States. His lifestyle was different from other pioneers of the time. He did not carry a weapon to protect himself from animals or Indians. Appleseed wanted white men and Indians to be friends. The art form is typical of its publication date in that bright, double-paged, color spreads are alternated with single-color, double-paged illustrations.

ABOUT THE AUTHOR-ILLUSTRATOR: Aliki Brandenberg, September 3, 1929- .
    Note: All book titles are written and/or illustrated under her pen name—Aliki. Children's literature resource material is referenced to Aliki, not Brandenberg. Her unusual name is reflective of her Greek family heritage.
    Aliki began her illustrating career while in elementary school. To be exact, as a kindergartner she remembers drawing 2 family portraits—hers and the picture of Peter Rabbit's

family. The 2 pictures were displayed and from that time on she was involved in her future career—art. She attended the Philadelphia Museum College of Art. After graduation, Aliki worked for the J. C. Penney Company in the display department in both New York City and Philadelphia. Later Aliki also was involved in freelancing in advertising and display art, painting murals, designing greeting cards, and teaching art and ceramics. After marrying Franz Brandenberg, they lived in Switzerland. At that time she visited the home of the legendary hero, William Tell. He became the subject of her first book, *The Story of William Tell*, published in 1960. Aliki has written and illustrated about 15 books of her own in addition to providing the illustrations for an additional 25 books written by other authors.

SELECTED ADDITIONAL TITLES BY THE AUTHOR-ILLUSTRATOR:

Corn Is Maize
Dinosaurs Are Different
Eggs
How a Book Is Made
Hush Little Baby
Keep Your Mouth Closed, Dear
My Five Senses
My Visit to the Dinosaurs
Three Gold Pieces
Weed Is a Flower—The Life of George Washington Carver
Wild and Woolly Mammoths

SELECTED ADDITIONAL TITLES BY THE ILLUSTRATOR:

Aunt Nina and Her Nephews and Nieces
Go Tell Aunt Rhody
I Once Knew a Man
Oh, Lord, I Wish I Was a Buzzard
One Day It Rained Cats and Dogs
This Is the House Where Jack Lives

Using the Book

Suggested Approach to the Book

Model Lesson #1

- Introduce the author-illustrator as an experienced artist who has illustrated a large number of books.

- Explain that Aliki has both written and illustrated her own books as well as illustrated books for her husband, Franz Brandenberg, and other writers.

- Select several books illustrated by Aliki and see if their style and color are identifiable as Aliki books in the same way that Robert McCloskey books are easily identified because of his illustration style.

Model Lesson #2

- Read the *Story of Johnny Appleseed* to the class.

- Show how the book is illustrated in 1-color and 4-color alternating, double-paged spreads.

- Compare this style with the monochromatic, sepia illustrations of McCloskey's *Make Way for Ducklings*. Can single-color illustrations in books be as effective as 4-color illustrations? Why or why not?

Model Lesson #3

- Some questions to explore with the class.

    1. Tell what kind of book you think this is going to be when you read the beginning, "Many years ago...."
    2. Why was Massachusetts the frontier in Johnny Appleseed's time?
    3. What were the roads like at the time of the story?
    4. Describe a covered wagon.
    5. People today frequently wear backpacks. What do you think they carry in them? What did Johnny Appleseed's pack contain?
    6. What kind of hat did he wear? Would you wear a hat like that today?
    7. Where did he sleep at night? When might you sleep outdoors?
    8. Tell about his meeting the bear family.
    9. Why were the Indians friendly to Johnny Appleseed?
    10. One year Johnny was afraid that all his trees would die. Tell what happened then.
    11. Can you learn the real name of Johnny Appleseed? The library media center can help you research the information.

Model Lesson #4

- Art appreciation through picture books: Compare the art style, color, drawing form, and kinds of information presented by Aliki with

    Gibbons, Gail, *Seasons of Arnold's Apple Tree*

Library Media Center Connections

1. Select and display books from the media collection on growing fruits.

2. Choose a number of different seasonal fruits and remove the seeds from each. Display the seeds in letter-marked containers. Ask students to identify each container. If the seed is not easily identified, have available reference books for students to use in locating correct answers. Seeds used in the lesson may include those from oranges, apples, pears, pomegranates, mangoes, peaches, plums, watermelons, honeydew melons and any other seeds available.

3. Use available media center reference books to find out about fruit and vegetable seeds. List and classify the seeds according to size ranging from the smallest to the largest.

Instructional Materials Connections

CHECpoint Systems, Inc., *Language Development Story Boards*
National Geographic Wonders of Learning Kit, *A Tree through the Seasons*
National Geographic Wonders of Learning Kit, *What Is a Seed?*

Theme Reading Connections: Apples and Fruit Trees

Barrett, Judi, *An Apple a Day*
Blocksma, Mary, *Apple Tree! Apple Tree!*
Brandenberg, Franz, *Fresh Cider and Apple Pie*
Bruna, Dick, *Apple*
Bulla, Clyde R., *Tree Is a Plant*
Cohen, Barbara, *Gooseberries to Oranges*
Greenaway, Kate, *A Apple Pie*
Hogrogian, Nonny, *Apples*
Kirkpatrick, Rena, *Look at Seeds and Weeds*; *Look at Trees*
McAffee, Sally, *My Orange Tree*
McMillan, Bruce, *Apples, How They Grow*
Mitgutsch, Ali, *From Seed to Pear*
Overbeck, Cynthia, *Fruit Book*
Pike, Norman, *Peach Tree*
Schnieper, Claudia, *Apple Tree through the Year*
Watson, Clyde, *Applebet* (alphabet)
Williams, Vera, *Cherries and Cherry Pits*

Activities to Connect Literature and Curriculum

ART

Make photograms using various kinds of fruit and their leaves.
Use apple halves and slices to create woodblock-like prints with tempera paints.
Dry apple slices and use for the faces of small puppets.
Draw an apple season tree. Divide art paper into 4 equal vertical sections. In each section, draw the shape of a dark brown tree trunk. Using the sponge art technique, dress the tree for 4 seasons—fall, orange colors and falling leaves; winter, white snow and leafless; spring, apple blossoms and spring green; and summer, fruit on the tree.

Plan a sketching lesson. Bring a bowl of apples and other fruit to the classroom. Present a simple lesson on form and encourage students to draw the still life composition. Mount on black construction paper and set up an art display of the class art.

Create a chronological order mural of the travels of Johnny Appleseed. Before beginning, list in order the places where he traveled on a piece of butcher paper or blackboard. This activity can be used to integrate cooperative learning. The places visited can be divided up, with 1 section of his travels assigned to each group for illustrating the mural. The group would be responsible for choosing how to illustrate its part of the class mural.

LANGUAGE ARTS

Write a story using the story starter, "What Happens to a Yellow Delicious Apple Lost in a Red Delicious Orchard?"

Pantomine parts of the *Story of Johnny Appleseed*.

Write a short version of the story and set it in the next century. Plan for the planting of apple trees in an outerspace station orchard. (*Note:* Disney World's EPCOT Center in Orlando, Florida, is already experimenting with simulated outerspace food growing processes. What does the acronym EPCOT stand for—Experimental Prototype City of Tomorrow.)

NUTRITION

Make several food items using apples. Choose from applesauce, baked apples, apple pie, applesauce cake, or apply brown betty.

Keep a total of the amount of money expended to purchase the necessary food items for each recipe. In math class, list the food items and the amount of money needed to purchase the ingredients and graph the cost of each cooking experience. Some groups may be able to compute the price of each food serving.

Discuss in class the number of calories of each food item. Explain that a calorie is a unit of energy. Talk also about the amount of exercise needed to use up the calories from the selected food item. Plan a short term class exercise program using this information.

SCIENCE

Label and illustrate a chart showing the different varieties of apples and their uses.

SOCIAL STUDIES

Could a modern day Johnny Appleseed story take place today? Explain your answer. What is a naturalist? Can you name a naturalist group today that is attempting to preserve the environment where you live? In your community are there any areas that have been set aside as parks?

Find out and report to the class about John Muir and the John Muir Trail. The University of California in San Diego has named a college in his honor, the John Muir College.

Beyond the Book

Guided Reading Connections across a Curriculum Rainbow: Biography

Aliki, *George and the Cherry Tree*
Aliki, *Many Lives of Benjamin Franklin*
Aliki, *Story of William Penn*
Aliki, *Weed Is a Flower*

Enriching Connections

FOR GIFTED STUDENTS

Go to the grocery store with a parent and make a list of the different kinds of apples and their price per pound. Are the prices the same or different for each variety of apple? Why?

Make a list of all the seasonal fruits that you would like to include in a family fruit salad. Ask permission to purchase the fruit and keep a record of how much each item cost. Add up the numbers for a total cost of the fruit purchased.

FOR PARENTS

Ask your child to retell the *Story of Johnny Appleseed* to you.

Are there any fruit orchards that you could visit? If not, locate the following information through books or an encyclopedia.

Try to learn how long it takes before the tree bears fruit.

How many years does the grower expect the tree to continue producing fruit?

What serious pests or diseases can cause the tree to die?

How much fruit does 1 tree produce?

What are some of the ways that the fruit is used?

POPCORN BOOK

Author: De Paola, Tomie
Illustrator: De Paola, Tomie
Publisher: Holiday House, 1978
Suggested Grade Level: K-3
Classification: Recreational and Motivational Materials
Literary Form: Picture book
Theme: Popcorn is good to eat and has existed for over 5,000 years.

About the Book

STUDENT OBJECTIVES:

1. Learn about a food that we eat today that existed when Christopher Columbus first saw the Indians wearing popcorn when he landed in the New World.

2. Classify the varieties of corn.

3. Recommend other uses for corn in the future.

SYNOPSIS: The *Popcorn Book* is a story within a story. Tony and Tiny, twin brothers, ask permission from their mother to pop corn. Tony gives directions for making popcorn while Tiny gives reference information about the history of popcorn. In the end they enjoy a treat of popcorn.

ABOUT THE AUTHOR-ILLUSTRATOR: Tomie De Paola, September 15, 1934- .

Tomie De Paola grew up in Meriden, Connecticut. From his comments, it was a good place to grow up. As a special convention speaker in 1987 at the American Association of School Librarians, Minneapolis, Minnesota, De Paola told about his love of books as a kindergarten student. He marched into class on the first day of school and told his teacher he was ready to read. (If he could read, he met the requirement for receiving a public library card in Meriden.) She explained that one did not learn to read until first grade. This information was upsetting to De Paola—he left school immediately, without permission, and went home to read a book to himself. He did get to apply for his library card shortly afterwards.

Of elementary school De Paola remembers, "Being an artist was easy. I just sat down and drew pictures—all over the place. By second grade, I was considered the 'best artist' by my teachers and classmates."* He also relates the story of the school librarian who traveled from school to school. He always wanted to help her load and unload books from her car. His thirst for books was unquenchable. The librarian recognized this need and set aside special books for him. His father would drive him once a week to the librarian's home to pick up his precious new books.

As a child he made special promises to himself, most of which he has kept. A few he didn't keep were to marry his babysitter or become a movie star. He did promise to always tell the truth to children. This he has done through the development of his many information books. It is a pleasure to hear De Paola speak because of his own special brands of truth and sincerity. For example, De Paola answers his student fan mail with a computer-generated form letter that includes a paragraph of personal input, and every letter is signed by him. When he was a child, he always tested the signature to see if it were real ink by wetting his finger to see if the ink would smear when he touched it. According to him, signatures must be signed in real ink.

Some of the information books that grew from his own life's experiences are *Nana Upstairs and Nana Downstairs*, *Watch out for the Chicken Feet in Your Soup*, *Oliver Button Is a Sissy*, and *Now One Foot, Now the Other*.

His art education includes a degree from Pratt Institute, New York City, and a master's degree awarded by California College of Arts and Crafts, Oakland, California. When he was graduated from college he was told by his professors that it was time for him to be "recognized." For 6 years he sought recognition by asking publishers to give him a contract to illustrate his first book. That struggle is past history, as De Paola has now illustrated over 100 books, of which 40 are titles he wrote himself. His writing falls into 3 distinct categories: retelling tales, information books, and those written about his childhood experiences.

In De Paola's work he must find the "inner eye" in order to see beyond the surface. This eye is the eye of imagination and is vital to his writing and illustrating. De Paola received the distinguished Caldecott Honor Medal for *Strega Nona* in 1975. The book was later adapted by him and presented as a play in the city of Minneapolis in 1987 as part of a special funding grant.

---

*Sally Holmes Holtze, ed., *Fifth Book of Junior Authors and Illustrators* (New York: H. W. Wilson, 1983).

SELECTED ADDITIONAL TITLES BY THE AUTHOR:

Big Anthony and the Magic Ring
Cloud Book
Clown of God: An Old Story
Fight the Night
Four Stories of Four Seasons
Legend of the Bluebonnet
Pancakes for Breakfast
Prince of the Dolomites
Quicksand Book
Strega Nona
Strega Nona's Magic Lessons

Using the Book

Suggested Approach to the Book

Model Lesson #1

- Present biographical material about Tomie De Paola to the class and explain that he cares very much about children and their stories because he had a very happy childhood, and that he has promised to continue writing and illustrating books for children to enjoy. Explain the word *prolific* and its relationship to the author-illustrator. De Paola has illustrated 100 books in his career. Some writers and illustrators need several years to produce and polish 1 work.

Model Lesson #2

- Read the *Popcorn Book* and share the illustrations with the class. Explain that this is an introduction to information books. Notice how Tomie De Paola presents information about the popcorn while the 1 brother is giving directions for making popcorn.

Model Lesson #3

- Some questions to discuss with the class:
    1. How is popcorn best stored? Why?
    2. Name the 3 types of corn.
    3. Who discovered popcorn? When?
    4. What was 1 of the first sights that Columbus saw in San Salvador?
    5. Tell about the finding of popcorn in a New Mexico bat cave.
    6. How old were the popcorn kernels in Peru? Could they still be popped?
    7. Explain how the Indians popped corn.
    8. What would you think of eating popcorn soup, as the Iroquois people did, or serving popcorn for breakfast with cream poured on it, as the colonists did?
    9. What is a popcorn "old maid?"
    10. How can you restore popcorn kernels that have been allowed to dry out?

Model Lesson #4

- Art appreciation through picture books: Compare the following books in terms of style, technique, and color of illustrations.

  De Paola, Tomie, *Cloud Book*
  Spier, Peter, *Peter Spier's Rain*

Library Media Center Connections

1. Use reference materials to discover information about popcorn. Ask the media center librarian to help you verify the fact presented by Tomie De Paola that 500,000,000 pounds of popcorn are eaten each year in the United States. Also try to learn if people in the Midwest still buy the most popcorn and whether Milwaukee and Minneapolis are the top popcorn consuming cities. Use both the *World Almanac* and *Information, Please Almanac* as resource guides to help you.

2. Compare another book on popcorn, David Woodside's *What Makes Popcorn Pop?* to the *Story of Popcorn.* How are they alike? Is there any additional or different information presented? Which book did you enjoy using the most?

Computer Connections

Developmental Learning Materials, *Comparison Kitchen*

Theme Reading Connections: Cooking

Better Homes and Gardens Editors, *Better Homes and Gardens Step-by-Step Kids'*
   Cookbook
Betty Crocker, *Betty Crocker's Cookbook for Boys and Girls*
De Brunhoff, Laurent, *Babar Learns to Cook*
Gibbons, Gail, *Too-Great Bread Bake Book*
Hoban, Lillian, *Arthur's Christmas Cookies*
Lindman, Maj, *Flicka, Ricka, Dicka Bake a Cake*
Tornborg, Pat, *Sesame Street Cookbook*

Activities to Connect Literature and Curriculum

ART

Use popcorn to create a winter landscape scene to illustrate the tall tale told about the summer heat. The heat was so severe that the corn roasted on the stalk and popped into the air, tricking the people into thinking it was winter instead of summer. The people put on their snow clothes and started shoveling popcorn.

HEALTH

To what food group does corn belong? Make a class chart and label the different kinds of corn available. Paste examples of corn on to the chart. List different ways corn may be used in cooking.

LANGUAGE ARTS

To encourage students to write humor, use the story starter, "I Woke up This Morning and It Was Snowing Pop Corn...."

Place a newspaper advertisement seeking to buy a popcorn farm. You will consider farms in outerspace, if the price is right.

Pop corn and bring a bowl to class. Give each student a piece. Assign a writing assignment of 1 paragraph to explain what popcorn is. Cluster words describing popcorn on the board as part of the activity.

Read selections of poetry from Lee Bennett Hopkins's *Munching: Poems about Eating.*

MATH

Estimate how many pieces of unpopped corn are in a 1-pound package. Graph both the estimate and actual amounts. Teach students that a method of estimation is to count the number of kernels in a half cup measure, then add or multiply the number of half cups in the pound by the number of kernels in the first cup.

Use a pint measuring container. Fill it with unpopped popcorn. Estimate how many pieces of popcorn it will hold. Fill the container with popped corn; the volume measurement will differ. Graph estimates and actual amounts that the container will hold.

Place a large square of butcher paper on the floor. Draw 3 lines an equal distance apart across the paper; draw 3 lines an equal distance apart down the paper. Tell students that you are going to pop corn with the container lid off. Predict how many pieces of corn will land in each section. Use a pen to record this information directly on the grid. Use a pen of a different color to record information about the actual number of pieces that landed on the squares when popcorn was popped. For this activity, establish safety rules before beginning the experiment.

An observation chart may also be developed.

1. How large is the seed?
2. What does it weigh?
3. Measure the kernel after popping and record the information.
4. What is the weight after popping?
5. What is the difference before and after popping?
6. Can you predict which kernels will be "old maids" by observation?

Beyond the Book

Guided Reading Connections across a Curriculum Rainbow: Algonkin and Iroquois Indians

Baker, Betty, *Little Runner of the Longhouse*
Bruchad, Joseph, *Iroquois Stories: Heroes and Heroines, Monsters and Magic*
Goller, Claudine, *Algonkians of the Eastern Woodlands*

Enriching Connections

FOR GIFTED STUDENTS

Pretend you are an explorer in the year 1612. Write a diary entry describing how the Iroquois Indians were first observed popping corn.

A popular food item today is gourmet popcorn. Invent several new flavors. Design a poster advertising the new flavors that you will feature in the store you own — the Popcorn Palace.

FOR PARENTS

Ask your child to tell you about the early discoveries of popcorn in the time of Christopher Columbus, in Peru, and in a bat cave in New Mexico.

Encourage your child to eat popcorn as a snack food instead of sweets.

Prepare popcorn as a family activity.

MAY I BRING A FRIEND?

Author: De Regniers, Beatrice Schenk
Illustrator: Montresor, Beni
Publisher: Atheneum, 1964
Suggested Grade Level: K-2
Classification: Core Materials
Literary Form: Picture book written in verse and with ink illustrations
Theme: We must be well mannered when we attend a party.

About the Book

STUDENT OBJECTIVES:

1. Dramatize *May I Bring a Friend?*

2. Generalize about which animals are compatible with each other in their natural environment.

3. Produce an area placement plan for animals in a zoo.

SYNOPSIS: We are invited to a week of parties. Not all the participants are on their best behavior. A fun book with good read-aloud verses.

ABOUT THE AUTHOR AND ILLUSTRATOR: Beatrice Schenk De Regniers, 1914- .
Beni Montresor, March 31, 1926- .

Beatrice Schenk De Regniers wrote her own biography within the framework of her bouncy *A Little House of My Own*. She is physically pictured as the little girl in the book who has a *Little House of My Own*. De Regniers is a very private person and wants children to have their marvelous private place in time. "I lived the first years of my life under the dining room table. Today it is hard for children. Now we have glass-topped dining room tables and no place to hide!" She tells us that if her book had not been published, she would have mimeographed it and put it on the back of cereal boxes. The message from the author to children is still clear.

Books are inside her and have to come out. She likes to think about her writing during the year and finalize the story on paper during her vacation time. Her favorite writing place is a quiet meadow, even if it is in the middle of Central Park. De Regniers is a New Yorker and loves art, music, and theater. *May I Bring a Friend?* won the Caldecott Award in 1965.

Beni Montresor grew up in Verona, Italy, and vividly remembers World War II. One morning he was sitting in his high school room and saw the enemy planes fly over the city. Moments later the bombs exploded and people were dead on the streets. He has never forgotten this picture of Verona.

His main work has been designing opera sets for the great opera houses of the world, including New York's Metropolitan and La Scala in Milan, Italy.

When asked to illustrate a children's book, he agreed. On thinking about it later, he had never owned a book as a child and the only Italian book for children he knew was *Pinocchio*! Since then Montresor has illustrated children's books, worked on movie sets as a costume designer for 30 movies, and continued his opera set designing. When you see his pictures, enjoy the fact that they are produced by a real knight! He was knighted by the Italian government in 1966 for his contributions to the fine arts.

SELECTED ADDITIONAL TITLES BY THE AUTHOR:

Bunch of Poems and Verses
It Does Not Say Meow
Laura's Story
Picture Book Theater: The Mysterious Stranger and the Magic Spell
Red Riding Hood
So Many Cats
This Big Cat and Other Cats I Have Known
Waiting for Mama

SELECTED TITLE WRITTEN WITH IRENE HAAS:

Little House of Your Own

SELECTED ADDITIONAL TITLES BY THE ILLUSTRATOR:

A Is for Angel
I Saw a Ship a-Sailing
Magic Flute
On Christmas Eve

Using the Book

Suggested Approach to the Book

Model Lesson #1

- Tell students about the author and illustrator. Explain that the animals in the story are not on their best behavior and that you are going to ask the class to name examples of poor manners. Read the story and enjoy the repetitive verse. Encourage students to participate in the story through oral language development.

Model Lesson #2

- List in sequence the animals who came to see the king and queen. Ask students if the animal drawings are representative of real animals and to share their feelings about the choice of colors used in the backgrounds. This is an opportunity to introduce the color wheel and the position of colors on it. Would another group of complementary colors work as well? Why?

Model Lesson #3

- Art appreciation through picture books: Compare the 2 parties and the manners of the guests in:

  De Regniers, Beatrice Schenk, *May I Bring a Friend?*
  Freeman, Don, *Dandelion*

Library Media Center Connections

1. Set up a display of circus zoo books from the media center collection. Include study prints, sound film strips, and other available materials.

2. What is the difference between a circus and a zoo? Explain.

3. Using materials from the media center display, make a list of all the circus and zoo animals pictured. Take this information back to class and integrate it into a math graphing lesson.

4. Divide the class into 2 study groups, 1 for zoo animals and 1 for circus animals. Assign each group to classify animals named in the zoo-circus animal lesson into the possible category of a zoo or circus animal. Next classify the animals by size. Illustrate them on a banner from the smallest to the largest animal.

Computer Connections

Unicorn Software, *Animal Kingdom*

Theme Reading Connections: Zoos

Amery, H., *What's Happening at the Zoo?*
Baskin, Leonard, *Hosie's Zoo*
Blance, Ellen, *Monster Goes to the Zoo*
Carle, Eric, *1, 2, 3, to the Zoo* (counting)
Carrick, Carol, *Patrick's Dinosaurs*
Fatio, Louise, *Happy Lion* Series
Grosvenor, Donna, *Zoo Babies*
Hoff, Syd, *Sammy the Seal*
Jacobsen, Karen, *Zoos*
Lobel, Arnold, *Holiday for Mr. Muster*
Rey, Hans, *Curious George Takes a Job*
Seuss, Dr., *If I Ran the Zoo*
Tester, Sylvia, *A Visit to the Zoo*

Activities to Connect Literature and Curriculum

ART

Create color wheels using primary, secondary, and complementary groups.
Do a watercolor wash on paper and draw animals in pen over the softly colored background.
Make a banner inviting guests to come to an animal festival.

LANGUAGE ARTS

Plan a program of poetry recitings and animal storytelling for a festival. Use *May I Bring a Friend?* as the theme and role-play the animal guests, who have now developed good manners. Use various sources of literature and ask the library media specialist to make suggestions of appropriate materials.

MATH

Graph the student responses from the media center lesson. List and record the animals named.
Poll students in another second grade class and compare their responses to the same lesson. Display the 2 graphs in the library media center.

NUTRITION

Plan a party menu to include appropriate natural snack foods like trail mix, fruit selections, and vegetables, including celery with peanut butter.

SCIENCE

Prepare a handout program for the animal festival and list both the student program and some class-researched information about zoo animals.

As a class project, if allowable, collect money through a second grade student art sale to adopt an animal at the local zoo. Visit the adopted animal as a class and learn about its care, feeding, habitat, and offspring from its keeper.

Design an ideal environment for a small zoo including 10 different animal species who will need a home. This could be presented as a large, student-produced bulletin board or as a folding panel display.

Name your zoo, and develop a flag and a logo.

Include a people cafe for visitors. Design a simple, original menu for the zoo cafe.

What kind of animal-related souvenir items would you like to sell in the gift shop?

What kind of special programs would you want to have for members of the "Animal Guild?" Work through this question in collaborative learning groups and report the best ideas.

Beyond the Book

Guided Reading Connections across a Curriculum Rainbow: Bad Behavior

Bemelmans, Ludwig, *Madeline and the Bad Hat*
Gantos, Jack, *Rotten Ralph*
Goodall, John, *Naughty Nancy*
Mayer, Mercer, *Applelard and Liverwurst*

Enriching Connections

FOR GIFTED STUDENTS

Plan and draw a seating chart for all the animals who were from the zoo in *May I Bring a Friend?* Who should sit next to each other, and who should not?

List the teatime food you would serve in order to meet the needs of all the animal guests. Illustrate the menu and make a copy of it for the tea table. Make place cards for each group of guests.

FOR PARENTS

Ask your child to list all the animals that might live in a zoo. Suppose the child is the director of the zoo and is in charge of the care and feeding of all the animals. What kinds of housing and food would each animal require? Brainstorm ideas.

*   *   *   *   *   *   *   *   *   *   *

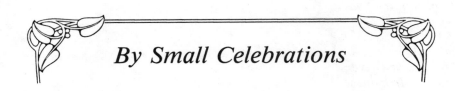

By Small Celebrations

GUNG HAY FAT CHOY

Author: Behrens, June
Photographs Compiled By: Behrens, Terry
Publisher: Children's Press, 1982
Suggested Grade Level: K-3
Classification: Core Materials
Literary Form: Nonfiction-information
Theme: Chinese New Year, an ancient rite celebrated today, is a time of good luck and happiness, feasting, family celebrations, and gift giving.

About the Book

STUDENT OBJECTIVES:

1. Describe the Chinese New Year celebration, Gung Hay Fat Choy.

2. Compare Gung Hay Fat Choy activities with traditional New Year's activities in the United States.

3. Explain the relationship of Gung Hay Fat Choy to a birthday party.

SYNOPSIS: *Gung Hay Fat Choy* is the story of a Chinese New Year celebration illustrated with colored photographs. The role of the good luck dragon is integrated into the information.

ABOUT THE AUTHOR: June Behrens, birthdate not available.
    June Behrens lives in Rancho Palos Verdes, a southern California suburb. For over 25 years she has written fiction and nonfiction books for students. She has written 60 books. Her wide-ranging expertise extends from a series of holiday books to 2 authoritative books on whales, *Whalewatch!* and *Whales of the World.*

SELECTED ADDITIONAL TITLES BY THE AUTHOR:

Can You Walk the Plank?
Feast of Thanksgiving

Fiesta!
Hanukkah
I Can Be a Truck Driver
I Can Be an Astronaut
Manners Book: What's Right, Ned?
Martin Luther King, Jr., the Story of a Dream
New Flag for a New Country
Powwow
Ronald Reagan: An All American
Sally Ride, Astronaut: An American First
Samoans!
Soo Ling Finds a Way
Who Am I?

Using the Book

Suggested Approach to the Book

Model Lesson #1

- Explain to students that they are going to learn about the Chinese New Year and the activities that are a part of it. June Behrens has written a photoessay book that will give an inside view of the John Yee family's celebration, including the lion's head parade.

Model Lesson #2

- Read *Gung Hay Fat Choy* to the class and show the photographs that accompany the story. Examine the cover. Why do you think there is a dragon's face? Look closely at the lettering. What does it say? There are New Year's greetings in 2 languages.

Model Lesson #3

- Some questions to discuss with the class:
    1. What are gongs and cymbals?
    2. How would you describe the dragon's head on page 6?
    3. Explain what Gung Hay Fat Choy means.
    4. Name 3 reasons to celebrate the Chinese New Year.
    5. Why do the Chinese add a year to their age on Chinese New Year even though it is not their birthday?
    6. Why is this "the grandest birthday party of all?"
    7. When is Gung Hay Fat Choy celebrated?
    8. What is different about the Chinese New Year calendar and those used by other people?
    9. List the names of the animals used in the Chinese zodiac. There are 12 zodiac signs.
    10. Why do they say that people born in a particular year will have the qualities of that animal?
    11. What things do the Chinese do to prepare for the New Year?
    12. Name a fruit that is the symbol of good luck.

13. What are the special colors of joy?
14. Why do children get to stay awake as long as they wish on New Year's Eve?
15. Explain *lai see*.
16. Why use firecrackers?
17. How do people act on the first day of the New Year?
18. How long may the celebration last?
19. What things might we see at a community carnival?
20. Tell about the lion dancers.

Model Lesson #4

- Art appreciation through picture books: Compare the following books in relationship to art, color, and text.

    Behrens, June, *Soo Ling Finds a Way*
    Lobel, Arnold, *Ming Lo Moves the Mountain*

Library Media Center Connections

1. Introduce reference keys to students. Design a key-shaped form with the following information on it.

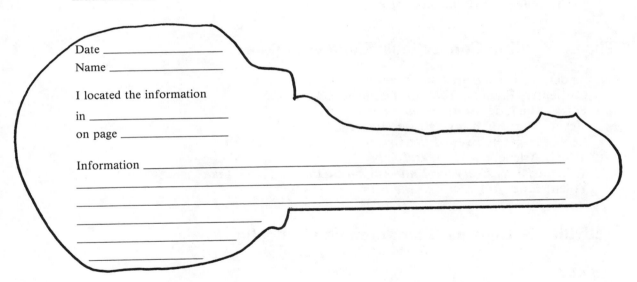

Date _____
Name _____
I located the information
in _____
on page _____
Information _____

Assign each student to fill out a reference key on a research topic from the following list. Start by using a dictionary:

abacus	fan	origami
China	fu dogs	pagoda
chop	getas	rice
chop suey	kimono	sampan
chopsticks	kite	yen
emperor	obi	

Each student should return to class with 1 reference key. Keys may be laminated and reused for other dictionary and encyclopedia work.

2. Make an illustrated chart in the shape of a circle of the Chinese zodiac calendar animals as follows:

Dragon — 1964, 1976, 1988, 2000
Serpent — 1965, 1977, 1989, 2001
Horse — 1966, 1978, 1990, 2002
Ram — 1955, 1967, 1979, 1991, 2003
Monkey — 1956, 1968, 1980, 1992, 2004
Rooster — 1957, 1969, 1981, 1993, 2005
Dog — 1958, 1970, 1982, 1994, 2006
Boar — 1959, 1971, 1983, 1995, 2007
Rat — 1960, 1972, 1984, 1996, 2008
Ox — 1961, 1973, 1985, 1997, 2009
Tiger — 1962, 1974, 1986, 1998, 2010
Rabbit — 1963, 1975, 1987, 1999, 2011

Ask each student to locate the year of his or her birth on the lunar calendar and design a modern day version of the zodiac animal pictured. A badge maker may be used to make individual student pins.

Theme Reading Connections: Chinese Folklore

Andersen, Hans Christian, *Nightingale*
Carpenter, Frances, *Tales of a Chinese Grandmother*
Flack, Marjorie, *Story about Ping*
Heyer, Marilee, *Weaving of a Dream*
Leaf, Margaret, *Eyes of the Dragon*
Mosel, Arlene, *Tikki Tikki Tembo*
Williams, Jay, *Everyone Knows What a Dragon Looks Like*
Yolen, Jane, *Emperor and the Kite*

Activities to Connect Literature and Curriculum

ART

Construct Chinese lanterns from cylindrical boxes (e.g., cereal, ice cream, salt). Remove the lid and cut rectangular or square openings out of the box to make lantern windows. Decorate tissue paper pieces with Chinese letters and designs. Glue tissue behind cut-out openings and add other decorations to the outside of the box.

In China the colors of red and orange are symbols of good luck. Make a colored, Happy New Year banner to hang at home with good luck letters and expressions.

Make paper bag dragon puppets:

Measure the bottom of a small, lunch-sized, brown bag.

Cut colored construction paper rectangles 2 inches larger than the bottom.

Design a dragon's face, color it, cut it out, and paste it to the bottom of the bag.

Design a *lai see*, a red money envelope.

Practice egg carton art by making dragons.

Use the bottom portion of an egg carton.

Cut the section into half lengthwise.

Cut off the first 2 sections.

Staple them to form the head and mouth of the dragon.

Cut 4 strips of green construction paper 2 inches by 11 inches.

Fold in half lengthwise and cut half circles, not cutting through the paper.

Unfold the strip and bend circle flaps up to represent scales.

Paste in overlapped strips across the egg carton to form the dragon's back.

Use fringed tissue paper to decorate underneath the dragon.

Add facial features as desired.

HEALTH

Discuss the pyramids of fruit served during the Chinese New Year. Name other foods that are included for this special time.

LANGUAGE ARTS

Write 2 Chinese New Year's greetings on red paper for your family or friends. Compare these greetings to the usual New Year's greeting cards.

The Chinese philosophy of life is that a Yin and a Yang exist. These are like balancing seesaws. They are opposites such as good and bad, sweet and sour, up and down. Make a list of all the opposites you can name. List them in 2 columns.

SOCIAL STUDIES

Show the film *I'm Going to Be the Lion's Head* to the class.

Plan a classroom dragon parade. Construct the head of papier mâché. Use old white sheets or brown butcher paper to design the dragon's body. Assemble musical instruments like drums, cymbals, and noise makers. Attach the head to the body and include the class in the dragon parade. Make music for the dragon march. If possible, coordinate this with Chinese New Year, which is between mid-January and mid-February each year, and parade through the school.

Add Chinese New Year to the school schedule of activities and share festival ideas, including the dragon parade, with other classes. Integrate this celebration with other ethnic holiday programs.

Beyond the Book

Guided Reading Connections across a Curriculum Rainbow: Chinese New Year

Cheng, Hou-Tien, *Chinese New Year*
Handforth, Thomas, *Mei Li*
Politi, Leo, *Moy, Moy*

Wallace, Ian, *Chin Chiang and the Dragon's Dance*
Young, Evely, *Tale of Tai*

Enriching Connections

FOR GIFTED STUDENTS

Write a story about the adventures of 2 Chinese pandas who are sent to a United States zoo to be placed on temporary display.

Make a list of all the books you can find in the library media center about dragons. Report orally on the story that interests you the most. Give a reason why you would recommend the book to someone else to read.

FOR PARENTS

Talk about your family's traditional New Year's activities and explain why these things are repeated each year. Ask your child which activities he or she would like to continue as an adult and why.

Plan a family outing to enjoy a meal at a Chinese restaurant. Try to eat with chopsticks. Explain that chopsticks are used instead of the knife and fork. Eating utensils have changed over the years. For interesting information about children's eating utensils in colonial times, go to the library and check out Ann McGovern's *If You Lived in Colonial Times.*

Purchase and assemble a Chinese kite or construct one of your own design. Go kite flying when the weather is appropriate.

SONG OF THE SWALLOWS

Author: Politi, Leo
Illustrator: Politi, Leo
Publisher: Charles Scribner's Sons, 1949
Suggested Grade Level: 1-5
Classification: Extended Materials
Literary Form: Picture book
Theme: The swallows will return to Mission San Juan Capistrano every year on March 19.

About the Book

STUDENT OBJECTIVES:

1. Describe a swallow.

2. Discover why the swallows return to the Mission every year on the same day.

3. Plan a fiesta.

SYNOPSIS: The story is of friendship between Julian, the old gardener and bell ringer at the Mission San Juan Capistrano, and Juan, a young school boy. One common link in the relationship is their love for the swallows who live at the Mission.

ABOUT THE AUTHOR-ILLUSTRATOR: Leo Politi, November 21, 1908- .

Leo Politi was born in Fresno, California, and spent his youth in Italy, where his parents had moved when he was 7. In Milan, Italy, Politi had the ideal art school environment. Opportunities were presented for him to sketch in the school gardens under the direction of a special teacher who found beauty in flowers, plants, trees, and animals in the school zoo.

When he returned to California as a young man in his twenties, he adopted as a place to work, study, and sell his sketches the small, quaint Mexican Olvera Street in Los Angeles. He loved it for all of its beauty, but feels today that it, like many other places, has become a place for tourists to visit.

He has very strong ties with several different cultural groups, as shown through his many picture books. Winning the Caldecott Medal in 1950 was an affirmation and assurance to him that he was doing the right kind of writing and illustrating for children.

Politi's creation of the *Song of the Swallows* resulted from a suggestion from his editor that he do a story about the Mission and its famous swallows. When he first visited the Mission, he learned that the old gardener and bell ringer for many years had recently died and was missed very much. Politi thought of all the school students who must have stopped and listened to the tale of the swallows and chose to write the story about the swallows and this old man.

Politi has illustrated several adult books recently, including a cookbook for the San Pedro (California) Public Library, *Around the World, Around Our Town, Recipes from San Pedro*, and 2 books illustrating California's own architectural style, *Bunker Hill Los Angeles* and *Redlands Impressions*.

SELECTED ADDITIONAL TITLES BY THE AUTHOR:

Boat for Peppe
Butterflies Come
Emmett
Juanita
Lito and the Clown
Little Leo
Mieko
Mission Bell
Moy, Moy
Mr. Fong's Toy Shop
Nicest Gift
Pedro, the Angel of Olvera Street
Rosa
St. Francis and the Animals

Using the Book

Suggested Approach to the Book

Model Lesson #1

- Tell children that this book is written and illustrated by a man who is very fond of California, the Golden State, and its early settlers, including the Mexican-American people. He likes sharing this Mission history with children across the United States as he feels that it is a very special story. Talk about your state's special name and what historical areas have been preserved that people can visit today.

Model Lesson #2

- Read the story aloud and share the softly colored pictures with the class. Plan to sing the "Mission Song" from *Song of the Swallows* with the class.

Model Lesson #3

- Questions to discuss with the students:
    1. Study the plan of the Mission. What is the Mission like?
    2. Who was Father Junipero Serra?
    3. Missions were described as "small villages." What kinds of things did the Indians do in the Missions?
    4. Why did a Mission need a barrack for soldiers?
    5. Describe the Mission gardens.
    6. Tell about the swallows who lived at the Mission.
    7. What did Juan do to get a better look at the baby birds in the nest?
    8. Where do the swallows go when they leave the Mission?
    9. What is a fiesta?
    10. What happens on March 19 every year at Mission San Juan Capistrano?

Model Lesson #4

- Art appreciation through picture books: Compare the style, color, and art presentation of

    Ets, Marie Hall, *Nine Days to Christmas*
    Politi, Leo, *Pedro, Angel of Olvera Street*

Library Media Center Connections

1. Select and share study prints and films of California missions with the class.

2. Show the class that *Pedro, Angel of Olvera Street*, is a book printed in both English and Spanish.

3. Talk about holiday celebrations such as fiestas, posadas, and other special days including legal holidays.

4. Plan a new holiday observation. What special event would you want to observe if you were in charge? Why? Announce the new holiday and plan for observation activities for the nation and for your home city. Would a new song be appropriate? What date would be set aside for the observation? Would a special person or group be honored? Would you want to issue a new postal stamp to commemorate the event? What special activities would you plan?

Theme Reading Connections: California

Carpenter, Allan, *California*
Edo, Terry, *Children's Yellow Pages: Orange County, 1986-87*
Fradin, Dennis, *California in Words and Pictures*
Ludwig and Bernal, *California Story and Coloring Book*
Raintree, *California*
Seablom, Seth H., *California Coloring Guide*

Activities to Connect Literature and Curriculum

ART

Illustrate a garden with trees, flowers, and water suitable for a swallow's home today.
Cut out pictures of birds from magazines and construct a class collage in the shape of a swallow.
Construct a cut-and-paste bulletin board mural of Mission San Juan Capistrano. Place it in the time of Father Serra.
Make swallow stick puppets.

LANGUAGE ARTS

Write a postcard to a friend and tell what you have learned about San Juan Capistrano. Draw a picture of the Mission on 1 side. Design a Mission stamp for your card.
Choose a Caldecott Medal or Honor book to read and make a report on it to your learning group. Select 1 person from your group to present a report to the class on a book.

MUSIC

Play Mexican cassette music tapes for the fiesta. Learn the "Mexican Hat Dance." Include a Mexican piñata for students to break. Students may construct individual piñatas during art class with the teacher's help.

NUTRITION

Plan a fiesta and serve a special lunch. Include tortillas on the menu and other Mexican food such as guacamole, Mexican rice, refried beans, and enchiladas. Ask for help from your school food services or from parents if you are not familiar with Mexican food preparation.
If the weather is cool, make and serve Mexican hot chocolate for a nutritious break.

SOCIAL STUDIES

Learn about the migratory route of the swallows to South America. Using desk maps, follow the travel route of the birds.

Pretend you are a radio or television announcer telling about the return of the swallows to Capistrano on March 19. Describe the waiting people and the colorful Mission in your announcement.

Draw an outline map of your state and include a picture of its official bird and flower. Mount the art on construction paper and display as an art project.

Beyond the Book

Guided Reading Connections across a Curriculum Rainbow: Parties

Asch, Frank, *Popcorn*
Blance, Ellen, *Monster Has a Party*
Cohen, Miriam, *Tough Jim*
De Paola, Tomie, *Popcorn Book*
Du Bois, William, *Bear Party*
Ets, Marie Hall, *Cow's Party*
Hutchins, Pat, *Surprise Party*
Zion, Gene, *Jeffie's Party*

Enriching Connections

FOR GIFTED STUDENTS

Research and report information about other birds that migrate. For the cover, draw pictures of the birds. Name the birds, describe their colors, tell how they build their nests, and tell about their babies and how they are fed.

FOR PARENTS

Take your child bird watching. Count the number of different bird species you "spot." Go to the library and check out a bird identification field guide. Identify the birds you saw on your walk and learn something about each one.

MR. RABBIT AND THE LOVELY PRESENT

Author: Zolotow, Charlotte
Illustrator: Sendak, Maurice
Publisher: Harper & Row, 1962
Suggested Grade Level: K-3
Classification: Core Materials
Literary Form: Picture book
Theme: Gifts to mothers are from the heart.

About the Book

STUDENT OBJECTIVES:

1. Classify objects by color.

2. Create a color collage of foods we eat.

3. Recommend additional ways to classify objects used in the color classification.

SYNOPSIS: A little girl seeks help from Mr. Rabbit in selecting the perfect birthday present. A rich conversation between 2 friends—Mr. Rabbit and the Little Girl—is recorded by the author.

ABOUT THE AUTHOR AND ILLUSTRATOR: Charlotte Zolotow, 1915- .
Maurice Sendak, June 10, 1928- .
Charlotte Zolotow did not study to be a teacher, but is interested in both education and reading. In the beginning of her career she worked as an editorial assistant for Harper's Publishing in the children's department. She had an opportunity to write her first book, *Park Book*, as a result of a memo she had written to her boss. She has written over 40 books in 24 years. These books are based on experiences with her 2 children, a son and a daughter. The *Storm Book* was written because of a visiting child's fear of a terrible, violent storm. She relates: "Writing came quite naturally to me. I can recall winning a silver pencil in grade three for a composition I wrote. Actually, all I could do was write," she laughs. "I couldn't add or subtract, nor could I remember names and dates!" *Mr. Rabbit and the Lovely Present* was named a Caldecott Medal Honor Book in 1963.
Biographical information on Maurice Sendak, illustrator, may be found in "Grade One," *Where the Wild Things Are.*

SELECTED ADDITIONAL TITLES BY THE AUTHOR:

Beautiful Christmas
Big Brother
Big Sister and Little Sister
Bunny Who Found Easter
But Not Billy

Hating Book
Hold My Hand
I Have a Horse of My Own
I Know a Lady
It's Not Fair
My Friend John
My Grandson Lew
New Friend
One Step, Two
Quarreling Book
Unfriendly Book
Wakeup and Good Night
When I Have a Little Girl
William's Doll

Using the Book

Suggested Approach to the Book

Model Lesson #1

- Present biographical material about Charlotte Zolotow and Maurice Sendak. Tell students that Charlotte Zolotow wrote the well-known story *William's Doll* and Maurice Sendak was the author-illustrator for another important children's book, *Where the Wild Things Are.*

- Read *Mr. Rabbit and the Lovely Present* to the class and share the fine illustrations.

Model Lesson #2

- Choose another Charlotte Zolotow book to read to the class.

Model Lesson #3

- Art appreciation through picture books: Compare the art technique, color, and story of

    Carle, Eric, *Secret Birthday Message*
    Flack, Marjorie, *Ask Mr. Bear*

Library Media Center Connections

1. Read a birthday story, such as

    Barrett, Judi, *Benjamin's 365 Birthday Hats*

2. Using media center materials, locate a listing of author's birthdays for this month.

3. Using the author birthday information, make a calendar for each month. Enter the birthday information on the appropriate date, add the birthdates of each class member,

the teacher, the principal, and favorite authors, and reproduce an illustrated calendar for each class member. This idea may be used as a schoolwide project listing each staff member's and student's birthday and selling the school calendar as a money-making project to purchase additional books to add to the library media center collection.

Theme Reading Connections: Birthdays

Asch, Frank, *Happy Birthday, Moon*
Averill, Esther, *Jenny's Birthday Book*
Brooke, Leslie, *Johnny Crow's Party*
Du Bois, William, *Bear Party*
Duvoisin, Roger, *Veronica and the Birthday Gift*
Freedman, Sally, *Monster Birthday Party*
Glovach, Linda, *Little Witch's Birthday Book*
Haywood, Carolyn, *Happy Birthday from Carolyn Haywood*
Hutchins, Pat, *Best Train Set Ever*
Keats, Ezra Jack, *Letter to Amy*
Krauss, Ruth, *Birthday Party*
Perl, Lila, *Candles, Cakes, and Donkey Tails: Birthday Symbols and Celebrations*
Seuss, Dr., *Happy Birthday to You*
Wiseman, Bernard, *Morris Has a Birthday Party*

Activities to Connect Literature and Curriculum

ART

Create the "World's Biggest Birthday Cake."* A large, class-sized cake can be constructed using cardboard and other instructional art materials available. Use 3-dimensional candles to list individual student's names in class and to record the exact birth date.

Individual mock birthday cakes can be made by mixing a small amount of water and Ivory Snow Flakes™ into paste. Spread the paste on to cottage cheese containers with lids. Continue the cake decorating by adding mini cake decorating flowers. These are made by using small tissue squares that are twisted with a pencil eraser and glued onto the carton top. Other artwork will complete the cake decorating.

LANGUAGE ARTS

Key vocabulary words for clustering and writing:

birthday	sugar
timer	crumb
cake	eggs
chocolate	wishes
flour	smell
hungry	song

Make up a story using the starter, "I Had the Biggest Birthday Party in the World...."
Write a thank you note for the "best ever birthday gift."

---

*Carol Greene, *The World's Biggest Birthday Cake* (Chicago: Children's Press, 1985).

MATH

Graph the birthday months of students in the class using an outline of a birthday cake.

MUSIC

Sing the "World's Biggest Birthday Song" with the class. Add pantomine movement to the music.

NUTRITION

Have a birthday party for the class and celebrate everyone's special day. Prepare a birthday cake or individual cupcakes for the party.

SCIENCE

Research the number of birthdays the following animals usually have:

elephant	tiger	turtle
dog	shark	
rabbit	eagle	

Beyond the Book

Guided Reading Connections across a Curriculum Rainbow: Gifts

Bunting, Eve, *Mother's Day Mice*
Martin, Sidney, *Calendar Crafts*
Wolf, Janet, *Best Present Is Me*

Enriching Connections

FOR GIFTED STUDENTS

Plan a celebration. The event need not be a traditional one. Be creative in planning the food, decorations, and event. Package all your sample drawings—invitations, menu, and program—in a birthday package.

FOR PARENTS

Tell your child that people celebrate birthdays in many different ways. On Chinese New Year, each Chinese person becomes a year older. Bar Mitzvah, the thirteenth birthday celebration, marks the entry of Jewish boys to the adult community. In France, the key to the house is given on the twenty-first birthday. In the United States, the eighteenth birthday is important because the person has reached what is considered to be "legal age." Go to the library and find a book that tells more about special birthdays and read the information together.

* * * * * * * * * * *

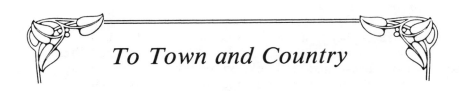

To Town and Country

LITTLE HOUSE

Author: Burton, Virginia Lee
Illustrator: Burton, Virginia Lee
Publisher: Houghton Mifflin Company, 1942
Suggested Grade Level: K-2
Classification: Core Materials
Literary Form: Picture book
Theme: The world is always changing and we must find ways to keep the best of things.

About the Book

STUDENT OBJECTIVES:

1. Retell the *Little House*.

2. Compare the different changes in environment around the Little House.

3. Predict other changes that will happen to the Little House in the future.

SYNOPSIS: The Little House is a lovely little country home for a family. The environment or neighborhood begins to change. Progress is seen all around. In fact, after a long period of years, the Little House is a part of a large city with a subway running underneath it, and an elevated train travels over it. Then another change occurs. Will the cycle of the Little House begin again?

ABOUT THE AUTHOR-ILLUSTRATOR: Virginia Lee Burton, 1909- .
　　Virginia Lee Burton grew up in Massachusetts, where her father was the first Dean of the Massachusetts Institute of Technology (MIT). Some of her early years were spent in California, where she studied both art and dance. Virginia worked very hard to win a dance contract. She was preparing to depart with the traveling ballet company when her father broke his leg and she had to remain behind. Fortunately for the readers of children's books, she turned to writing and illustrating books for children.

Like many writers, her first book was not a success. It was the story of a tiny speck of dust and when she read it to her 4-year-old, he fell asleep. She then discarded it! It is interesting to note that she field-tested her books on her own children. Today's writers and illustrators feel that their children are not good critics and do not ask their children's opinions about stories they write. Virginia wrote for her children and their interests.

As an art form, the work of Virginia Lee Burton stimulates our feelings. Her books are like a ballet and display a great fluidity of motion. She uses circles and curves as graceful lines that represent happiness, serenity, and comfort. Her diagonal lines represent sudden changes in the environment and unpleasant happenings.

Three of the books represent her home town, Gloucester, Massachusetts. The house in *Little House* is the home of the Burton family; Mike Mulligan's shovel was first seen in the basement of the Gloucester High School; and Katy of *Katy and the Big Snow* was the town's faithful snow plough. The *Little House* was awarded the 1943 Caldecott Medal for the Best Picture Book of the Year.

SELECTED ADDITIONAL TITLES BY THE AUTHOR:

Choo Choo
Emperor's New Clothes
Katy and the Big Snow
Maybelle, the Cable Car
Mike Mulligan and His Steam Shovel

Using the Book

Suggested Approach to the Book

Model Lesson #1

- Discuss the biographical materials of Virginia Lee Burton. Tell how sometimes our lives are changed by unexpected events. What if Virginia's father had been able to have someone else stay with him when he broke his leg? Do you think Virginia might have still "found" her art talents and published so many important children's books? Why?

Model Lesson #2

- Read *Little House*. Pay particular attention to the style of the art and the use of swirls and circles to show time and happiness. Notice when progress infringes on the Little House. Think about progress in your town. Are any big changes being planned? What are they? What changes will result from the plan? Ask your parents about changes in their environment which they consider to be negative. Why?

Model Lesson #3

- Some questions to explore with the class:
    1. Carefully examine the end papers. They resemble a wallpaper border. Why do you think the artist chose this format to show progress?

2. List the different modes of transportation shown on the 2 end pages. Also, see if you can list other modern changes that are happening around the Little House.
3. Notice the daisy circle dedication. Can you find out who Georgie Dorgie is? Ask your school library media specialist to help you learn something about the author-illustrator using reference books.
4. Describe the Little House as it is on the opening page of the book.
5. Looking at the "sun" pages, 2-3, tell how the illustrator creates a happy mood for the Little House.
6. On page 4 a moon calendar is pictured. Explain the different moons.
7. How can you tell what season it is for the Little House? List the 4 seasons on a sheet of butcher paper and brainstorm for responses.
8. Progress begins on page 14. Why did Virginia Lee Burton use dark lines and colors to represent the building of a highway?
9. Looking at page 16, you see many houses that are alike. The Little House is now surrounded by new houses. Is there any available land left?
10. What has happened to the Little House on page 19?
11. On pages 22-34, describe the changes in city transportation.
12. How does the Little House get to leave the city?
13. Compare the opening and closing pictures of the Little House.

Model Lesson #4

- Integrate a Caldecott picture book study unit with the Little House. Research the history of the Caldecott Medal. Learn when the Honor Medals were first awarded. Study the award seal. Who is on the horse? Why was it selected as the symbol of this special award?

- Distribute a reading list of Caldecott Medal and Honor books. Assign the reading of a book from the list as a class project.

- Pretend that you have just won the Caldecott Medal for this year. Illustrate your own ABC book of school items.

- Ask each student to make a new book jacket for his or her ABC book. Display the artwork as if hung in an art gallery. Attach a Caldecott seal to each cover. (Source for purchasing seals is the American Library Association.) Explain to students that when an illustrator wins the Caldecott award, the selling price of his art sold in galleries escalates. Have each student assign an imaginary price for purchasing art through the art gallery display. Role-play the opening of the art exhibit of Caldecott cover art. Design a program and list all the class artists.

Model Lesson #5

- Art appreciation through picture books: Compare the art style, colors, and pictures of the following:

    Burton, Virginia Lee, *Little House*
    Mendoza, George, *Need a House? Call Ms. Mouse*

Library Media Center Connections

1. Display all the Caldecott Medal and Honor books from the library media collection. Include a poster picturing all the winners as a visual guide to titles that students might want to read.

2. Set up a Caldecott activity learning center. (Several commercially produced centers are available from Dennison Company and Book Lures.)

3. Poll students and ask which is their favorite Caldecott book. Send the information generated back to the classroom to be used in graphing their responses. Display the information in the media center and encourage other classes to participate in polling student responses and adding their graphs to a media center display. Information could also be graphed to reflect a school profile.

Instructional Materials Connections

Random House publishes literature materials relating to Caldecott winners.

Computer Connections

Head Start, *Talk about a Walk*
Random House, *City and Country Opposites*
Weekly Reader, *Stickybear Town Builder*

Theme Reading Connections: Houses

Barton, Bryon, *Building a House*
Brown, Margaret Wise, *House of a Hundred Windows*
Crompton, Margaret, *House Where Jack Lives*
De Regniers, Beatrice, *Little House of My Own*
Fisher, Aileen, *Best Little House*
Hoberman, Mary Ann, *House Is a House for Me*
Krauss, Ruth, *Very Special House*
Mayer, Mercer, *Little Monster at Home*
Miles, Betty, *House for Everyone*
Murphy, Shirley, *Tattie's River Journey*
Nussbaum, Hedda, *Animals Build Amazing Houses*
Pienkowski, Jan, *Homes*
Scarry, Richard, *Is This the House of Mistress Mouse?*
Schulz, Charles, *Snoopy's Facts and Fun Book about Houses*
Seuss, Dr., *In a People House*
Shapp, Martha, *Let's Find Out about Houses*
Watanabe, Shigeo, *I Can Build a House*
Wildsmith, Brian, *Animal Homes*
Zelinsky, Paul, *The Maid and the Mouse and the Odd-Shaped House*

Activities to Connect Literature and Curriculum

ART

Draw a diagram of your room. Decorate it with a new theme.

Plan to replace the row houses shown on page 17 with new designs. What would you want them to look like? Draw several new exterior "faces" that you would use in updating the homes.

Construct a model of an ultramodern home that you would like to live in.

If you could be a school architect, what would your classroom look like? Explain your choices.

Design a set of house "paper dolls" and cut them out using the folded-paper technique.

LANGUAGE ARTS

Write your own Little House story. Think about setting it in the year 2000 and write about the house you live in today and the changes that might happen.

Write a poem about houses.

Compose a real estate advertisement to sell the Little House.

List some of the new features to be found in houses today. Can you anticipate what things may be standard equipment in the future that are luxury items today? Let your imagination fly. Be fluid and flexible in brainstorming ideas as a class.

MATH

Look at the classified ads of a newspaper and list some of the prices of homes shown for your city. List the numbers chronologically from the smallest to the largest as a class project. (Round off 3 zero places, if necessary.) Also count how many homes are available in your area. Graph the information.

MUSIC

Listen to recorded music about cities including *New York, New York* and *Around the World in 80 Days*.

NUTRITION

Plan an international salad luncheon that includes many different ingredients that represent the many different people who live in a city and make it a good place to live. Include Greek or Italian olives; Swiss, American, and provolone cheese; kidney beans; and fresh vegetables as a beginning. Serve French, Italian, or pita bread to add a foreign flavor.

SOCIAL STUDIES

Using the Little House book, trace the changes in transportation and communication. Do you think Virginia Lee Burton liked changes or progress? Why? Share picture examples.

Can you share any new technology or inventions that you have seen on television?

Beyond the Book

Guided Reading Connections across a Curriculum Rainbow: Transportation

Arnold, Caroline, *How Do We Travel?*
Boyer, Edward, *River and Canal*
Crews, Donald, *School Bus; Truck*
Gibbons, Gail, *New Road!*; *Tunnel*
Scarry, Richard, *Richard Scarry's Cars and Trucks and Things That Go*
Steele, Phillip, *Land Transport around the World*
Zaffo, George, *Big Book of Real Airplanes*

Enriching Connections

FOR GIFTED STUDENTS

Watch television news programs for a week and record any new technology or inventions presented. Chart the information and give your own opinion about the value of the new idea.

Plan a new housing development and include community services and recreation areas. Draw a diagram of your development including the buildings, streets, and landscaping.

FOR PARENTS

Can you find any examples of Little Houses whose environment has changed over the years? Ask your child to draw a picture for you of a Little House that still exists in your community.

MISS RUMPHIUS

Author: Cooney, Barbara
Illustrator: Cooney, Barbara
Publisher: Viking, 1982
Suggested Grade Level: K-3
Classification: Core Materials
Literary Form: Picture book
Theme: We should all make the world more beautiful in some way through our own efforts.

About the Book

STUDENT OBJECTIVES:

1. Define what beauty is, including abstract forms.

2. Classify things that are beautiful and things that are ugly.

3. Recommend a plan to provide beautiful places for people in the future.

SYNOPSIS: Miss Rumphius is instructed by her grandfather that she is to leave something beautiful to the world through her life. She traveled the world, came home to live by the sea, and did leave her mark of beauty for future generations.

ABOUT THE AUTHOR-ILLUSTRATOR: Barbara Cooney, 1917- .

Barbara Cooney and her twin brother were born in Brooklyn, New York, and spent their childhoods on Long Island and in Maine. Her mother was an artist, and she describes her career choice as an easy one because she was always surrounded by tubes of paint, paper, and brushes. She attended Smith College in Massachusetts; she still lives in Massachusetts today in a 16-room house.

Barbara Cooney has been illustrating since college. She feels she is a romantic and draws only things that she knows. In fact, she worries because her books "look just like me." She admits to liking "elegant, beautiful, interesting things, whether trees or houses, or pebbles or dishes or jewelry or clothes—the things must be really delicious."*

She enjoys traveling and has visited France, Spain, Switzerland, Ireland, England, and St. Lucia and Haiti in the Caribbean. Perhaps *Miss Rumphius* is a composite of Barbara Cooney.

Her book *Chanticleer and the Fox* was awarded the 1959 Caldecott award as was *Ox-Cart Man*, a poem by Donald Hall, in 1980. Barbara Cooney had become fascinated by the chickens owned by her neighbor. Some of them were moved to her yard where she could further observe them. She watched them and drew authentic sketches of their body movements. The rooster in the opening pages is a colorful example of her eye for detail. The herbs featured in the Chaucer tale were ones in her own garden. *Ox-Cart Man* is illustrated in the style of primitive art.

SELECTED ADDITIONAL TITLES BY THE AUTHOR-ILLUSTRATOR:

Little Brother and Sister
Little Juggler
Little Prayer

SELECTED ADDITIONAL TITLES BY THE ILLUSTRATOR:

Christmas in the Barn
Courtship, Merry Marriage, and Feast of Cock Robin and Jenny Wren
Little Fir Tree
Mother Goose in French
Mother Goose in Spanish
Owl and the Pussy Cat

---

*Lee Bennett Hopkins, *Books Are by People* (Chicago: Citation Press, 1969).

Plant Magic
Snow White and Rose Red
Where Have You Been?
Wynken, Blynken and Nod

Using the Book

Suggested Approach to the Book

Model Lesson #1

- Present biographical information about Barbara Cooney. Tell students that her writing and illustrating career spans 50 years and that she has illustrated over 100 picture books. She is a unique illustrator, and like Robert McCloskey, Marcia Brown, Leo and Diane Dillon, and Chris Van Allsburg, has received 2 Caldecott Medals for a best-illustrated picture book of the year. Explain that after she won the Caldecott Medal for *Chanticleer and the Fox* she changed her art technique from scratchboard to other techniques. Observe that the 2 Caldecott award books and *Miss Rumphius* are quite different from each other.

Model Lesson #2

- Read *Miss Rumphius* to students and share the informative pictures. Ask the class if they can identify where she traveled. Also note that the book is dedicated to St. Nicholas, patron saint of children, sailors, and maidens.

Model Lesson #3

- Some questions to discuss with the class:
    1. What is a "Lupine Lady?"
    2. Describe the home of Alice in the city by the sea.
    3. What is a ship's figurehead?
    4. Why do you think ships' figureheads are women?
    5. What did grandfather tell Alice that she must do when she grew up?
    6. What did Alice do as a librarian? Would you like to be a librarian?
    7. What did Alice's name become when she grew up?
    8. Describe the conservatory in the park.
    9. Can you tell from the pictures what kinds of places Miss Rumphius visited?
    10. Why did she return home?
    11. Tell how the wind helped spread the beautiful blue lupine flowers.
    12. What idea did the wind give Miss Rumphius?
    13. Compare her to Johnny Appleseed.
    14. Why do you think people called her "That Crazy Old Lady?"
    15. Who is telling the story of Miss Rumphius? How do you know?

Model Lesson #4

- Art appreciation through picture books: Compare the story, art, and viewpoint of

    Aliki, *Story of Johnny Appleseed*
    Cooney, Barbara, *Miss Rumphius*

Library Media Center Connections

1. Miss Rumphius was a librarian, and this is an excellent opportunity to introduce students to the activities of their school media center. Arrange a schedule agreeable to the classroom teacher and invite small groups to visit the library and assist the librarian for a half hour activity such as selecting new books, processing new books, or developing and planning a display.

2. Prior to the student groups visiting the library, present a class lesson on alphabetizing. Pretend that an alphabet train is in the station with 26 cars attached. Using placards of the 26 letters, have students line up behind the initial letter of their last names. If several students are within 1 letter, use the opportunity to teach second-letter alphabetizing. Announce the departure of the alphabet train from the media center en route to the classroom.

3. The group media center activity might include an introduction to the shelving of easy fiction books. The librarian should explain that these books are placed on the shelf according to the initial of the author's last name. Explain to the students that they can pretend that they have just written a book and it is going to be placed on the library shelf. Have the students show where their own books would be shelved. Allow students to shelve books as part of the visit.

Computer Connections

Head Start, *Alphabetizing*

Theme Reading Connections: Flowers

De Paola, Tomie, *Legend of the Bluebonnet*
Fisher, Aileen, *And a Sunflower Grew*
Heller, Ruth, *Reason for a Flower*
Lerner, Carol, *Flowers of a Woodland Spring*
Lobel, Arnold, *Rose in My Garden*
Mitsumasa, Anno, *King's Flower*
Selsam, Millicent, *First Look at Flowers*
Steig, William, *Rotten Island*

Activities to Connect Literature and Curriculum

ART

Create a "Garden of Books" bulletin board. Use butcher paper to construct a garden including snails, butterflies, bees, grass, and trees. As a reading incentive, encourage students to add a flower to the garden every time they complete reading a library book. The centers of the flowers are the book titles. Integrate biology into the garden also.

HEALTH

Talk about the needs of older people. Include grandparents in the class discussion. What do they do with their leisure time? Are they retired or working?

LANGUAGE ARTS

Write a letter to Miss Rumphius and explain what things you consider to be beautiful. Predict what you might do to make the world a lovely place.

MATH

Give each student a wildflower seed packet to plant in a corner of the back yard as his or her own "something beautiful." Predict how many seeds are in a wildflower package and how many seeds will actually grow at home in the student's yard. Ask for continuing observations of the seed growth and flowering. Each student should keep individual observation records on a form designed by the teacher.

SCIENCE

Grow a rock garden of narcissus in the classroom. Keep an observation chart of the growth and flowering of the bulbs. Tell students that the narcissus is called the "water fairy" by the Chinese people. Are there any other paper-like flowers? Talk about other bulbs that can be grown in dish gardens and vases.

Tell the students to imagine that they are architects of a large city skyscraper project. People must be provided with gardens for relaxation and beauty. Design a rooftop garden that would be available for strolling and resting. Before beginning, think about trees, lawns, butterflies, flowers, quiet music, and a tea party.

SOCIAL STUDIES

Help the students trace on a world map or globe the travel route of Miss Rumphius.

Beyond the Book

Guided Reading Connections across a Curriculum Rainbow: Ships and Sailing

Crews, Donald, *Harbor*
Holling, Holling C., *Seabird*
Locker, Thomas, *Sailing with the Wind*
Smith, Boyd, *Seashore Book*
Van Allsburg, Chris, *Wreck of the Zephyr*
Willard, Nancy, *Voyage of the Ludgate Hill*

Enriching Connections

FOR GIFTED STUDENTS

Using a *Scott United States Stamp Catalog*, locate stamps that have as their theme the beautification of America. Be sure to locate the special series that began when President Johnson's wife, Lady Bird Johnson, called the nation's attention to the need for an environmental program.

Design a new "America the Beautiful" stamp for the Postal Service.

List other ways to achieve beauty in the world.

FOR PARENTS

Discuss with your child the things that you think make the world a more beautiful place to live. What improvements would you like to see? Explain why. Plan to make something in your own personal environment nicer with the help of your child.

TALE OF PETER RABBIT

Author: Potter, Beatrix
Illustrator: Potter, Beatrix
Publisher: F. Warne and Co., 1902
Suggested Grade Level: K-2
Classification: Core Materials
Literary Form: Picture book illustrated with watercolors
Theme: You can get in trouble when you disobey a parent.

About the Book

STUDENT OBJECTIVES:

1. Describe the adventure of Peter Rabbit in Mr. McGregor's garden.

2. Predict what steps Mr. McGregor might take to catch Peter Rabbit next time.

3. Sketch Mr. McGregor's garden plan.

SYNOPSIS: Peter Rabbit is warned to stay away from Mr. McGregor's garden by his mother. Peter disobeys and is almost caught. Next time he might not be able to escape. This story presents a lesson and is quietly, authentically illustrated.

ABOUT THE AUTHOR-ILLUSTRATOR: Beatrix Potter, 1866-1943.
Beatrix Potter grew up quietly with a younger brother and parents who were very strict disciplinarians. From the time she was very young, she sketched animals in their natural

settings as one of her vacation pleasures. The parents took the children on long, 3-month vacations to Scotland and the Lake District from their home in London.

Her first drawings of Peter Rabbit were sent to the sick, 5-year-old son of her former governess in 1893. She tried to get her stories published, but was unsuccessful. This was possibly because materials from women were not widely published at that time. Remember that she lived during the Victorian era, so named after the then queen of England, Victoria. Her own family were typically wealthy Victorians—they had received a large cotton inheritance. Even Mr. Potter, a lawyer, did not find it necessary to practice law to earn money.

Beatrix Potter did get her book published! She paid the sum of £11 to Warne and Co. to privately print 250 copies of the small format book. With the success of this printing, her future as 1 of the great English illustrators was assured. Warne then published 6,000 copies of *Tale of Peter Rabbit* in 1902 and it has since been translated into 12 languages.

With her future assured, which was unique for a woman of her day, Beatrix Potter was able to purchase her own neighboring farm, Hilltop, near Sawrey in the Lake Country. It and the surrounding country were the background for her naturalistic writing and illustrating. The home may be visited today in order to gain more insight into her life and work and see the environment from which her watercolor pictures evolved.

Biographers always portray Beatrix Potter as a quiet person who enjoyed watching animals close up; putting them in their natural habitat; and writing about the food, clothes, and homes of her animal friends.

An odd twist to her life that must be added is that she did eventually marry a neighboring lawyer. At age 47, her parents refused her request to be married and she rebelled and did what her heart directed. After her marriage, Beatrix Potter left writing and illustrating children's books and turned to sheep raising, which she continued until the end of her life.

SELECTED ADDITIONAL TITLES BY THE AUTHOR-ILLUSTRATOR:

Tailor of Gloucester
Tale of Benjamin Bunny
Tale of Flopsy Bunnies
Tale of Jemima Puddle-Duck
Tale of Johnny Town-Mouse
Tale of Mr. Jeremy Fisher
Tale of Mrs. Tiggy-Winkle
Tale of Pigling Bland
Tale of Squirrel Nutkin
Tale of Tom Kitten
Treasury of Peter Rabbit and Other Stories

Using the Book

Suggested Approach to the Book

Model Lesson #1

- Relate the Beatrix Potter biographical information to students. Explain that it was very important to her that the book be comfortable and fit right into the little hands of readers. Therefore, the small book size was her choice.

- Read the *Tale of Peter Rabbit* and share the small pictures. It may be helpful to have several library copies available for students to read later. The *Treasury of Peter Rabbit and Other Stories* is a larger book.

Model Lesson #2

- Select and read another Beatrix Potter story.

Model Lesson #3

- Art appreciation through picture books: Compare the art form, color, and story in

    Bianco, Margery Williams, *Velveteen Rabbit*. Illustrated by Michael Hague
    Potter, Beatrix, *Tale of Peter Rabbit*

Library Media Center Connections

1. There are a number of foods and herbs mentioned in the *Tale of Peter Rabbit*. Use a large hand magnifying glass or the opaque projector to locate these foods in the book. List them on a sheet of paper. Help the students find a use for each herb in reference books. Have them explain these uses to the rest of the class as the pictures are projected.

2. Using Beatrix Potter books from the media center, identify, list, and classify all the different animals she has illustrated in her pictures.

Theme Reading Connections: Gardening

Barrett, Judi, *Old MacDonald Had an Apartment House*
Brown, Marc, *Your First Garden Book*
Carlson, Nancy, *Harriet and the Garden*
Creative Education, *Indoor Gardens*
Davidson, Amanda, *Teddy in the Garden*
De Jong, Meindert, *Nobody Plays with a Cabbage*
De Paola, Tomie, *Four Stories for Four Seasons*
Fujikawa, Gyo, *Let's Grow a Garden*
Galland, Sarah, *Peter Rabbit's Gardening Book*
Keeping, Charles, *Joseph's Yard*
Moncure, Jane, *See My Garden Grow*
Oechsli, Helen, *In My Garden*
Rockwell, Anne, *How My Garden Grows*
Rylant, Cynthia, *This Year's Garden*
Westcott, Nadine, *Giant Vegetable Garden*

Activities to Connect Literature and Curriculum

ART

As a class project, make a "Peter Rabbit Visits Mr. McGregor's Garden" mural. Begin with blue sky, green grass, brown dirt. Plant 3-dimensional construction paper vegetables in sections and rows. Add a cold frame and storage shed to make it a typical British garden. Include Mr. McGregor and Peter Rabbit in their appropriate places. See math activity section for integration of vegetable planting.

Create a carrot bookmark for mother's favorite cookbook. This may be a student Mother's Day activity. Use construction paper or felt. Attach a green raffia carrot top for authenticity.

Construct Peter Rabbit finger puppets. Use a half circle of paper stapled to form a cone. Glue in a round paper strip to form a finger hold. Dress Peter Rabbit as appropriate using scraps and construction paper.

CITIZENSHIP

Select class members who are good citizens for the Peter Rabbit Club. List their names on a classroom Peter Rabbit Citizenship Honor Roll and award Peter Rabbit buttons made with a badge maker (a machine that can be used by hand to produce buttons with pins on the back).

LANGUAGE ARTS

Beatrix Potter first illustrated Peter Rabbit when she sent the drawings and story to an ill, 5-year-old child. Illustrate a blank white sheet of paper with Beatrix Potter characters and write a letter to a special friend telling about Beatrix Potter and her special animal friends.

Pretend that you are Peter Rabbit and are writing a letter to a Potter character to come and visit you. Who would you choose to visit the class for an afternoon? Why?

MATH

Use the information generated in the media center activity about the number of different animals Beatrix Potter drew in her picture books. This information is the source material for a class math graphing lesson. List the names of the various animals illustrated. Ask students to tell which ones they found. Record these student answers and then plot on a chart using the bar graph technique.

NUTRITION

Make a cole slaw from cabbage. Grate the cabbage with a food processor and mix with a small amount of vinegar, sour cream, and poppy seeds. A small amount of sugar will diminish the acidity of the vinegar. As part of the fun, use another cabbage head and cut the bottom to make a level base. Add carrots for ears and other vegetables for the face and present as a cabbage head puppet decoration for the classroom.

Make a nutritious Shaggy Carrot Cookie for a snack treat.

What kinds of good dishes can you create from Mr. McGregor's garden? List them in a miniature cookbook with illustrations.

SCIENCE

Sketch Mr. McGregor's garden plan. Reread the book for information. Before beginning the sketch, list the names of plants growing in the garden. Next research the growing and space requirements for each plant variety. Ask help from the media specialist in the media center. Incorporate the information into your sketch. Color the plants as identification marks of planting sections and rows.

Beyond the Book

Guided Reading Connections across a Curriculum Rainbow: Rabbits

Adams, Adrienne, *Easter Egg Artists*
Aesop, *Hare and the Tortoise*
Balian, Lorna, *Humbug Rabbit*
Brown, Margaret Wise, *Runaway Bunny*
Fisher, Aileen, *Listen, Rabbit*
Gag, Wanda, *ABC Bunny*
Hogrogian, Nonny, *Carrot Cake*
Peet, Bill, *Huge Harold*
Potter, Beatrix, *Peter Rabbit's Puzzle Book* (devised by Colin Twinn)
Seuss, Dr., *Eye Book*

Enriching Connections

FOR GIFTED CHILDREN

Decide the measurement of land needed for Mr. McGregor's garden. Would it fit into a backyard or is the land required really large as the area seemed to Peter Rabbit? Explain your answer.

How many seed packs would be required to plant the garden? Go to a nursery with a parent and learn the prices of seed packages. How much money would be needed to purchase the necessary seeds?

Plant some seed packs in containers at home. When they become baby plants, transplant them to an appropriate place in the garden. Show your class the products of your home garden.

Peter Rabbit had to wiggle out of his new blue jacket in order to escape Mr. McGregor. Design a jacket for Peter. Think carefully about the color and design. Make a prototype jacket and ask other students what they think of the color and design. If modifications are required, redesign the jacket. Display all the new jacket designs as artwork.

FOR PARENTS

Discuss with your child some reasons for obeying family and school rules. Include aspects of personal safety, explaining that like Peter Rabbit, we may not understand the reasons for the rules, but it is best if we obey them. Relate this to street traffic laws and talking to strangers on the street. This is also an opportunity to talk about secrets that should not be kept, such as child abuse.

*   *   *   *   *   *   *   *   *   *   *

Grade Three

EXTENSIONS

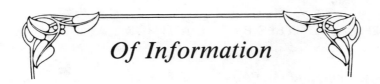

Of Information

BANANAS
From Manolo to Margie

Author: Ancona, George
Illustrator: Ancona, George
Publisher: Clarion, 1982
Suggested Grade Level: 3-5
Classification: Core Materials
Literary Form: Photoessay
Theme: It takes many helping hands to grow bananas, ship them to market, and deliver them to the consumer.

About the Book

STUDENT OBJECTIVES:

1. Describe a banana plant and its product.

2. Categorize the steps necessary to grow, ship, and market bananas.

3. Locate the title page, table of contents, and glossary in a book.

SYNOPSIS: Manolo's family grows bananas in Honduras and ships them to market so Margie in the United States can enjoy a ripe banana for a snack. Photographs are traditionally worth a thousand words and tell the story well.

ABOUT THE AUTHOR-ILLUSTRATOR: George Ancona, birthdate not available.
    George Ancona is a children's author who has perfected the photoessay book. He researches a subject and then takes photographs to tell the story. In *Bananas: From Manolo to Margie* he learned about his subject by visiting a banana plantation, or *finca*, and observing and photographing the Velez family. He continued the story of the shipping of bananas to market and ultimately to Margie in the city.

151

SELECTED ADDITIONAL TITLES BY THE AUTHOR:

Dancing Is
Freighters: Cargo Ships and the People Who Work Them
Handtalk
Helping Out
I Feel: A Picture Book of Emotions
It's a Baby!
Monster Movers
Monsters on Wheels
Sheep Dog
Team Work

Using the Book

Suggested Approach to the Book

Model Lesson #1

- Explain to students that there are many ways to use pictures to illustrate a story, including ink drawings, as in McCloskey's *Make Way for Ducklings*, Ezra Jack Keats's collage technique, and the felt-tipped marker art of Bernard Waber's *Ira Sleeps Over*.

- The students had an opportunity to meet another photoessayist earlier. Can they identify her? She was introduced through her alphabet and counting books. Do they remember Tana Hoban and her books for little children? Share some of her photoessay concept books with the class now.

Model Lesson #2

- Read *Bananas: From Manolo to Margie* to the class.

  1. Does Manolo look like children in your class? Why?
  2. Find Honduras on the map. Why is the country of Honduras frequently in the news?
  3. Where were bananas first discovered some 500 years ago?
  4. How did the bananas come to the New World?
  5. What area of the world exports two-thirds of the world's bananas?
  6. What is Manolo's father, who cares for banana plants, called?
  7. What language do you think the word *bananero* is?
  8. Do bananas grow on trees? Why?
  9. Describe a banana plant.
  10. How long does it take the fruit to mature and ripen?
  11. How many bananas are usually on a stalk, and how heavy is the stalk?
  12. What is the work of a *protejedor*?
  13. Why are the banana stalks covered with plastic bags?
  14. Why do you think Manolo and his sister wear white shirts or dresses?
  15. What is a *cortero*?
  16. Why do you think it takes 2 weeks to get the fruit from the *finca* to the market?

17. What is the name of the Indian bread that the Velez family has for dinner? Have you ever eaten a tortilla?
18. What happens to the bananas in the packing plant?
19. Tell what work Manolo's mother does as a packer.
20. How many boxes of bananas will a man load into the train box car?
21. What is a reefer?
22. Tell what the inspector does at dockside.
23. How many boxes of fruit will it take to fill the ship? Can you imagine such a large number of boxes?
24. What will be the job of the pilot who meets the ship after its journey from Honduras?
25. Complete the story of the journey of the bananas after being unloaded from the ship.

Model Lesson #3

- Read and practice pronouncing the Spanish words included in the glossary. Introduce the glossary as an important part of a book. Explain that a book that gives factual information is called a nonfiction book.

Model Lesson #4

- Compare the following photoessay books:

  Ancona, George, *Bananas: From Manolo to Margie*
  Miller, Jane, *Seasons on the Farm*

Library Media Center Connections

1. Collect materials and set up an interest center on Honduras. Include map materials, sound film strips, and available realia including study prints on the growing of bananas.

2. Would it be better to ship bananas by air freight instead of by ship? Would the swift delivery be as important as the increased cost of shipping? Why? Which way would you ship bananas if you were in charge of getting *Bananas: From Manolo to Margie*?

3. Design a shipping plan to send summer Georgia peaches to New York and California. What means of transportation would you choose for each delivery? Remember that peaches do not have a "long life." Also, are there any ways in which the peaches could be frozen or processed at the point of origin? Explain.

Theme Reading Connections: Photography

Forbes, Robin, *Click: A First Camera Book*
Freeman, Tony, *Photography*
Leen, Nina, *Taking Pictures*
Mitchell, Barbara, *Click! A Story about George Eastman*
Willard, Nancy, *Simple Pictures Are Best*

Activities to Connect Literature and Curriculum

ART

Create a banana art bulletin board for open house. Using construction paper, create a bunch of bananas and attach a Polaroid™ print of each child to his or her banana. Name the board "Our Classroom Bunch."

Make papier-mâché bunches of bananas to hang in the kitchen at home.

Using information from the book about the size and structure of a banana plant, construct one from materials available in your art department.

CITIZENSHIP

Award good citizenship banana awards. Call them "Top Bananas."

LANGUAGE ARTS

Observe the colored photograph opposite the map of Central America in the book. Have students cluster for prewriting words that they think describe the photograph. Write 1 brief paragraph to present a feeling about the sea of banana plants.

Write a letter to Manolo and ask him questions about his family and school. Give some facts about your family and school. Illustrate the letter with drawings of your own family and a picture of your school.

MUSIC

Introduce South American songs. Music is available on cassette.

NUTRITION

Prepare a special banana nutrition snack. Slice bananas into 1-inch chunks. Insert a toothpick and dip into lemon juice to prevent darkening. Dip into sour cream that is room temperature and has been stirred. Use the toothpick to roll the chunk in canned coconut. Enjoy.

Banana nut bread with cream cheese is another baking suggestion.

Banana chunks may also be dipped into chocolate hard sauces for ice cream.

Another possibility is to use bananas as part of a fruit platter with a light dipping sauce.

SCIENCE

Present a photoessay of the growing of a local food product.

SOCIAL STUDIES

Write a research report on bananas. Present the information on a chart using a 1-page format.

Beyond the Book

Guided Reading Connections across a Curriculum Rainbow: Hispanic Culture

Behrens, June, *Fiesta!*
Ets, Marie Hall, *Gilberto and the Wind*; *Nine Days to Christmas*
Felt, Sue, *Rosa Too Little*
Fraser, James, *Los Posadas*
Hitte, Kathryn, *Mexicallie Soup*

Enriching Connections

FOR GIFTED STUDENTS

Draw a pictorial graphic map to show bananas traveling from plantation, to shipping, and final market delivery.

Locate in a cookbook a recipe for a banana dish that you have not tasted before, and ask permission to help make it for your family.

Write a poem about a banana using the limerick form.

FOR PARENTS

As part of the media center lesson, ask your child to think about the different ways in which peaches are sold in the store—fresh, frozen, dried, and canned. How could each one be used in home food preparation? Name as many variations as possible.

THE POST OFFICE BOOK
Mail and How It Moves

Author: Gibbons, Gail
Illustrator: Gibbons, Gail
Publisher: Thomas Y. Crowell Company, 1982
Suggested Grade Level: 2-5
Classification: Extended Materials
Literary Form: Information book in picture format
Theme: A piece of mail is processed many times between sender and receiver.

About the Book

STUDENT OBJECTIVES:

1. Recognize that the process of mailing and delivering a letter is complex.

2. Explain the process of mailing a letter to a friend in another city.

3. Write friendly letters to other class members using a classroom mailbox system.

SYNOPSIS: A letter is mailed and delivered. But in the process it will be weighed, sorted, transported, culled, canceled, coded, binned, boxed, and sorted once again.

ABOUT THE AUTHOR-ILLUSTRATOR: Gail Gibbons, birthdate not available.

Gail Gibbons was born and grew up in Illinois, where she went to school and was graduated from the University of Illinois with a major in graphic design. She has had experience as a television artist, freelance artist, and designer. Her real love is creating children's books. She started writing, illustrating, and binding her books together with yarn at 8 years of age. Today Gail Gibbons is an important author-illustrator of information books illustrated with diagrams and cut-away views.

"How does it work?" is always a question for this author-illustrator. When writing a book, Gail Gibbons investigates her subject thoroughly and experiments. For example, when writing *Clocks and How They Go*, she took a pendulum and wind-up clocks apart to see how they functioned. When working on *Trucks*, she asked a truck driver she had just met to show her how his car carrier truck worked in loading and unloading cars.

SELECTED ADDITIONAL TITLES BY THE AUTHOR:

Boat Book
Check It Out: The Book about Libraries
Clocks and How They Go
Deadline! From News to Newspapers
Department Store
Fire! Fire!
From Path to Highway: The Story of the Boston Post Road
Halloween
Milk Makers
Missing Maple Syrup Sap Mystery
New Road!
Paper, Paper Everywhere
Playgrounds
Seasons of Arnold's Apple Tree
Sun Up, Sun Down
Thanksgiving Day
Too-Great Bread Bake Book
Tool Book
Trains
Trucks
Tunnels
Up Goes the Skyscraper!
Weather Predictions

Using the Book

Suggested Approach to the Book

Model Lesson #1

- Introduce the author-illustrator as a person who researches and experiments with ideas before writing a book. Gail Gibbons has written a number of information books on a variety of subjects.

- Ask students to select and read a book written and illustrated by Gail Gibbons as preparation for a future class assignment.

Model Lesson #2

- Read *Post Office Book* and share the illustrations with the class. Carefully look at the style of illustrations that have been used. What is distinctive about them? Also note the use of the perforations similar to those on a stamp as borders for the cover and on an information page. This study of a service-oriented business may be integrated with a community services study unit.

Model Lesson #3

- Some questions to discuss with the class:
    1. What information do addresses and zip codes provide?
    2. Name 2 places where mail may be mailed.
    3. Who is a letter carrier?
    4. Do you think mail is still hand-sorted today? Why?
    5. What is an area post office? Which is the nearest area post office to your home?
    6. Explain the work of a culling machine. Do you know that small strawberries are called "culls?" Why do you think they are called that?
    7. Tell how a computer helps to move the mail.
    8. Why is it important to use a zip code when mailing letters?
    9. Retell the story of George Washington's first air mail letter.
    10. What is the world's most popular hobby? Why?

Model Lesson #4

- Art appreciation through picture books: Compare the art of Gail Gibbons with the following 2 artists who have written about mail or the post office.

    Ahlberg, Janet, and Allan Ahlberg, *Jolly Postman or Other People's Letters*
    Haley, Gail, *Post Office Cat*

Library Media Center Connections

1. Establish pen pals for the class with a different school. Plan to exchange several letters during the semester, particularly at holiday times. If possible, exchange student pictures between the pen pals.

2. As a culminating activity, plan for students to meet at a host school for a classroom visit and possibly have lunch together or engage in sports activities.

3. Some school systems today have an electronic bulletin board system that students may use to exchange computer mail. Fullerton School District (1401 W. Valencia Dr., Fullerton, CA 92633) is one such school district.

Computer Connections

Milliken Publishing, *Milliken Word Processor*

Instructional Materials Connections

Good Apple, *Communicating*

Theme Reading Connections: Mail

Bell, Norman, *Letter to Linda*
Keats, Ezra Jack, *Letter to Amy*
Maury, Inez, *My Mother the Postal Carrier*
Petersen, Johanna, *Careers with the Postal Service*
Roth, Harold, *First Class! The Postal System in Action*
Seuss, Dr., *On Beyond Zebra*

Activities to Connect Literature and Curriculum

ART

Design a new stamp to be included in the Postal Service's continuing series of LOVE stamps.

Create a banner to illustrate the travels of a letter deposited in a neighborhood letter box and later delivered to the president of the United States (Pennsylvania Ave., Washington, DC).

Secure a collection of canceled stamps and suggest that the class sort and classify them by value, color, and subject depicted. A web or cluster is an appropriate way to report student findings.

LANGUAGE ARTS

Plan to implement a letter writing unit with the class. Every student should write and mail a letter a day for a week through classroom mail. The rules are simple: the letter must be appropriate, well written, dated, and signed by the writer.

Establish a mail box system by using a large, decorated box for depositing letters and smaller, decorated milk carton mail boxes for receiving each student's mail. Students should mail letters at specified times during the day. Mail pick up by the teacher-postal carrier should be scheduled and a time schedule announced on the mail box. Student mail deliveries will be by overnight, "express" mail.

February is an appropriate month to implement this unit, as it can be combined with Valentine's Day activities.

Research and draw the illustrations for an information book on a subject of your choice. Use the Gail Gibbons book that you read at the beginning of the unit to stimulate ideas. Do not use the same ideas as those in the book, but develop some new materials that you think would be useful for other class members to use.

SCIENCE

The Postal Service issued 2 series of stamps in sheet format that included all the state birds and flowers. Through collaborative learning groups, list the names of the birds and flowers by state. There will be duplicate listings, as several states may have adopted the same bird or flower. Can you determine how many different flower and bird stamps have been actually issued? A postage stamp catalog will help, and you can ask your local post office stamp agent to confirm your findings.

SOCIAL STUDIES

Discuss with students changes in communications from the time of the clipper ships to the Pony Express, the role of trains in mail delivery, and modern day air mail and trucking services. Some students may wish to do additional reading on the subject. Ask them to share their research information through oral reports by role-playing typical communications figures.

Draw cross-section views of your home and street. Illustrate as many means of communication as possible. Some starter ideas are the postal carrier delivering mail, someone pushing the doorbell to deliver flowers, a clock on the kitchen wall, a television in the family room, and a radio in your bedroom.

Start a Ben Franklin stamp club for students interested in collecting United States stamps. Information on how to do this is available through the local United States Post Office in your community. It is also possible to invite a post office employee to speak to your class on the Postal Service and its history.

Explain to students that letter writing is an important art in Japan and that each year during October the Japanese postal service issues a special letter writing stamp. Ask a Japanese stamp collector to show the class issues of the letter writing stamp. Research and design a Japanese letter writing stamp for issuance in October of this year. *Note:* The Japanese theme is usually selected from famous works of art.

Beyond the Book

Guided Reading Connections across a Curriculum Rainbow: Communication

Arnold, Caroline, *How Do We Communicate?*
Billings, Charlene, *Fiber Optics: Bright New Way to Communicate*
Bowman, Kathleen, *New Women in Media*
Charlip, Remy, *Handtalk*
Nordstrom, Ursula, *Secret Language*
Schulman, Janet, *Big Hello*
Sundene, Wood, *Messages without Words*

Enriching Connections

FOR GIFTED STUDENTS

Use an encyclopedia to look up the subject communications. List all the forms of communications you can identify through pictures and photographs. If help is needed, ask the library media specialist to help you start the research project.

FOR PARENTS

Ask your child to join you in a "communications walk." Take a pencil and pad and list every form of communications that can be identified as you make a room-by-room survey of your home or walk around the neighborhood. When the list is completed, ask your child to "look again" and predict new communications forms that may be in use when he or she owns a home. Put the information in an envelope, address the envelope to your child, seal with candle wax, date, and store with your personal papers as a family time capsule to be opened in 20 years.

TALKING LEAVES,
THE STORY OF SEQUOYAH

Author: Kohn, Bernice
Illustrator: Valli
Publisher: Prentice-Hall, 1969
Suggested Grade Level: 3-6
Classification: Core Materials
Literary Form: Biography presented in picture form
Theme: Through hard work and ingenuity, people find solutions to problems.

About the Book

STUDENT OBJECTIVES:

1. Retell the *Story of Sequoyah*.

2. Describe the difference between an alphabet and a syllabary.

3. Evaluate the usefulness of a syllabary for the Cherokee Indian tribe.

SYNOPSIS: Sequoyah, a Cherokee Indian born in the eighteenth century, devised a syllabary, a sign for each of the Cherokee language sounds. This was a miracle of language and allowed the Cherokees to begin reading and writing within several weeks. They were even able to write letters and share tribal news immediately.

ABOUT THE AUTHOR AND ILLUSTRATOR: Bernice Kohn, June 15, 1920- .
Valli, no birthdate available.

Bernice Kohn was born in Philadelphia, Pennsylvania. She attended the University of Wisconsin and lives in New York City.

Sequoyah invented a system of writing for the Cherokee tribe. Sequoyah was born in Tennessee of a white father and an Indian princess. His father was respected by the tribe; the tribe had favored the unusual marriage. His father eventually returned home, leaving Sequoyah to be raised by his mother within the tribe.

As an adult, Sequoyah met many white people and was fascinated by their "talking leaves." As an Indian serving in the United States Army, he observed a messenger carrying what resembled a white leaf to the commanding officer. The officer looked at it, nodded his head and said, "We'll see about that." Sequoyah wanted to share the "talking leaves" with his own people from that moment on. He worked for 12 years to solve the problem of language while transcribing all his work on birch bark with pieces of charcoal. He did overcome the difficulties and completed his language work in 1821.

He tried to mediate the problem between the government and the Indians who had been forced to go to a new reservation in the territory of what is now the state of Oklahoma. In the Statuary Hall in the United States Capitol, it is his figure that represents Oklahoma. Sequoyah died in Mexico while searching for some Cherokees to whom he wanted to teach the syllabary.

SELECTED ADDITIONAL TITLES BY THE AUTHOR:

Bat Book
Beachcomber's Book
Echoes
Light
Telephones

Using the Book

Suggested Approach to the Book

Model Lesson #1

- Present a brief biography of Sequoyah to the class. Also relate that he was an extremely important Cherokee Indian who did much to advance his tribe's literacy. Explain that the giant Sequoia trees and Sequoia National Park in California are named after him. He wanted to preserve the history of his tribe and set about to create a system of writing for his own people that would enable them to both read and write in a matter of weeks. His work was phenomenal for this time period. Sequoyah earned the respect of the president of the United States, who honored him with an annual gift of $500.00. This amount of money was a very large sum in the early nineteenth century.

Model Lesson #2

- Read the story about Sequoyah and his famous "talking leaves" to the class. Draw a time line on the blackboard and include some important milestones of communications history. Include the work of Sequoyah. Students can research the dates of important events during the library media center lesson.

Model Lesson #3

- Some questions to discuss with the class:
    1. Examine the title page and explain what the Indians are doing.
    2. Can you guess what "talking leaves" are?
    3. Why didn't people know the dates when Indians were born or died?
    4. Why did Wuh-teh stay with the tribe when Sequoyah's father went back to his own family?
    5. Name some of the things that Sequoyah learned to do.
    6. What did he discover in the army camp that was to change his life?
    7. Tell about the discovery of language.
    8. What is a syllabary?
    9. Tell about the Cherokee Tribal Council meeting.
    10. According to the book, what was the first literary prize given in the United States?

Model Lesson #4

- Compare this story to the story of Pocahontas in terms of art form and technique through the book written and illustrated by

    D'Aulaire, Ingri, and Edgar D'Aulaire, *Pocahontas*

Library Media Center Connections

1. Assist students in using an encyclopedia to research the broad topic communications. Let them explore the lesson through pictures because of the vast amount of material available on this subject.

2. Ask students to list a few important dates of discoveries in the field of communications. They should return to class with their notes and be able to complete a communications timeline with the classroom teacher.

3. Support the class lesson with available study prints and sound film strips.

Computer Connections

Tom Snyder Productions, *Timerliner*

Theme Reading Connections: Sequoyah and the Cherokee Indians

Bealer, Alex, *Only the Names Remain: The Cherokees and the Trail of Tears*
Bleeker, Sonia, *Cherokee: Indians of the Mountains*
Lepthien, Emilie, *Cherokee*
Oppenheim, Joanne, *Sequoyah, Cherokee Hero*
Patterson, Lillie, *Sequoyah: The Cherokee Who Captured Words*
Stein, R. C., *Story of the Trail of Tears*
Underwood, Tom, *Cherokee Legends and the Trail of Tears*

Activities to Connect Literature and Curriculum

ART

Create an Indian sand painting design in a glass container with a cover. Small baby food jars work quite well. Carefully layer different textured materials to create a simple design. Use sand, charcoal, small seeds, beans, peas, and other available items. Do not shake. Place cap over materials when layering is completed.

Weave an Indian design using different yarn textures.

Produce Indian art designs on pieces of sandpaper. The rough texture makes an interesting background for art.

Use the timeline prepared in class as a bulletin board display.

LANGUAGE ARTS

Produce individual student clusters or webs about Sequoyah and the Cherokees.

Use the web for prewriting activities. Prepare a 1-page report about Sequoyah. Attach the web as an additional reference source. Students may also review materials that are listed in the library card catalog and include them as part of the web.

Compose a poem about Sequoyah and record it on a cassette tape with appropriate Indian music in the background.

Record a diary entry as an army commanding officer who just has learned about Sequoyah's syllabary and its use by the Cherokee tribe.

MUSIC

Introduce students to American Indian chant music through cassette recordings. Write your own class background music to be played during the reading of the original poem composed in language arts class.

SCIENCE

Tell the class about the Indian medicine man and some of the herbs used by the Indians.

Try writing the alphabet on tree bark with charcoal.

SOCIAL STUDIES

Trace on a United States desk map the infamous Trail of Tears. Explain the movement of Indians to Oklahoma by the United States government.

Brainstorm what other solutions might have been possible at the time. Role-play the meeting in Washington, D.C., between the government and Sequoyah.

Pretend that you are Sequoyah and have returned to see the United States today. What do you think he would say and feel? Report to the class orally.

Sequoyah wore a silver medal around his neck. It was very important to him because it was a gift from his people. What do you think it was like? Describe a Medal of Achievement that the United States could bestow on him today.

Make a model of the type of tent the Cherokees took with them. Check the resource material available through the library media center.

Beyond the Book

Guided Reading Connections across a Curriculum Rainbow: Sign Language

Cody, *Iron Eyes, Indian Talk: Hand Signals of the North American Indians*
Hofsinde, Robert, *Indian Sign Language*

Enriching Connections

FOR GIFTED STUDENTS

Write a letter to a class friend. Invent your own pictorial Indian language. Share copies of your language with other class members.

Work together as a committee and develop a single picture symbol language. When the committee has reached consensus regarding a pictorial language, make a chart and explain the symbols to other members of the class.

FOR PARENTS

Ask your child to retell the *Story of Sequoyah* to you.

Help your child construct a timeline of his or her life from birth to the present date. Relate special family events that will add meaning to the timeline.

Develop a simple family tree with your child's input. When it is completed, ask the child to provide the illustrations. Combining the family tree and timeline documents into a personal book will provide the child with a feeling of family pride and unity.

*   *   *   *   *   *   *   *   *   *   *

Into the Animal Kingdom

BUNNICULA
A Rabbit-Tale of Mystery

Author: Howe, Deborah
    Howe, James
Illustrator: Daniel, Alan
Publisher: Atheneum, 1981
Suggested Grade Level: 1-5
Classification: Recreational and Motivational Materials
Literary Form: Modern fantasy
Theme: Vampires stalk the earth, and when discovered, must be "done in."

About the Book

STUDENT OBJECTIVES:

1. Retell the story of *Bunnicula*.

2. Point out facts that would make you believe that Bunnicula is a vampire.

3. Decide if Bunnicula is in fact a vampire who sleeps all day and must drain vegetables of their juices at night.

SYNOPSIS: A tiny rabbit is found in a movie theater under unusual circumstances by the Monroe family. He is taken home and strange things begin to happen—a tomato in the refrigerator turns white and when sliced has no juice and is dried out. Is there a vampire rabbit loose in the home?

ABOUT THE AUTHORS AND ILLUSTRATOR: James Howe, August 2, 1946- .
                                            Deborah Howe, August 12, 1946-1978.
                                            Alan Daniel, birthdate not available.

Both James and Deborah Howe were graduated with degrees in theater from Boston University. Deborah Howe worked as an actress, model, and children's record and tape recording artist. James Howe has been involved in the theater as a director, producer, and agent for both writers and actors.

SELECTED ADDITIONAL TITLES BY JAMES HOWE:

Case of the Missing Mother
Day the Teacher Went Bananas
How the Ewoks Saved the Trees: An Old Ewok Legend

SELECTED ADDITIONAL TITLE BY DEBORAH HOWE:

Teddy Bear's Scrapbook

Using the Book

Suggested Approach to the Book

Model Lesson #1

- Plan to read the book aloud to the class. Explain to students that this will be the first example of a short novel that has been introduced to them and will be read in chapters. It is a fantasy story that is make believe and could not really happen. There are no vampires, but they make for exciting reading.

Model Lesson #2

- Locate Transylvania (in Romania) on a map of Eastern Europe and explain that there still remains an old castle that is said to have belonged a long time ago to a Count Dracula. Curious tourists still visit the castle, but none has ever seen a vampire there. Talk about titles of royalty and ask students to give examples. Cluster the titles on the board as a prewriting activity. Keep the list for a future language arts activity.

Model Lesson #3

- Read several passages from the classic adventure story, *Treasure Island*, which Scholarly Cat is reading in *Bunnicula*.

Model Lesson #4

- Art appreciation through book illustrations: Compare the animal illustrations in the following 2 books:

  Cleary, Beverly, *Ramona and Her Father*
  Howe, Deborah, and James Howe, *Bunnicula*

Library Media Center Connections

1. Present a lesson to students on how to locate fiction and nonfiction books that are shelved in a place other than the "easy" section or story hour corner. Explain that fiction books are shelved according to the last name of the author. Give each student a "reference key" with a fiction author's name and title written on it. Ask that students take the key and return to you with the key and book. Check for accuracy and repeat the exercise several times.

2. Using the same "reference key" idea, introduce nonfiction books that are located through a call number. Use transparencies to show examples of a book's author, title, and subject cards. Ask students to locate the book and return the reference key for verification.

3. Finally, ask students to check each other's "reference keys" for correctness.

Computer Connections

Micro Power and Light, *Library Skills*

Theme Reading Connections: Dogs

Anderson, J. I., *I Can Read about Dogs*
Herriot, James, *Only One Woof*
Posell, Elsa, *Dogs*
Radlauer, Ruth, and Ed Radlauer, *Dog Mania*
Selsam, Millicent, and Joyce Hunt, *First Look at Dogs*

Activities to Connect Literature and Curriculum

ART

Construct a model of Count Dracula's castle in Transylvania.
Create miniature model design sets of rooms in Dracula's castle.
Design a cut-and-paste mural of castles. Place into the landscape design at least 10 famous castles of the world. Use an encyclopedia to begin learning about different castles of the world.
Organize a contest and award prizes for the most original and scariest Dracula "puppets" created by drawing on a student's hand with stage makeup.

HEALTH

Research the myths concerning vampires and their blood-drinking habits. When did people first begin believing in such figures? Can you learn why?
Integrate the body and its blood supply as a science lesson component. How much blood does our body contain? How is blood used by our complex body machinery? What is a transfusion? Explain the types of blood used. Who first classified blood into types? When? Why? What are some diseases of the blood? How is science finding new cures for them?

LANGUAGE ARTS

Using the model room stage sets of the castle and puppet hands, present an original Dracula play.
Write a letter to Dracula and ask him to be the next Grand Marshal of the Rose Bowl Parade on New Year's Day in Pasadena, California, or at a parade in your local community. Ask him to suggest an appropriate parade theme.

Write the beginning to an adventure story in 1 paragraph. Polish your work until it reads like the opening paragraph in a good book.

Using several adventure paragraphs written by students, write cumulative tales. Pass an adventure tale down each row and ask students to add 1 well-written paragraph to the story starter. The last student will write the closing paragraph. Read the stories aloud for class enjoyment.

Write an original fantasy story. Work as a team and exchange stories with your partner, read each other's work, and make suggestions to improve the writing. Students are not required to make the recommended changes, but should consider them. It would also be helpful if the fantasy stories could be written and later edited on a computer with a word processing program. Research states that students tire of writing and rewriting manuscripts and write better when corrections are easily made.

SOCIAL STUDIES

Learn more about the Count Dracula castle. When was it built? How many rooms does it have? Is it in an eerie setting? How many people visit it each year?

Read about a court jester. What kind of jokes would he have told? What was his fate if he did not make people laugh?

Beyond the Book

Guided Reading Connections across a Curriculum Rainbow: Castles

Clarke, Richard, *Castles*
Gee, Robyn, *Living in a Castle*
Goodall, John, *Story of a Castle*
Macaulay, David, *Castle*
Odor, *Learning about Castles and Palaces*
Unstead, R. J., *See Inside a Castle*

Enriching Connections

FOR GIFTED STUDENTS

Using an encyclopedia, identify 5 famous castles. Using a fact sheet that you design, compare and contrast them. Present the information in an orderly manner. Include pictures of the castles for comparison purposes.

Read and report on one of America's most famous places, the Randolph Hearst Castle in San Simeon, California. Several years ago, *Life* magazine presented a feature story on the castle and pictured William Randolph Hearst, the owner, having lunch in the knight's dining room. He was using paper napkins and had a bottle of catsup on the table in front of him!

FOR PARENTS

Ask your child if he or she would rather live in a 500-year-old castle or in your present-day home. Why? Can you brainstorm together and name some people who have lived in castles? Do you think anyone will be living in a castle in 500 years? Why?

Next time you have an opportunity to go to the beach, build a sandcastle together. Make it as distinctive as possible, with turrets and spires.

LEO THE LATE BLOOMER

Author: Kraus, Robert
Illustrator: Aruego, Jose
Publisher: Windmill, 1971
Suggested Grade Level: 2-4
Classification: Extended Materials
Literary Form: Picture book
Theme: We don't all grow and develop at the same pace, but in our own time and way.

About the Book

STUDENT OBJECTIVES:

1. Describe, according to the story, a "late bloomer."

2. Dramatize *Leo the Late Bloomer.*

3. Justify Leo's behavior.

SYNOPSIS: Leo, an adorable little tiger cub, does not seem to do anything right. His mother says things will be all right in time. His father wants to know when that will be. Leo does things in his own way and in his own time.

ABOUT THE AUTHOR AND ILLUSTRATOR: Robert Kraus, June 21, 1925- .
Jose Aruego, August 9, 1932- .

Robert Kraus was born in Milwaukee, Wisconsin, and was already a published illustrator by age 11. He had his first cartoon published on the children's page of the *Milwaukee Journal.* Cartoons were his art form and several were purchased by the *Saturday Evening Post* magazine. After finishing art school in New York, he began to do cartoons and covers for *The New Yorker* magazine. *Junior, the Spoiled Cat* was his first published book. He works by sketching the pictures and writing the story at the same time. Kraus explains that after writing 20 books and working 20 years with *The New Yorker* magazine, he started his own publishing company, Windmill Books. His reason for this was that there were many fine artists who had not published children's books, but could, if given an opportunity. Windmill published *Roland, the Minstrel Pig* and *CDB!* by William Steig, the *Norman Rockwell Storybook,* and other best sellers.

How could anyone not be enchanted with the pen name of Robert Kraus—he writes some materials under the signature Eugene H. Hippopotamus.

Jose Aruego is still amazed that he has become a children's illustrator. His home was in Manila, Philippines, where he grew up in a household filled with animals—"3 horses, 7 dogs and their puppies, 6 or 7 cats and their kittens, a backyard filled with chickens and roosters, a house of pigeons, frogs, tadpoles and ducks in our miniature rice paddies that had a lot of water lilies, and 3 very fat pigs that belonged to my sister."* He delights in the fun of illustrating books for children and laughs over the funny animals he creates. He has illustrated many books for children, both by himself and in cooperation with his former wife, Ariane Dewey. The Philippines government honored him with an award for the country's most outstanding artist abroad.

SELECTED ADDITIONAL TITLES BY THE AUTHOR:

Another Mouse to Feed
Big Brother
Boris Bad Enough
Daddy Long Ears
Detective of London
Good Night Little One
Herman the Helper
I, Mouse
Ladybug! Landbug!
Little Giant
Littlest Rabbit
Mert the Blurt
Milton the Early Riser
Noel the Coward
Owliver
Rebecca Hatpin
Springfellow
Three Friends
Trouble with Spider
Whose Mouse Are You?

SELECTED ADDITIONAL TITLES BY THE ILLUSTRATOR:

Another Mouse to Feed
Boris Bad Enough
Crocodile's Tale
Good Night
Herman the Helper
If Dragon Flies Made Honey
King and His Friends
Lizard Song
Look What I Can Do
Mert the Blurt
Milton the Early Riser

---

*Doris de Montreville and Elizabeth D. Crawford, eds., *Fourth Book of Junior Authors and Illustrators* (New York: H. W. Wilson, 1978).

Never Say Ugh to a Bug
Noel the Coward
One Duck, Another Duck
Owliver
Pilyo the Piranha
Three Friends
We Hide, You Seek
Where Does the Sun Go at Night?
Whose Mouse Are You?

Using the Book

Suggested Approach to the Book

Model Lesson #1

- Introduce the author and illustrator as artists who have produced a large number of children's works as author and illustrator, respectively. Share the pen name of Kraus with the students. Look carefully at Aruego's funny animals that make him laugh.

Model Lesson #2

- Read *Leo the Late Bloomer* to the class. Ask them if they know what a "late bloomer" is. Enjoy the pictures with the class. Explain that there are 3 friends, *Leo the Late Bloomer*, *Herman the Helper*, and *Milton the Early Riser* who have had books written about them. They meet together in 1 storybook called *Three Friends*. Students may want to join them in their adventures through reading.

Model Lesson #3

- Some questions to ask students:
    1. Look at the opening page and sympathize with poor Leo, who could not do anything right. Have you ever had a day when you felt like Leo looked? Tell the class about it.
    2. Name the things that Leo could not do that the other animals could. Look at the pictures to formulate your answers.
    3. What did Leo's father want him to do?
    4. Tell what little Leo did.
    5. List the things Leo did while his father was not watching.
    6. What happened when Leo bloomed?
    7. What did Leo say?

Model Lesson #4

- Art appreciation through picture books: Compare the art of the following books starring *Leo the Late Bloomer*

    Kraus, Robert, *Leo the Late Bloomer*
    Kraus, Robert, *Three Friends*

Library Media Center Connections

1. Research tigers, pandas, and octopuses through available materials in the library media center. Choose to report on one.

2. Questions that will need explaining are:

   What are the physical characteristics of the animal?

   Where is its native habitat? (Find and label the native habitat on a world map.)

   What food does it eat?

   How many young are usually born to the mother and what kind of care do they receive?

   What kind of problems may the animal encounter?

   Who are its enemies?

   What is a typical day for the animal like?

3. Plan to integrate the research unit with an introduction to the library media center card catalog. Explain to students that research skills are like a treasure hunt. There are many prizes possible, but it takes careful searching to find the best material available. Use the card catalog as a treasure box to locate all the possible sources of material.

4. Teach students to evaluate each source they locate with a critical eye. Have them answer all the questions listed above about the animal they have chosen. Have students write a simple 1-page report incorporating the answers to the questions.

Computer Connections

Unicorn Software, *Animal Kingdom*

Theme Reading Connections: Solitude

Hallinan, P. K., *Just Being Alone*
Hayes, Geoffrey, *Bear by Himself*
Henkes, Kevin, *All Alone*
Keyser, Marcia, *Roger on His Own*

Activities to Connect Literature and Curriculum

ART

Plan a classroom jungle theme mural and include Leo, Herman, and Milton in the scene. Use the research information from the library media center lesson to plan the habitat, food sources, number of young, and predators.

Study some jungle scenes as painted by the well-known French artist Rousseau.

Have students create their own funny animals.

LANGUAGE ARTS

Pretend that you are an animal zoo keeper and have been sent to Africa to observe your animal in its native environment. Make diary entries for a week about your animal. Information from library media center research may be used in this format in lieu of a written report.

Write a letter back to the zoo director and report on your progress concerning animal observations.

SCIENCE

Make all the plans necessary to ship several of your animals back to the zoo. Plan for the zoo to have a suitable display area available when they arrive as well as adequate food supplies.

Beyond the Book

Guided Reading Connections across a Curriculum Rainbow: Tigers

Cajacob, Thomas, and Theresa Burton, *Close to the Wild*
Green, Carl, and William Sanford, *Bengal Tiger*
Hoffman, Mary, *Animals in the Wild*
Hogan, Paula, *Tiger*
Hunt, Patricia, *Tigers*
McClung, Robert, *Last of the Bengal Tigers*
Torgersen, Don, *Lion Prides and Tiger Tracks*

Enriching Connections

FOR GIFTED STUDENTS

In a shoe box, make a miniature jungle scene of an endangered animal's home.

List as many endangered species as possible. Draw a picture of each animal and use it to mark its habitat on a world map.

What kind of plans would you make in order to secure financial help for a worldwide animal protection program? Who should give help and why?

FOR PARENTS

Using pandas as an example, talk with your child about the problems of animals in the wild. In the case of pandas, like many other animals, civilization is encroaching on their living space. As homes are built, land is lost to animals and they die because they cannot find food and shelter any longer. Also, the food supply is not dependable. The bamboo that is food for the pandas blooms sometimes at irregular intervals. When this happens, the pandas do not always have enough to eat and not all pandas survive.

FABLES

Author: Lobel, Arnold
Illustrator: Lobel, Arnold
Publisher: Harper & Row, 1980
Suggested Grade Level: 3-5
Classification: Core Materials
Literary Form: Fables
Theme: Lessons of life are presented through fables.

About the Book

STUDENT OBJECTIVES:

1. Recognize the literary form of a fable.

2. Retell a fable.

3. Develop a new fable and state the moral.

SYNOPSIS: Arnold Lobel, a noted illustrator, presents 20 animal fables complete with original art.

ABOUT THE AUTHOR-ILLUSTRATOR: Arnold Lobel, May 22, 1933- .
   Arnold Lobel was born in California of parents who in the 1930s were seeking an impossible pot of gold at an inopportune time. The parents returned home to Schenectady, New York, where Arnold grew up. His memories of childhood are sad ones, as his parents divorced and he was very ill and remembers spending long periods in the hospital. His health improved as a teenager, and he realized then that he wanted to become an artist.
   Later, he was graduated from the Pratt Institute in Brooklyn, where he met his wife, Anita. She is also a noted children's writer and artist. Throughout the early years, they worked independently at home in the same studio and served as each other's critics. Recently they have collaborated successfully on several titles.
   Ideas for Lobel's books have come from his own childhood memories rather than from observing his children. "I never try my ideas out on children—they should see the finished performance, not the rehearsal."* "Mr. Lobel describes himself as a 'confident illustrator. But when it comes to the writing of the stories for my books, my approach is far more cautious and apprehensive.' Cautious or confident, the results are always a perfect meld of pictures and text."** He is a diversified author-illustrator and is well known for his series of Frog and Toad books, which have received the following awards:

---

*Lee Bennett Hopkins, *Books Are by People* (Chicago: Citation Press, 1969).
**Arnold Lobel, *Fables* (New York: Harper & Row, 1980), jacket flap.

Frog and Toad Are Friends (1970), Caldecott Honor Book

Frog and Toad Together (1972), Newbery Honor Book

Holiday for Mr. Muster (1962), one of *New York Times* list of best illustrated books of the year

Fables (1980), Caldecott Medal book 1981

SELECTED ADDITIONAL TITLES BY THE AUTHOR-ILLUSTRATOR:

Book of Pigericks
Days with Frog and Toad
Frog and Toad All Year
Giant John
Grasshopper on the Road
Lucille
Ming Lo Moves the Mountain
Mouse Soup
Mouse Tales
On the Day Peter Stuyvesant Sailed into Town
Owl at Home
Small Pig
Uncle Elephant

SELECTED ADDITIONAL TITLES BY THE AUTHOR, ILLUSTRATED BY ANITA LOBEL:

How the Rooster Saved the Day
On Market Street
Rose in My Garden
Treeful of Pigs

Using the Book

Suggested Approach to the Book

Model Lesson #1

- Introduce Arnold Lobel as an author-illustrator who is diversified in his art techniques and choice of subjects. Explain that as an illustrator he views himself as competent, but as a person who must work very hard to write children's books. Ask students how many of his Frog and Toad series books they have read. List the titles and graph their responses.

Model Lesson #2

- Read aloud and share the art depicted in several fables. Allow time after reading to discuss the moral of each fable.

Model Lesson #3

- Continue to read fables aloud and share the art. Involve the class in discussing the fables and their morals.

Model Lesson #4

- Art appreciation through picture books: Compare the story and art styles of Arnold Lobel and that of Arthur Rackham, who was a famous book illustrator of another era.

    Lobel, Arnold, *Fables*
    Rackham, Arthur, *Aesop's Fables*

Library Media Center Connections

1. Select, read, and list the titles and authors, if known, of 5 fables.

2. Instruct students to cluster or web the titles and the dates of publication. Classify the titles into publication date categories within the web.

3. Design a front and back cover for your favorite fable book that needs a new cover. Mount new cover pages back-to-back and make mobiles or attach with a string to the ceiling of the library media center in order to encourage the reading of fables.

Theme Reading Connections: Fables

Aesop, *Aesop for Children* (Winter Milo, illustrator)
Aesop, *Aesop's Fables* (Ann McGovern, editor)
Aesop, *Caldecott Aesop—Twenty Fables*
Andersen, Hans Christian, *Emperor's New Clothes*
Bagley, Victor, *La Fontaine's Fables in Modern Clothes*
Bird, E. J., *Ten Tall Tales*
Galdone, Paul, *Three Aesop Fox Fables*
Lionni, Leo, *Frederick's Fables*
Miller, Edna, *Mousekin's Fables*
Parry, Marian, *City Mouse-Country Mouse and Two More Mouse Tales from Aesop*
Stevens, Janet, *Tortoise and the Hare: An Aesop Fable*

Activities to Connect Literature and Curriculum

ART

Design sandwich boards like fable book jackets to wear in a "Fable Parade."

Create a selection of fable bookmarks that can be reproduced and given to the library media center for schoolwide distribution when students check out books. Each one should be signed and dated by the student artist.

Using the techniques illustrated in *On Market Street*, make an alphabet letter using objects that begin with the same letter. Exhibit the unique letter representations in the library media center. Award prizes for the most unique presentation and the most complex materials used in the project.

LANGUAGE ARTS

Select and practice telling fable stories. Arrange for students to tell fables in other classrooms.

Write and illustrate a new fable with a moral.

Compare fables as presented by several illustrators and writers. Students may make initial presentations in collaborative learning groups and then select a person from each group to share a new fable with the class.

NUTRITION

As a class project, list food items mentioned in fables. Plan a nutritious snack using some of these foods. For example, Arnold Lobel mentions apples, candy, crab, lobster, bean soup, brussels sprouts, mashed potatoes, and other foods.

Ask the school food service to plan a "Fable Luncheon" to be scheduled on the same day as the "Fable Parade."

SCIENCE

Use the Lobel fable, *Frogs at the Rainbow's End*, to explore science. The frogs are rushing to the place where the rainbow ends. It is a dark cave where a snake lives. The snake swallows all the frogs in a gulp.

Do snakes usually eat frogs?

How does a snake eat its prey?

Why do snakes have curved teeth?

How do poisonous snakes inject their venom into their victims?

SOCIAL STUDIES

March in a "Fable Parade" and wear the sandwich boards constructed during the art activity to advertise your favorite fable. Choose appropriate music for the parade. Distribute bags of popcorn to the parade watchers. Invite parents and younger brothers and sisters to the event. Distribute a parade program written by the students.

Beyond the Book

Guided Reading Connections across a Curriculum Rainbow: Pigs

Allard, Harry, *There's a Party at Mona's Tonight*
Blegvad, Lenore, *This Little Pig-A-Wig*
Brooks, Walter, *Freddy Goes Camping*
Goodall, John, *Adventures of Paddy Pork*
Lavine, Sigmund, *Wonders of Pigs*
McPhail, David, *Pig Pig* Series
Orbach, Ruth, *Apple Pigs*

Peet, Bill, *Chester the Worldly Pig*
Scott, Jack, *Book of Pigs*
Steig, William, *Amazing Bone*
Winthrop, Elizabeth, *Sloppy Kisses*

Enriching Connections

FOR GIFTED STUDENTS

Using index cards, read and compile an annotated bibliography of Arnold Lobel's books. Make an interesting statement about each book. Organize a student file in the library media center of annotated bibliographies about important authors and illustrators, starting with the Lobel cards.

FOR PARENTS

Discuss adages, colloquial expressions, and fable morals with your child. Some examples are:

When it rains, it pours.

It's thundering and the old man's snoring.

The early bird gets the worm.

Save the best for last.

A stitch in time saves nine.

A penny saved is a penny earned

Sticks and stones will break my bones, but names will do me no harm.

Add examples you remember from your childhood.

*   *   *   *   *   *   *   *   *   *   *

COLUMBUS

Author: D'Aulaire, Ingri
         D'Aulaire, Edgar
Illustrator: D'Aulaire, Ingri
         D'Aulaire, Edgar
Publisher: Doubleday and Company, 1955
Suggested Grade Level: 3-6
Classification: Extended Materials
Literary Form: Picture book with a masterful researched text
Theme: The story of Columbus's discovery of the New World is timeless.

About the Book

STUDENT OBJECTIVES:

1. Interpret information about the 4 voyages of Christopher Columbus.

2. Compare the support given by the king and queen to Columbus on each of the 4 voyages.

3. Plan a voyage of exploration to today's frontier, "the Ocean."

4. Analyze the problems of being a pioneer explorer in any field.

SYNOPSIS: Columbus made 4 voyages from Spain to the New World. This version of the Columbus story is a biographical presentation and points out the many hardships involved in being an explorer in the 1400s.

ABOUT THE AUTHORS-ILLUSTRATORS: Edgar D'Aulaire, September 30, 1898-1986.
                              Ingri D'Aulaire, 1901-1980.
    Ingri D'Aulaire was born Ingri Mortenson in Kongsberg, Norway. Her father was a government official, and she remembers moving from one government townhouse in town to the next. Her summers were fun and she spent them on her grandfather's estate, which was in an area similar to Vermont.

Edgar D'Aulaire laughed about his birth certificate, because it lists his place of birth as the official residence of his parents—Campoblenio, Switzerland. He was actually born in a hospital in Munich, Germany.

The couple met in art school in Paris, France, and were married a year later. Their work took them to many places, including New York City. They fell in love with the city and were able to return as immigrants to the United States.

The art form perfected by the couple was lithography. When they began working with lithography, it was a tedious art form, requiring that the picture be drawn on a stone with a crayon. There was no way to correct mistakes; the work had to be started again. Critics of their work say that they began to perfect their art form with the book *George Washington*, which is considered to be crude in art application, and were at their best with the publication of the picture book *Abraham Lincoln*. *Abraham Lincoln* was researched extensively, as all their books were. To collect information, the D'Aulaires would visit each place and "pitch our tent wherever he had been staying, to smell the same flowers, be bitten by the same bugs, and have the same thunderstorms burst over our heads." Their research and illustrations were rewarded in 1940 with the announcement that *Abraham Lincoln* had been awarded the third Caldecott Medal.

The research for *Columbus* spanned 2 years while they traveled to every spot described in the book. They drove from Italy to Spain, visited Genoa, and did more research by traveling even to the La Rabida Cloister. Another trip took the D'Aulaires to the Caribbean to see the islands through the eyes of the explorer, Columbus.

After traveling so far and sketching so much, the pair returned home to the United States and took 1 more year to combine the research and sketches in the classic book we still treasure today as a resource guide to one explorer's voyages.

Seven biographical books were written and illustrated by the D'Aulaires. Included are portraits of George Washington, Abraham Lincoln, Leif Ericson, Pocahontas, William Cody, Benjamin Franklin, and Columbus. In the 1960s they turned their talents to mythology and produced the definitive *D'Aulaires' Book of Greek Myths and Norse Gods and Giants*.

SELECTED ADDITIONAL TITLES BY THE AUTHORS-ILLUSTRATORS:

Animals Everywhere
Children of the Northlights
Don't Count Your Chicks
East of the Sun and West of the Moon
Nils
Ola
Terrible Troll Bird
Wings for Per

Using the Book

Suggested Approach to the Book

Model Lesson #1

- Present the attached biographical materials and explain the methodology used by the D'Aulaires to research materials for their books. Examine the cover of the book. Why do you think Columbus is holding an orange and looking at a butterfly on the other side of the fruit? Support your answers with reasons. The question will be answered when the book is read aloud.

Model Lesson #2

• Read the story of Columbus aloud. Allow 2 class sessions to complete the book. Relate the fine art to the text.

Model Lesson #3

• Some questions for class discussion:
    1. Describe the map printed before the story begins.
    2. Examine the title page. What ideas do we have about the book from these pictures?
    3. Retell the story of the childhood of Columbus.
    4. Tell how Columbus decided that the world was round.
    5. Did he think that people in China walked upside down?
    6. How did Columbus survive the wreck of his ship?
    7. What were the fairy tale lands of the Far East supposed to look like?
    8. What was the shape of maps in Portugal at that time?
    9. Describe the king and queen of Spain and their response to Columbus's request to sail under their names.
    10. Take turns in class telling about the 4 voyages he made.
    11. What was Columbus like as an old man? Why? Could he have been different? Why?

Model Lesson #4

• Art appreciation through picture books: Compare the art of the D'Aulaires with this contemporary biography of Columbus:

    Ventura, Piero, *Christopher Columbus*

Library Media Center Connections

1. Plan to display Columbus books from the media center collection. Other books about explorers may be included. Include stories about space explorations also.

2. Plan an "Explorer's Week" program and display books, study prints, models, and available materials. Supplement with appropriate films.

3. Since we believe that we have mapped, photographed, and explored all the land masses in the world, can you propose a way to preserve undeveloped land such as the swampy Everglades of Florida, the deserts of New Mexico, or the Rocky Mountains of Colorado? Note that the areas named are watery, very hot, or extremely cold.

Instructional Materials Connections

National Geographic sound filmstrip, *People behind Our Holidays*

Computer Connections

Intellectual Software, *Map Reading Skills*

Theme Reading Connections: Columbus

Bains, Rae, *Christopher Columbus*
Foster, Genevieve, *Year of Columbus 1492*
Fritz, Jean, *Where Do You Think You're Going, Christopher Columbus?*
Gleiter, Jan, *Christopher Columbus*
Golden Press, *Voyages of Christopher Columbus*
Gross, Ruth, *Book about Christopher Columbus*
Johnson, Spencer, *Value of Curiosity: The Story of Christopher Columbus*
Knight, David, *I Can Read about Christopher Columbus*
Parker, Margot, *What Is Columbus Day?*
Richards, Dorothy, *Christopher Columbus Who Sailed On!*
Weil, Lisl, *I, Christopher Columbus*

Activities to Connect Literature and Curriculum

ART

Construct a cut-and-paste mural of Columbus arriving in the New World. Include water, ships, jungle, birds and flowers, and Indians.

Create replicas of Columbus's ships using ice cream shop banana split boats. Give a prize for the most authentic model.

Draw a picture from the viewpoint of Columbus looking out from the deck of the *Santa Maria*. Use imagination to gain the best view.

Construct the lead ship, the *Santa Maria*, using a milk carton.

LANGUAGE ARTS

Pretend that you are a cook who sailed with Columbus. Write a letter home describing the voyage. Be sure to tell about the food and eating conditions aboard the vessel.

As part of the media center "Explorer's Week," write and publish a newspaper set in 1492. Brainstorm and use the words generated as part of the newspaper assignment.

Using the outline design of a ship with a large sail, write a poem about discoveries and write the message on a sail.

Pretend you are a sailor and the ship is being attacked; send a message in a bottle asking for help.

MATH

Find out about the ships and supplies used on each voyage. Remember that the ships were about the size or just slightly larger of a modern day mobile home—50 feet long.

MUSIC

Listen to cassette tapes of music about the sea and sailors.

NUTRITION

Columbus sailed to find the spice route. Why? List the spices by name and graph, by number of students, the spices that class members have tasted. Which spices are the favorites? Why? Place 10 different spices in containers labeled with letters. Challenge students to identify each one by sight and smell.

SCIENCE

Discuss the need for spices to preserve food at the time of Columbus.

SOCIAL STUDIES

"Interview" Columbus on tape as he prepares to leave on his first voyage.
"Interview" Columbus when he arrives in the New World.
"Interview" Columbus when he has retired from the sea and is an old man.
Combine the three interviews into a special news program. Use sound effects if possible.

Beyond the Book

Guided Reading Connections across a Curriculum Rainbow: Explorers

Artman, John, *Explorers*
Fradin, Dennis, *Explorers*
National Geographic, *Books for Early Explorers, Series 5*
Sandak, Cass, *Explorers and Discovery*
Taylor, Mark, *Henry the Explorer*

Enriching Connections

FOR GIFTED STUDENTS

Plan a new outerspace discovery expedition. You are captain of the *Adventure*. Pick your staff, choose your transportation, and plan food and other details. Remember to keep a captain's log of the planning.

FOR PARENTS

Tell your child about early space exploration. Talk about the sacrifices that people have made to obtain information on outerspace. Explain that we have suffered the loss of people in space exploration, including astronauts and the first teacher in space. Explain that sometimes people give a great deal of themselves to be on the frontier of discovery. Columbus had goals and plans as an explorer, too. What kind of information do you think we can have as a result of space shuttles in the future?

JACK JOUETT'S RIDE

Author: Haley, Gail
Illustrator: Haley, Gail
Publisher: Viking, 1973
Suggested Grade Level: 3-5
Classification: Core Materials
Literary Form: Historical fiction
Theme: Liberty in the United States has been won through the bravery of many people.

About the Book

STUDENT OBJECTIVES:

1. Recall the ride of Jack Jouett to save colonial leaders from British capture.

2. Compare the rides of Jack Jouett and Paul Revere.

3. Plan the delivery of a modern-day warning message.

SYNOPSIS: Jack Jouett was resting outside the Cuckoo Tavern when he observed British soldiers galloping down the only road to Charlottesville, Virginia. There slept Thomas Jefferson, Patrick Henry, Benjamin Harrison, and Thomas Nelson, all signers of the Declaration of Independence. They had to be warned!

ABOUT THE AUTHOR-ILLUSTRATOR: Gail Haley, November 4, 1939- .
Gail Haley grew up in Shuffletown, North Carolina, in a hard but beautiful environment. The people held quilting bees, saved flour sacks to make dresses and children's toys, plowed the fields, and pumped their water from wells. Life was difficult, but peaceful. She wandered through the fields barefooted creating a world of fantasy for herself.
Her father was art director of the *Charlotte Observer*, and she had many opportunities to observe the newspaper world when she visited his office. As she has said, "In the art department and pressrooms I soaked up the exciting smells and sounds of the graphic arts. I've had printer's ink and rubber cement in my veins ever since."*

---

*Doris de Montreville and Donna Hill, eds., *Third Book of Junior Authors* (New York: H. W. Wilson, 1972).

Gail Haley illustrated 6 books for other authors before she was able to sell her first manuscript. She works in various art media and chooses the one most appropriate to the text. She does not explain everything in her books, but wants the reader to have an opportunity to use his or her own imagination to complete the visual picture.

She is a master at wood block printing. She chose that art form for her Caldecott Medal book, *A Story, A Story*, an African folktale. It was also the medium she chose for her first, privately printed book, *My Kingdom for a Dragon*. She bound and sold the 1,000 copies of this book herself.

SELECTED ADDITIONAL TITLES BY THE AUTHOR-ILLUSTRATOR:

Go Away, Stay Away
Green Man
Noah's Ark
Post Office Cat

Using the Book

Suggested Approach to the Book

Model Lesson #1

- Introduce the author-illustrator to the class as an artist who uses different materials and techniques to illustrate her work. Explain that she has received a Caldecott Medal for *A Story, A Story*, an African folktale, and a Kate Greenaway Award, England's most prestigious award given to illustrators, for *Post Office Cat*.

Model Lesson #2

- Before beginning the book, read to the class the research information cited by Gail Haley in the beginning of the book. Explain that she has thoroughly researched the information in order to retell the story.

- Read the Henry Wadsworth Longfellow poem, "Paul Revere's Ride," to the class. Compare it with the verse presentation of *Jack Jouett's Ride*. How are the two works alike and what differences are identifiable? Do you think one was easier to write than the other? Explain your reasons.

- Closely examine the wood block illustrations. They are different than other art that we have examined. What impression does the art leave on the reader? Explain that the wood blocks are carved by the illustrator and that each color is printed separately. Wood block printing represents a strong sense of power and dynamic color. Is this an appropriate use of materials and colors for a book about an event in the early days of a new country that had just declared its independence? Look how the cover illustration extends across the front and back covers of the book. Why is this effective?

Model Lesson #3

- Some questions to discuss with the class:

    1. Look at the first illustration. Does it relate a feeling of what the book will be about?
    2. How does the title page establish the feeling of time and history?
    3. By looking at the picture, describe the Cuckoo Tavern. What was the function of a tavern during the colonial period?
    4. Why do you think Gail Haley used a red hat in a black picture?
    5. Who were the Green Dragoons? Do you see Jack Jouett in the picture? Look closely for them in later illustrations. Can you see them among the trees? They are all the same color—green.
    6. Whom did the colonists need to fight against for freedom? Name them.
    7. Describe the night ride of Jack Jouett. How was it different from Paul Revere's ride, which happened earlier?
    8. Tell about the 3 stops that the British made earlier in the evening.
    9. Who was Tarleton?
    10. What did he mean by the statement, "On to Charlottesville, Dragoons; bigger game is yet ahead!"
    11. What did the ferryman do for Jack Jouett?
    12. Describe the scene that greeted Jack Jouett at Monticello.
    13. What message did he deliver to the people of Charlottesville?
    14. Tell the story about how he helped General Stevens, who was wounded.
    15. What are "epaulets and braid?"
    16. What is an epilogue?

Model Lesson #4

- Art appreciation through picture books: Compare the African folklore presentations through art and story of the following Caldecott Medal artists:

    Brown, Marcia, *Once a Mouse*
    Haley, Gail, *A Story, A Story*

Library Media Center Connections

1. As an introduction to the lesson, show examples of art materials such as tubes of oil paint, watercolors and brushes, felt-tipped pens, chalk, and wood blocks. Show children's book illustrations, art study prints, and student classroom artwork as examples of art techniques used today.

2. Select 10 books that are Caldecott Medal books and list the art media used to integrate the story text. Is it possible to identify all of the art forms of the 10 titles selected? Do not be concerned if you cannot decide what art form was selected. It is not always easy to tell what kind of materials and art technique were used. Sometimes you obtain this information through research about the author. Students should work in teams and help each other to make choices.

Theme Reading Connections: Wood Block Printing

Brown, Marcia, *All Butterflies* (alphabet); *How, Hippo*
Carle, Eric, *All about Arthur* (alphabet)
Clifton, Lucille, *Everett Anderson's Year*
Emberley, Ed, *Drummer Hoff*
Frasconi, Antonio, *See and Say, a Picture Book in Four Languages*

Activities to Connect Literature and Curriculum

ART

Design and print a greeting card using the wood block technique. If cutting linoleum is too difficult for students, substitute styrofoam, vegetables, or cardboard. Use your best lettering to print the greeting.

Begin to think in terms of art materials selected and techniques that are used to illustrate children's books. Plan a bulletin board display and include examples of student art and magazine pictures that are representative of art styles and techniques. Label the examples.

Ask a guest artist to come and talk to the class about the materials and techniques an artist can choose for a picture.

LANGUAGE ARTS

Write a class poem about *Jack Jouett's Ride* that rhymes. Display a copy of it on the classroom bulletin board and include examples of wood block printing.

Record the poem using appropriate background sounds. The sounds of horse hooves may be made by striking coconut shells on a table top. Students can make breathing sounds for the running horse. "Voice unders" can be added for the ferryman, the servant at Monticello, and townspeople by students speaking softly away from the microphone.

SOCIAL STUDIES

Brief research topics that may be assigned follow:

colonial life	Tarleton	Patrick Henry
King George	Jack Jouett	Thomas Jefferson
Green Dragoons	Monticello	General Stevens
Charlottesville	Declaration of Independence	Paul Revere

Beyond the Book

Guided Reading Connections across a Curriculum Rainbow: United States History

Dalgliesh, Alice, *Fourth of July Story*
Peterson, Helen, *Give Us Liberty: The Story of the Declaration of Independence*
Phelan, Mary, *Fourth of July*
Richards, Norman, *Story of the Declaration of Independence*; *Story of Monticello*

Enriching Connections

FOR GIFTED STUDENTS

Plan a dinner for the founding fathers and signers of the Declaration of Independence. Draw a seating chart and list the names of the dinner guests. Where in the library would you look to find the names of the signers of the Declaration of Independence listed?

Design a special menu card for the event and include the dinner menu you selected. What will the room look like? Sketch the dining room, table setting, and clothing to be worn.

An appropriate reference book, *First Ladies' Cook Book* (Parent's Magazine, 1982) has excellent color photographs of the table settings, room decors, and menus representative of each of the presidents of the United States. Use this book as a primary resource guide.

FOR PARENTS

In today's newspaper, can you find an example of someone who is fighting for personal or political freedom? Ask your child to read the clipping and explain how he or she feels about the issue. Should the person or persons continue to fight for his or her rights? Give reasons.

LITTLE HOUSE IN THE BIG WOODS

Author: Wilder, Laura Ingalls
Illustrator: Williams, Garth
Publisher: Harper & Row, 1932; pictures revised, 1953
Suggested Grade Level: 2-4
Classification: Core Materials
Literary Form: Historical fiction
Theme: Life as a pioneer settler in the late 1800s was hard work everyday except on Sunday.

About the Book

STUDENT OBJECTIVES:

1. Locate Wisconsin, the setting of the *Little House in the Big Woods*, on a map.

2. Classify work that had to be performed by the family by the 4 seasons.

3. Compare the Wilder family life with your family life today.

SYNOPSIS: *Little House in the Big Woods* is a story about the Wilder family and their life as viewed through a calendar year. The 13 chapters provide a circular perspective of the existence of a pioneer family in early United States history.

ABOUT THE AUTHOR AND ILLUSTRATOR: Laura Ingalls Wilder, February 7, 1867-1957.
Garth Williams, 1912- .

The series of autobiographical Little House books reflects the pioneer spirit of America from one person's viewpoint, Laura Ingalls Wilder. Even though she did not begin writing until middle age, Laura Ingalls Wilder has had a profound affect on children's literature. She chronicled her own life story from her first book, *Little House in the Big Woods*, when she was 5, through a series of 6 more stories. The original title proposed for the first book in 1920 was "When Grandma Was a Little Girl," which eventually became *Little House in the Big Woods*.

Other titles in the series are *Little House on the Prairie*, telling about the first of many moves that the Wilder family would make; *On the Banks of Plum Creek*, describing life in Minnesota where the family moved after being forced to vacate their previous home by the United States government; *By the Shores of Silver Lake*, in which Mary has now become blinded by scarlet fever and Pa works on the developing railroad; and the last 3 books in the series, *Long Winter*, *Little Town on the Prairie*, and *These Happy Golden Years*, centered around their home in DeSmet, South Dakota.

Laura Ingalls Wilder tells us: "Great improvements in living have been made because every American has been free to pursue his happiness, and so long as Americans are free they will continue to make our country ever more wonderful."*

Garth Williams is a prominent illustrator known for his work in *Stuart Little*, *Charlotte's Web*, and the reissue of the Laura Ingalls Wilder books in the 1950s. He is equally well known for his Golden Book illustrations, where he has recreated animals through their human qualities. *Baby Farm Animals* and the *Big Golden Animal ABC* feature pictures that present animals who are rich in the personification of people.

Garth Williams has illustrated over 60 book titles, and like many children's book illustrators has been engaged in other art forms including architecture, theater scenery, poster design, murals, sculpture, and textile design.

SELECTED ADDITIONAL TITLES BY THE ILLUSTRATOR:

Amigo
Bedtime for Frances
Chester Cricket's Pigeon Ride
Chicken Book
Do You Know What I'll Do?
Emmett's Pig
Fox Eyes
Little Giant Girl and Elf Boys
Over and Over
Rabbit's Wedding
Sky Was Blue
Three Little Animals
Wait Till the Moon Is Full

---

*Stanley J. Kunitz and Howard Haycraft, eds., *Junior Book of Authors* (New York: H. W. Wilson, 1951).

Using the Book

Suggested Approach to the Book

Model Lesson #1

- Tell children that both the author and the illustrator are well-known people who have written and illustrated books for children. Present the attached biographical material. They will recognize the book titles and the art style.

Model Lesson #2

- Read *Little House in the Big Woods* aloud in 13 installments. Enjoy each chapter. Explain that the book begins in the fall and will proceed through 3 other seasons, and that the story will end with the coming of fall again and the storing of the crop for winter.

- Point out the descriptions of clothing, food, housing, and travel that are inherent to the book. Compare and contrast the life style of the Wilders with that of children in the class today, who live in a high-tech age of modern conveniences and swift modes of transportation.

Model Lesson #3

- Art appreciation through picture books: Compare the art style of Garth Williams and that of Barbara Cooney, who also presented a slice of early American life in *Ox-Cart Man*, a farm book viewed through the 4 seasons.

     Hall, Donald, *Ox-Cart Man*
     Wilder, Laura Ingalls, *Little House in the Big Woods*

Library Media Center Connections

1. Using different chapters of *Little House in the Big Woods*, assign teams of students to rewrite a chapter in diary form from the viewpoint of the mother, who writes the family history every night before retiring.

2. Illustrate sections of the diary account, design an appropriate cover for the writings, and present the finished product as a completed diary for the year 1872-1873.

3. Reproduce a copy of the diary for each student in the class.

Theme Reading Connections: Farms

Arnow, Jan, *Hay from Seed to Feed*
Azarian, Mary, *Farmer's Alphabet*
Booth, Eugene, *On the Farm*
Demuth, Patricia, *Joel: Growing Up a Farm Man*
DeWitt, Jamie, *Jamie's Turn*

Harkonen, Helen, *Farms and Farmers in Art*
Provensen, Alice, and Martin Provensen, *Town and Country*; *Year at Maple Farm*
Rudstrom, Lennart, and Carl Larsson, *Farm*

Activities to Connect Literature and Curriculum

ART

Present a cut-and-paste mural of the locations of the 7 Laura Ingalls Wilder homes.

Make decorated paper bonnets for the girls and hats for the boys to wear during a Laura Ingalls Wilder theme day.

Ask students to sketch the attic of the Wilder home and all the food products stored there from the descriptions in *Little House in the Big Woods*.

HEALTH

Research and make a list of the "bitter" herbs and cooking herbs stored in the attic for medicine and food.

LANGUAGE ARTS

Choose your favorite chapter in the book and design a book cover that best illustrates the material in the chapter. Put the best covers in plastic jackets and cover some worn copies of the library books with them.

Read another book in the Little House series. Tape a 3-minute book report that you would use for a radio spot to encourage other students to read the book as part of Children's Book Week in November.

A Laura Ingalls Wilder award has been established to honor an outstanding author for his or her work in children's literature once every 5 years. Nominate some authors. Organize a political campaign to select a winner. Reach a class consensus about the person you would like to nominate. This may be organized as an all-school project, and voting may be implemented through a simplified computer program in the library media center. Each class may decorate its classroom door to promote its choice of candidate.

Write a letter to the Laura Ingalls Wilder committee and submit your author nomination.

MUSIC

Listen to selected theme tapes of Western folk music.

Beyond the Book

Guided Reading Connections across a Curriculum Rainbow: The West

Ames, Lee J., *Make Twenty-Five Felt Tip Drawings Out West*
Bierhorst, John, *Ring in the Prairie*
Gammell, Stephen, *Git Along, Old Scudder*

Levine, Ellen, *If You Traveled West in a Covered Wagon*
McCall, Edith, *Steamboats to the West*

Enriching Connections

FOR GIFTED STUDENTS

Create a pictorial map of the United States. Trace on it the travels of the Wilder family from the *Little House in the Big Woods* to *These Happy Golden Years*.

Build a covered wagon model and include figures of the Wilder family and their animals crossing the prairie. Display these craft projects in the library media center.

Advertise for pioneers to join your wagon train west from Carthage, Missouri.

FOR PARENTS

Share with your child your family heritage. Are there any historical figures or pioneer settlers that you know about in your history? Draw a family tree for your child and challenge him or her to fill in the parent and grandparent entries as well as the information about brothers and sisters.

*   *   *   *   *   *   *   *   *   *   *

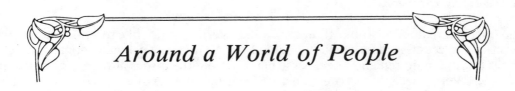

Around a World of People

WHY MOSQUITOES BUZZ
IN PEOPLE'S EARS

Author: Aardema, Verna
Illustrator: Dillon, Leo
            Dillon, Diane
Publisher: Dial, 1975
Suggested Grade Level: 1-4
Classification: Core Materials
Literary Form: Picture book
Theme: A series of events, once set in motion, must continue to the end.

About the Book

STUDENT OBJECTIVES:

1. List the events of the story in sequence.

2. Explain the meaning of the literary form tall tale.

3. Write a tall tale about 1 of the animals in *Why Mosquitoes Buzz in People's Ears*.

SYNOPSIS: Mosquito began telling a tall tale to Iguana. Iguana did not enjoy the story and grumped away after putting sticks in his ears to avoid hearing any more of this tale. What happened next caused many problems for the jungle animals.

ABOUT THE AUTHOR AND ILLUSTRATORS: Verna Aardema, June 6, 1911- .
                                     Leo Dillon, March 2, 1933- .
                                     Diane Dillon, March 13, 1933- .
       Verna Aardema was the third of 9 children in the family. She remembers how much she hated doing the housework and dishes. She was a bookworm and wanted to read! She doesn't remember being noticed by her family until she made an "A" on a poetry assignment. Her mother said she was just like her great-grandfather. Great-grandfather could not find a

quiet place to read, so he took "thinking" walks. Verna did not like to walk and so substituted a visit to the cedar swamp which lay behind her New Era, Michigan, home. There she told stories to other children and later, while her sister did the dishes at home, started composing new ones. Verna became a professional writer in 1973, after she retired from teaching journalism. Since then she has been writing and telling the African folktales she enjoys so much.

Leo and Diane Dillon were born 11 days apart in Brooklyn, New York, and Glendale, California, respectively. They met while attending Parsons School of Design, New York, where they were fierce competitors until they married. They view themselves as believers in magic—the magic of illustrating children's literature. They explain that they came to children's illustrating following work with adult book jackets, album covers, and in advertising. Those artworks had to tell the story in a single picture, while children's book illustrations evolve page after page and reach a culminating point. The illustrators delight in adding elements not found in the text.

The Dillons are the first illustrators to win the Caldecott Medal 2 years consecutively. They were named for *Why Mosquitoes Buzz in People's Ears* in 1975 and for illustrating Margaret Musgrove's *Ashanti to Zulu: African Traditions* in 1976. The art presentations are quite different—*Mosquitoes* is illustrated in vibrant pastel colors, and *Ashanti* is in the subtle earth tones of the African landscape. In accepting the Caldecott Award, the Dillons remarked: "We believe that the role of the illustrator is not simply to duplicate the text, but to enlarge on it, to restate the words in our own graphic terms."*

SELECTED ADDITIONAL TITLES BY THE AUTHOR:

Bringing the Rain to Kapiti Plain: A Nandi Tale
Half-a-Ball-of-Kenki: An Ashanti Tale
Ji-Nongo-Nongo-Means Riddles
Oh, Kojo! How Could You? An Ashanti Tale
Riddle of the Drum: A Tale from Tizapanh
Vinganance and the Tree Toad
What's So Funny, Ketu? A Nuer Tale
Who's in Rabbit's House?

SELECTED ADDITIONAL TITLES BY THE ILLUSTRATORS:

Ring in the Prairie: A Shawanee Legend
Song of the Boat
Songs and Stories from Uganda
Who's in Rabbit's House?

Using the Book

Suggested Approach to the Book

Model Lesson #1

- Introduce the author as a lady who loves to tell and write African folktales. Explain to students that you will be sharing several of her books, including *Bringing the Rain to Kapiti Plain* and *Oh, Kojo! How Could You?* in order to examine her African tales.

---

*John C. Stott, *Children's Literature from A to Z* (New York: McGraw-Hill, 1984).

- Present the biographical information available about Leo and Diane Dillon. Tell the class that they are a married couple who love illustrating books for students. They feel that they can and do provide a special kind of magic through illustrations. They do not think adults should simplify things that are written and illustrated for children.

Model Lesson #2

- Read and share the dramatic art that accompanies *Why Mosquitoes Buzz in People's Ears*. Look at the style and see if you can see any resemblance to other artists such as Tomie De Paola. You may notice a certain freedom of motion to the design and the use of loops and more loops of color separated by white space and then interwoven into the picture. It almost appears to be a handwork of yarn threads. The art appears simplistic in structure, but, in fact, is very complex. The Dillons explain that their artwork for *Why Mosquitoes Buzz in People's Ears* was a combination of watercolors airbrushed onto the paper, pastels hand-applied, and india ink. Paper cutting was also used.

Model Lesson #3

- Some questions to discuss with the class:
    1. How could 1 mosquito cause so much trouble?
    2. Look carefully at the title page. What is the farmer holding in his hand? Who is watching?
    3. Describe the opening of the story.
    4. Tell the tale in sequence.
    5. What does Owl do in her sorrow?
    6. What animals are pictured in the night scene?
    7. Who was blamed for all the misfortunes? Why?
    8. Where was the mosquito when questions were being asked?
    9. What does the mosquito still say today?
    10. What still happens to mosquitoes today?

Model Lesson #4

- Art appreciation through picture books: Compare the art of the following 2 Caldecott award books that were illustrated by the Dillons, but written by different authors.

    Aardema, Verna, *Why Mosquitoes Buzz in People's Ears*
    Musgrove, Margaret, *Ashanti to Zulu: African Traditions*

- Ask students to discuss the comment by the Dillons that the artwork should not only restate the text, but enlarge on it. What can they see in the illustrations that is not stated in the story?

Library Media Center Connections

1. Plan "Africa Week" in the library media center. Ask students to participate in the following ways:
    - One group of students can list the materials available for the unit by using the card catalog as a reference source and selecting materials that are suitable for the media center display. They may decorate the display area with appropriate materials and study prints.

- Assign another student group to make a large model of an African house that could serve as a student art gallery during the week.

- A third group may construct simple musical instruments.

- The fourth group may create examples of African art to be displayed in the house.

- Students in the final group may construct a physical map of the continent using a flour-salt formula mix.

Theme Reading Connections: Africa

Adamson, Joy, *Elsa*
Aruego, Jose, *We Hide, You Seek*
Arundel, Jocelyn, *Land of the Zebra*
Fatio, Louise, *Happy Lion in Africa*
Feelings, Muriel, *Jambo Means Hello*

Activities to Connect Literature and Curriculum

ART

Create African animal head masks from brown paper grocery bags to represent the animals illustrated in *Why Mosquitoes Buzz in People's Ears*. Save them for use in language arts class.

Use paper rolls and cartons to create African animals. For patterns and additional directions refer to the following books:

Hardiman, George W., and Theodore Zernich, *Art Activities for Children*
Toney, Sara D., *Smithsonian Surprises*

HEALTH

Learn about African food through cookbook research. Bring a cookbook to class and read the ingredients for a dish that interests you. Compare the African dish to your favorite food. How are they alike? Different?

LANGUAGE ARTS

Present *Why Mosquitos Buzz in People's Ears* as a class play. Use the paper bag head masks created in art as costumes. Design a play program and illustrate it appropriately with African art. Present the play for other classes on request.

MATH

Read Muriel Feeling's Swahili counting book, *Moja Means One*. If you were born in Africa and had not gone to school, how would you count? Devise a new number system to be used for counting.

SCIENCE

List the wild animals that the travel group would want to see. Mark the locations of animal habitats on a map, using animal pictures.

Using index cards, design a format and present a capsule profile of each animal that might be seen on a photography safari. Organize and classify the cards so that a traveler could take the packet along in a flight bag.

Research and present a report on wildlife preserves in Africa. Identify their locations on a map of Africa.

SOCIAL STUDIES

Establish a simulation activity for the class. Role-play the job of a travel agent who has a group that wishes to travel to Africa to observe wildlife and whose members belong to the local zoological society. Plan the trip for the group using student travel agents and travel agency brochures. Travel agencies will usually give outdated brochures to schools on request.

Explain travel schedules and documents that are required.

Draw the travel route planned for the group on a desk map of Africa.

Explain time zones to the travelers who are flying by plane.

Plan an appropriate travel wardrobe to be purchased.

Beyond the Book

Guided Reading Connections across a Curriculum Rainbow: African Folktales

Aardema, Verna, *Bimwill and the Zimwi*
Brown, Marcia, *How, Hippo!*; *Shadow*
Bryan, Ashley, *Adventures of Aku*
Dayrell, Elphinstone, *Why the Sun and the Moon Live in the Sky*
Dolch, Marguerite, *Animal Stories from Africa*
Domanska, Janina, *Tortoise and the Tree*
Grifalconi, Ann, *Village of Round and Square Houses*
Guy, Rosa, *Mother Crocodile*
Haley, Gail, *A Story, A Story*
McDermott, Gerald, *Anansi the Spider*

Enriching Connections

FOR GIFTED STUDENTS

Read *Anansi the Spider*, by Gerald McDermott. Imagine that Anansi had 7 sons instead of 5. What could those 2 spider sons have done to be included in the story of Anansi? The story tells why we have the moon each night. Can you write an Anansi tale that explains the sun's existence? Illustrate your tale in an art style like Gerald McDermott's, if possible.

FOR PARENTS

Ask your child to retell *Why Mosquitoes Buzz in People's Ears.*
Play an African "bean" game with your child. Take turns asking 10 questions about Africa, its animals, culture, geography, and folktales. Collect a bean for each correct answer. When the game is over, the person who has the most beans wins the round. Use an encyclopedia or a book about Africa to make up questions and find answers.

CRICKET SONGS

Author (Translator): Behn, Harry
Illustrator: Sesshu and other Japanese masters
Publisher: Harcourt, Brace & World, 1964
Suggested Grade Level: 3-6
Classification: Core Materials
Literary Form: Poetry
Theme: Through poetry we see a world of beauty

About the Book

STUDENT OBJECTIVES:

1. Write and memorize a poem written in haiku form.

2. Compare poetry written in haiku, rhyme, and nonrhyming form.

3. Select examples of haiku for a student poetry anthology.

SYNOPSIS: *Cricket Songs* is a collection of Japanese haiku illustrated with the artwork of the great masters of Japan.

ABOUT THE AUTHOR (TRANSLATOR): Harry Behn, 1898-1973.
   Harry Behn was born in McCabe, Arizona, in a town which later became a ghost town. His stories frequently tell tales of the Apache Indians with whom he grew up. He vividly remembers Prescott, Arizona, with its fort. It was always a mystery whether the fort was supposed to protect the townspeople from the Indians or the Indians from the townspeople.
   After he was graduated from Harvard, he lived with the Blackfoot tribe of Montana for a year. He translated his love of Indian legends and culture into books that include the *Painted Cave*, which was about the search by a courageous Indian boy among gods and animals to find his true name.
   Behn accomplished many things in his life: he started a little theater in Phoenix, Arizona; was a scholar in Sweden; wrote scenarios for Hollywood movies; taught at the University of Arizona; and organized a broadcasting company. He was amused that doing what he loved, writing books and composing poetry, could be called an occupation.

Behn's works are set in New England or the Southwest, areas where he has lived and worked, and deal with children and their sense of time. Time is measured by clocks in *Golden Hive*, by the children's time in *All Kinds of Time*, and by the time cycle of nature in *Cricket Songs*.

Cricket Songs has been highly praised by critics. "Each of [the poems] is, he has stated, 'an experience of illumination,' and each fulfills his criteria for a good poem: 'Anything or any experience, to become a poem, must be presented with a careful incompleteness of information.' "*

SELECTED ADDITIONAL TITLES BY THE AUTHOR (TRANSLATOR):

Crickets and Bullfrogs and Whispers of Thunder
More Cricket Songs
What a Beautiful Noise

Using the Book

Suggested Approach to the Book

Model Lesson #1

- Introduce the biographical materials about Harry Behn. Tell students that he translated the haiku and that each must have exactly 17 syllables.

Model Lesson #2

- Explain a syllable to the class. Using the blackboard, divide words into syllables. This can be an integrated lesson on using the dictionary and locating examples of syllabicated word forms.

Model Lesson #3

- Read a selection from *Cricket Songs* to the class. Present the accompanying artwork and explain that the art is by some of Japan's great artists. Ask how they relate to the black-and-white work and to the poetry. Colored art prints are available of many of the black-and-white book pictures. Ask students if they can identify which of the pictures has been reproduced as a Japanese stamp. Use a Japanese stamp catalog to match the pictures. When was the stamp issued? For what reason?

Model Lesson #4

- Read other haiku by another writer to the class.

---

*John C. Stott, *Children's Literature from A to Z* (New York: McGraw-Hill, 1984).

Model Lesson #5

- Art appreciation through picture books: Compare the artwork and photographs used to illustrate the following haiku books. Which do you like better? Why?

    Atwood, Ann, *Haiku: The Mood of the Earth*
    Behn, Harry, *Cricket Songs*

Library Media Center Connections

1. Explain to students that poetry is like food: We all have our own tastes. The library media center will offer a sampling of many poetry forms. Select books that have rhyme and nonrhyming verse forms, including haiku and cinquain, ballads and sonnets, and limericks. Introduce poetry anthologies.

2. Ask students to find a poem they like. They should copy their choices and take them back to class. The teacher will graph the types of poetry selected by students through a classroom poll.

3. Encourage students to further develop their oral language skills by reading the poems aloud in small listening groups.

Computer Connections

Learning Well, *Poetry Express*

Theme Reading Connections: Haiku

Atwood, Ann, *Haiku — Vision in Poetry and Photography*
Mizumura, Kazué, *Flower Moon Snow: A Book of Haiku*

Activities to Connect Literature and Curriculum

ART

Illustrate poems written by students using dried grasses and flowers glued on to a paper backing.

Poems may also be illustrated using watercolor paints or felt-tipped marking pens.

Using tempera paint, sponge-paint construction paper with color and allow to dry. With a straw, blow paint onto the dried, sponge-painted paper lightly with black tempera paint that has been thinned. The art will look like Japanese calligraphy.

LANGUAGE ARTS

Present a selection of small materials that can be displayed on a table in the classroom. Include "things of beauty" such as pretty beads or costume jewelry, sea shells, mineral rocks, colored photographs, and pieces of luxurious fabrics. Allow each student to take a Polaroid™

picture of an item from the group. Mount the photograph on a half sheet of colored construction paper. Write a poem about the "item of beauty" and mount it on the construction paper with the photograph.

Classify the favorite poems copied in the library media center by poetry form. Graph the information for students.

Ask each student to input and print out his or her favorite poem as a computer exercise. Illustrate each poem and collect them into a classroom anthology.

Create "Paint Pot" poems by cutting words from different magazines, arranging them into poems, and gluing them onto construction paper.

Select 8 or 10 haiku for an interest center. Ask students to illustrate the poems as they wish.

Listen to a music cassette tape and write poetry reflective of the music. Sounds of waves could be used to establish atmosphere. Turn off the classroom lights and ask students to shut their eyes and listen quietly to the sounds. After an appropriate listening time, ask students to open their eyes and quietly write about the wave sounds they have just heard.

Cluster on the board with the class words that describe each of the 4 seasons. Use this activity as a prewriting exercise. Ask students to work as a committee in their learning groups and to compose a haiku about a season of the year.

Teachers should be aware that children's literature research states that many students do not like poetry because of the abstract levels of thinking that it requires. Plan to share poetry as a class and do not require that students execute examples of every poetry form. Make it fun and integrate the book *Poems Make Pictures, Pictures Make Poems* by Giose Rimanelli (Pantheon, 1972). Suggest that students read many different poems as appetizers before selecting a main course poetry class project.

MUSIC

Compose pentatonic music using tone blocks. Use the notes A, C, D, E, and G only. These particular notes will sound like oriental music. Read a haiku aloud and compose the accompanying music. Write the music composition down so that other students may play it. For additional directions, consult materials about the Orff method of teaching music.

Beyond the Book

Guided Reading Connections across a Curriculum Rainbow: Poetry

Frost, Robert, *Swinger of Birches: Poems of Robert Frost for Young People*
Karp, Naomi, *Nothing Rhymes with April*
Koch, Kenneth, and Kate Farrell, *Talking to the Sun: An Illustrated Anthology for Young People*
Prelutsky, Jack, *New Kid on the Block*; *Random House Book of Poetry*
Stevenson, Robert L., *Child's Garden of Verse*

Enriching Connections

FOR GIFTED STUDENTS

Write an original poem that can be written like a picture.

Prepare a "Poem in a Can." Decorate a lidded coffee can as a character or to represent a scene. Write a poem and store it inside the can. Put another item into the can, such as a finger puppet, a set of paper dolls, a pretty feather, an interesting rock, or an animal picture that you have selected to create a mood about your poem. Begin to share your poem with the class by showing the can's design, read or recite the poem, and conclude with your own prop from inside the container. Put everything back in the can for a future reading.

FOR PARENTS

Ask your child to read and tell you about poems from a poetry book of his or her selection. Read an appropriate poem that you like to your child.

Play a rhyming word game. You begin and the child responds. Begin with examples such as *hi-bye*, *hello-jello*, *tall-wall*. See how many pairs you can complete together. Then let the child begin the game. Keep score.

FOOL OF THE WORLD
AND THE FLYING SHIP

Author: Ransome, Arthur
Illustrator: Shulevitz, Uri
Publisher: Farrar, Straus & Giroux, 1968
Suggested Grade Level: 1-3
Classification: Recreational and Motivational Materials
Literary Form: Picture book
Theme: Each person has a special place reserved in the world.

About the Book

STUDENT OBJECTIVES:

1. Describe the *Fool of the World*.

2. Paraphrase *Fool of the World and the Flying Ship*.

3. Evaluate the behavior of the Czar toward the *Fool of the World*.

SYNOPSIS: The *Fool of the World* is representative of the universality of folktales and contains many common elements such as stories about royalty, peasants, a quest for a suitable husband for a princess, magic, impossible tasks, a supernatural figure to make the tasks come true, and humor.

ABOUT THE AUTHOR AND ILLUSTRATOR: Arthur Ransome, 1884-1967.

Uri Shulevitz, February 17, 1935- .

Arthur Ransome grew up in England. His favorite recreation as a child and in the days of his retirement, many years later, was fishing in the same lakes that his father and grandfather had fished before his birth. He was a prominent children's writer in England and in 1936 was awarded the Library Association Carnegie Medal, comparable to the United States's John Newbery Medal, for *Pidgeon Post*.

He was a newspaper correspondent in World War I and later wrote stories about the Russian Revolution for his home town newspaper. He was later expelled from Russia for political reasons, but had fortunately collected many of that country's folktales, which were published in 1916 as *Old Peter's Russian Tales*. The *Fool of the World and the Flying Ship* is a tale from that book. This story, retold by Arthur Ransome and illustrated by Uri Shulevitz, was awarded the Caldecott Medal in 1969 for "the most distinguished American picture book for children."

Uri Shulevitz was born in Warsaw, Poland, and saw the horrors of war as a child. His family were forced to flee and were homeless, wandering for many years because of the war. They eventually moved to Paris. His favorite activity was wandering through the bookstalls which line the Seine River. At age 15 the family moved again, this time to Israel. In Israel, he went to school and held many jobs, working as a rubber stamp maker, house painter, carpenter, and dog license seller in Tel Aviv's City Hall.

Shulevitz emigrated to New York in 1959 and began studying art at Brooklyn College. He began to illustrate books and later wrote them as well. In regard to writing, he has said: "First, one has to have something to say. This may appear in one's mind in pictures, not necessarily in words, very much as in a film or comic strip. As I was to discover, the picture book is a medium in which words and pictures complement each other without repetition."*

SELECTED ADDITIONAL TITLES BY THE ILLUSTRATOR:

Dawn
One Monday Morning
Rain Rain Rivers
Soldier and Tsar in the Forest: A Russian Tale
Treasure

Using the Book

Suggested Approach to the Book

Model Lesson #1

- Introduce the author and illustrator as people who cocreated a beautiful folktale that is as enjoyable today, if not more so with its complementary artwork, as it was when initially

---

*Doris de Montreville and Donna Hill, eds., *Third Book of Junior Authors* (New York: H. W. Wilson, 1972).

published some 50 years ago. Indicate to students that other Russian materials will be introduced during this study unit and to look for differences in the cultures of Russia and the United States.

Model Lesson #2

- Read the *Fool of the World and the Flying Ship* to the class.

- Share the art with students. Ask if they can tell you why the flying ship is like a certain model of boats seen in history books.

- Study the artwork in detail as the *Fool of the World* flies over the fields. Ask students to tell what they see in the pictures. These snapshot views will add to reading comprehension as the story progresses. Look at pictures of peasants in the fields, people on the road, and a tiny windmill.

Model Lesson #3

- Retell the story in class and assign students to take the parts of various people who are invited to accompany the *Fool of the World*, as well as his parents, the old man, and people who live in the Czar's castle. There will be enough parts for all students in the class to participate in this oral language development exercise.

Model Lesson #4

- Art appreciation through picture books: Compare the illustrations and story of the following 2 versions of the same story:

  Harris, Rosemary, *Flying Ship*
  Ransome, Arthur, *Fool of the World and the Flying Ship*

Library Media Center Connections

1. Collect all the books that relate to Russia and make them available for student reference use.

2. Ask students to explore the collected materials, which should include study prints, sound filmstrips, and available realia.

3. Students should choose an interesting topic about Russia to share with another student in a different class. The format for sharing the information may be in the form of a videotape presentation, a cassette recording, a multiple series of diary entries, postcards and letters, newspaper stories, or any additional, approved method.

Theme Reading Connections: Russia

Haskins, Jim, *Count Your Way through Russia*
Lyle, Keith, *Take a Trip to Russia*
Singer, Isaac, *When Shlemiel Went to Warsaw*
Watson, Jane, *Soviet Union: Land of Many Peoples*

Activities to Connect Literature and Curriculum

ART

Create a mural as a product of the folktale unit. Divide the mural into 3 vertical imaginary parts. In the first section, place the modern city of Leningrad, with an emphasis on the canals and Peter the Great's "Window on the West." In the middle part, draw the agricultural areas as seen from the viewpoint of the *Fool of the World and the Flying Ship* and the people who were invited to join him on his trip. End the journey in section 3 with Moscow and its onion-like building spires.

LANGUAGE ARTS

Present the *Fool of the World* as a school play complete with costumes, scenery, and background music.

Identify and list all the elements of a folktale that are included in the *Fool of the World and the Flying Ship*.

Write a new ending for the story. Imagine that the Czar breaks his word and will not allow his daughter to wed the *Fool of the World*. What would happen if war were declared on the Czar? Who do you suppose would win?

NUTRITION

Mix and bake loaves of Russian black bread as an introduction to the foods of Russia.

SOCIAL STUDIES

Study a map of Russia and locate Leningrad and Moscow.

Look at a world map and find the closest land point between the United States and Russia. How many miles separate these 2 countries?

Talk about agreements between countries in regard to air traffic and other issues. Should the number of Pan American and Aeroflot flights between Russia and the United States be equal? Should the number of employees at each foreign embassy in the United States and Russia be the same? What restrictions, if any, should be placed on workers who are assigned to a foreign embassy in the United States or Russia?

Examine the dust jackets of the following books about Russia and compare and contrast their visual appearances.

> Harris, Rosemary, *Flying Ship* (illustrated by Errol Le Cain)
>
> Isele, Elizabeth, *Frog Princess* (illustrated by Michael Hague)
>
> Maxym, Lucy, *Russian Lacquer Legends and Fairy Tales*
>
> Prokofiev, Sergei, *Peter and the Wolf* (adapted from the musical tale and illustrated by Erna Voigt)
>
> Stanley, Diane, *Peter the Great*

Choose 1 of the books listed above to read and present a brief oral report in collaborative learning groups.

Learn about Russian folk toys that are available today. Why do you think that they are usually made of wood?

Beyond the Book

Guided Reading Connections across a Curriculum Rainbow: Russian Folktales

Brown, Marcia, *Stone Soup*
Domanska, Janina, *Turnip*
Isele, Elizabeth, *Frog Princess*
Robbins, Ruth, *Baboushka and the Three Kings*
Tolstoy, Aleksei Nikolaevich, *Great Big Enormous Turnip*

Enriching Connections

FOR GIFTED STUDENTS

Make a hand puppet of the *Fool of the World* or the *Frog Princess* and practice telling the story until you are confident and ready to present the story to students in another class. You may also consider the "Puppet in a Can" idea. Decorate a coffee can to use as an attention getting device to begin your presentation. Open the can later to highlight another idea of the presentation. Choose the kind of puppet you think will work best from among a fabric figure, a paper bag kind, a finger puppet, a stick puppet, or even a bread dough form.

FOR PARENTS

Listen to your child retell the *Fool of the World and the Flying Ship*. It is a very difficult tale with a number of sequences of events.

Share a favorite fairy tale from your life. Which story was your favorite? What elements in it made it special to you?

Make up a tale that you can practice telling to each other at bedtime.

CROW BOY

Author: Yashima, Taro
Illustrator: Yashima, Taro
Publisher: Viking, 1955
Suggested Grade Level: 2-3
Classification: Core Materials
Literary Form: Picture book
Theme: There is something special about every person.

About the Book

STUDENT OBJECTIVES:

1. Explain the school behavior of Chibi.

2. Role-play the parts of Chibi and other students in a Japanese school.

3. Invent a story that explains why Chibi spent so much time alone in school and without friends.

SYNOPSIS: *Crow Boy* is the story of a boy who is lonely in school because he is "different" and no one seems to care about him. At the end of the story he participates in the school talent show and exhibits an amazing talent. His lonely feelings are portrayed through meaningful crayon and ink illustrations.

ABOUT THE AUTHOR-ILLUSTRATOR: Taro Yashima, 1908- .

Taro Yashima, a pseudonym for Jun Atsushi Iwamatsu, has illustrated 3 picture books that have received Caldecott Honor awards. Taro Yashima has explained that *Taro* means "healthy boy" and *Yashima* means "eight islands of old Japan."

The son of a Japanese country doctor and his assistant, he was orphaned very young. He lost his mother when he was in first grade and his father 3 years later. While in elementary school, he decided to become an artist. Taro's father reminded him in his will to follow his dream and become an artist. After what appears to be a very stormy and volatile young adulthood, Yashima and his wife left Japan to study art in the United States. They left behind their 5-year-old son. Unfortunately, war broke out between Japan and the United States and they were not able to locate the child for 10 years. Yashima had chosen to aid the United States government and chose his new name when he and his wife worked for the war effort.

He explains that he did not begin illustrating children's books until the 1950s when his son was located and brought to the United States. During that time a daughter was born, and Taro was struggling with stomach ulcers. His early books were written and illustrated for his daughter, Momo. *Umbrella*, a gift for her eighth birthday, is about a little girl in New York City who is given an umbrella and rain shoes and waits impatiently for rain. Other books, such as *Momo's Kitten* and *Youngest One*, are also about her childhood.

The themes that are expressed by Taro Yashima are about life in Japan and revolve around children who grow through their experiences.

SELECTED ADDITIONAL TITLES BY THE AUTHOR-ILLUSTRATOR:

Plenty to Watch
Seashore Story
Village Tree
Youngest One

SELECTED ADDITIONAL TITLE BY THE ILLUSTRATOR:

Soo Ling Finds a Way (written by June Behrens)

Using the Book

Suggested Approach to the Book

Model Lesson #1

- Share the biographical material about Taro Yashima and the books he has written and illustrated. Explain that he was born in Japan, but is listed in biographical sketches as an American. He became a United States citizen after leaving Japan. Tell students that it takes courage to support a government in time of war against one's former homeland. Discuss reasons that people may have for leaving their country and building a new life in another country.

Model Lesson #2

- Read *Crow Boy* to the class and share the artwork. Point out that the art technique is crayons, just like those they use in class.

Model Lesson #3

- Some questions to discuss with the class:
    1. Look at pages 4-5. Find the missing boy. Notice the contrast between the teacher, students, and the little boy. Notice that in all the pictures Chibi is lonely and alone. When students respect him, he moves to the center of the drawing. Explain why.
    2. What does Chibi mean?
    3. Look at the pictures and locate the position of Chibi in the art.
    4. List the ways that Chibi found to be alone.
    5. What was the lunch brought by Chibi each day?
    6. Describe the new teacher. Note the dedication of the book, to a former teacher of Taro Yashima.
    7. What did Mr. Isobe do about Chibi that was different from what the original teacher had done?
    8. What things did Mr. Isobe display in the classroom that were Chibi's?
    9. Describe the voices of the crows.
    10. What made the students and parents cry?
    11. What award did Chibi receive at graduation?
    12. Describe Chibi's home.
    13. What good-bye did Chibi give people when he made the turn on the mountain road?
    14. How do you think he felt then?
    15. Notice the last page. Describe the feeling you have about the art. Why?

Model Lesson #4

- Art appreciation through picture books: Compare the work of the following 2 illustrators through pictures and stories:

    Matsuno, Masako, *Red Clogs*
    Yashima, Taro, *Umbrella*

Library Media Center Connections

1. Learn about crows by using reference books.

2. Compare crows to your state bird.

3. Create a "U-Write" filmstrip about crows. Choose appropriate background music for the filmstrip. Begin a filmstrip collection of student-made materials. Process the material, add cards to the card catalog, and store the films in the library media center.

Theme Reading Connections: Japanese Folktales

Matsutani, Miyoko, *How the Withered Trees Blossomed*
McDermott, Gerald, *Stonecutter: A Japanese Folk Tale*
Morimoto, Junko, *Inch Boy*
Mosel, Arlene, *Funny Little Woman*
Yagawa, Sumiko, *Crane Wife*

Activities to Connect Literature and Curriculum

ART

Construct a crayon, cut-and-paste mural of Chibi's school and home.
Use crayons on cloth to create a wall hanging.
Crayon rubbings are also effective art projects. Outline the picture using a pencil. Place the thin paper with the outlined sketch over a rough surface. Use crayons to fill in the outline. Vary the texture by changing the surface over which the crayon is rubbed.
Make and decorate a paper folding fan in the Japanese style.

HEALTH

People in the United States consume a large amount of potatoes, while people in Japan grow and eat large quantities of rice. Find out the amounts of potatoes and rice consumed per person in each country. Ask the library media specialist to help find a reference source for this information.

Plan 2 menus using the 4 basic food groups. One should include rice or a rice product and the other, potatoes.

LANGUAGE ARTS

Write a letter to Chibi and invite him to come and visit your school. Tell him something that would make him feel welcome.

MATH

Japanese currency is called *yen*. Draw pictures of the coins that are used in Japan and share them with the class. How many yen does it take to equal $1.00? Make a chart of the changing value of the yen and the dollar for a month. This information is printed in the financial section of the daily newspaper.

SCIENCE

Make a list of Japanese vegetables and plants. Classify them by color of plant product. Make a chart and label the 4 headings "Seed," "Length of Growing Time," "Plant," and "Product." Under each heading, supply samples of the plant seeds, facts about the growing time, and a colored picture of the plant and its product. Seed catalogs are an excellent source of materials.

SOCIAL STUDIES

Make a salt and flour relief map of the 8 islands of old Japan referred to by Taro Yashima. Combine 3 parts salt and 1 part flour with enough water to bring the solution to the consistency of dough. Model the dough on a sheet of heavy cardboard. Use watercolors to complete the map.

Create miniature models of a United States and a Japanese classroom.

Beyond the Book

Guided Reading Connections across a Curriculum Rainbow: Teachers

Allard, Harry, *Miss Nelson Is Missing*
Arnold, Caroline, *Where Do You Go to School?*
Beckman, Beatrice, *I Can Be a Teacher*
Cone, Molly, *Mishmash and the Substitute Teacher*
Feder, Paula, *Where Does the Teacher Live?*

Enriching Connections

FOR GIFTED STUDENTS

Find out how schools in the United States differ from those in Japan.
Design a kimono and obi sash using a Japanese motif.

FOR PARENTS

Explain to your child that there are many cultural differences between people of the United States and Japan. The Japanese have had many influences on the United States. A few of these are flower arrangement, Japanese food including sushi and tempura, automobile designs, televisions, videocassette recorders, and furniture. Using today's newspaper, have your child find things that might relate to Japanese design or culture in the United States.

*   *   *   *   *   *   *   *   *   *   *

From an Illustrator's Palette

ISLAND OF THE SKOG

Author: Kellogg, Steven
Illustrator: Kellogg, Steven
Publisher: Dial, 1973
Suggested Grade Level: 3-4
Classification: Extended Materials
Literary Form: Picture book
Theme: Freedom is a hard-won privilege.

About the Book

STUDENT OBJECTIVES:

1. Define the concept of privilege.

2. Identify the freedoms of people in the United States.

3. Develop a list of student school responsibilities.

SYNOPSIS: A group of mice living in an antique store find that their lives are being endangered by cats and dogs. They decide to leave their home and sail away in a miniature model ship. Like the pilgrims who landed on Plymouth Rock, they must overcome an obstacle—the skog.

ABOUT THE AUTHOR-ILLUSTRATOR: Steven Kellogg, October 6, 1941- .
    Steven Kellogg has spent most of his life in Connecticut, a state he loves. His desire to be an artist began with his close relationship with his grandmother and the hours he spent listening to the stories of her childhood in the late nineteenth century. He loved her room, which was cluttered with prize treasures. Those images are apparent today in his art and writing.
    After graduating from the Rhode Island School of Design, he won a European Honors Fellowship and was able to spend a semester in Florence, Italy. He remembers "living in that

magic city as one of the most meaningful and wonderful times of life."* One of his favorite books is the *Island of the Skog*.

SELECTED ADDITIONAL TITLES BY THE AUTHOR-ILLUSTRATOR:

Best Friends
Can I Keep Him?
Chicken Little
Mysterious Tadpole
Mystery of the Flying Orange Pumpkin
Mystery of the Magic Green Ball
Mystery of the Missing Red Mystery
Mystery of the Stolen Blue Paint
Paul Bunyan
Pecos Bill
Pinkerton, Behave!
Ralph's Secret Weapon
Rose for Pinkerton
Tallyho, Pinkerton!

SELECTED ADDITIONAL TITLES BY THE ILLUSTRATOR:

A, My Name Is Alice
Day Jimmy's Boa Ate the Wash
How Much Is a Million?
Jimmy's Boa Bounces Back
Ten-Alarm Camp Out

Using the Book

Suggested Approach to the Book

Model Lesson #1

- Introduce Steven Kellogg as an author-illustrator who enjoys producing books for children. Closely examine the illustrations, as he has included many fine details that foreshadow the story.

Model Lesson #2

- Read the *Island of the Skog* and share the art with the class. Do not share the cover picture until the lesson is completed because the skog is pictured hiding in the tree in the upper lefthand corner. Read the story to the class until they reach the "Island of the Skog." Stop at that point in the story and ask students to both describe and draw a picture of the skog. When the activity is completed, finish reading the story until the point that the skog is

---

*Doris de Montreville and Elizabeth D. Crawford, *Fourth Book of Junior Authors and Illustrators* (New York: H. W. Wilson, 1978).

illustrated. Stop at this point and ask students to draw a final sketch of the skog. To complete the lesson, show the skog as illustrated by Steven Kellogg. Examine the book cover and point out that the illustration covers both the front and back of the book cover.

Model Lesson #3

- Questions to ask the students:
    1. Examine the title page illustrations with the class. Describe the activities of the cat and mice. Look at the window sign. Why is the store name spelled backwards?
    2. Describe in detail the model ship, the *Flying Rose.*
    3. What is National Rodent Day?
    4. Tell about the celebration activities that the mice planned.
    5. Why did the mice think that they should stay in their holes?
    6. What decision did the mice reach as a group?
    7. Describe the ship's departure.
    8. Why did the weather turn colder for the ship's passengers?
    9. Were the mice wise to unload their possessions and then spend the night on the ship?
    10. Do you think that the mice went on a modern-day voyage of exploration?

Model Lesson #4

- Art appreciation through picture books: Compare the presentation of number concepts in the following books:

    Kellogg, Steven, *How Much Is a Million?*
    Slobodkin, Louis, *Millions and Millions and Millions!*

Library Media Center Connections

1. Plan a research project using the theme "Alone on an Island." Ask each student to choose an island to learn more about and make an oral report to the class. Facts to research:

    What is the size of the island?

    What is its geographical location?

    How many people live on the island?

    What is the climate?

    How do the people dress?

    What language do they speak?

    What foods do the people like to eat?

    Describe the houses.

    What are schools like?

    What special holidays are observed?

Computer Connections

HRM Software, *Voyages of Discovery*
Rand McNally, *Unlocking the Map Code*

Theme Reading Connections: Islands

Brown, Margaret Wise, *Little Island*
De Brunhoff, Laurent, *Babar's Visit to Bird Island*
McCloskey, Robert, *Time of Wonder*
Steig, William, *Rotten Island*
Yorinks, Arthur, *Heh, Al*

Activities to Connect Literature and Curriculum

ART

Make papier-mâché life-sized heads that can be worn by students. The heads may be imaginary monsters representing skogs. Plan a parade and ask each student to wear an adult's coat or other large garment and the monster head.

Construct a model ship like the one the mice sailed on. Use banana split containers from an ice cream store. Hold a contest to see which one, crewed by miniature mice constructed from walnut shells or other materials, stays afloat the longest time.

Plan and make an Old World map of the *Island of the Skog.*

HEALTH

List foods that would be appropriate to take on an around-the-world sailing voyage today. Think about supplies that would provide a balanced diet.

MATH

Compute the mileage around the world by ship. Find out how many miles per day a sailing ship could sail. How many days would a ship voyage around the world take? Inquire about how long cruise ships take to sail the same route today under power. How many miles would a jet liner log on a nonstop flight around the world? If refueling was not a problem, how long would the jet actually be in the air?

SOCIAL STUDIES

List 25 islands in the world and label them on a world map.

Create a ship's log with all the entries for the voyage of the *Flying Rose.*

What shipboard jobs would the mice need to do? Who would assign the jobs?

If you were moving permanently to a new island home in the Pacific Ocean, what things would you want to bring with you that might be considered sentimental choices? List 10 possessions that you would want to take with you.

Explain the science of navigating a sailing ship. What instruments would you need?

Beyond the Book

Guided Reading Connections across a Curriculum Rainbow: Traveling

Cooney, Barbara, *Miss Rumphius*
De Brunhoff, Jean, *Travels of Babar*
Demi, *Adventures of Marco Polo*
Goodall, John, *Paddy Goes Traveling*
Ventura, Piero, *Christopher Columbus*; *Marco Polo*

Enriching Connections

FOR GIFTED STUDENTS

Read Jules Verne's *Twenty Thousand Leagues under the Sea* or an edited version and list experimental things from the book that have become realities in today's world.

Design a prototype of a modern-day sailing ship suitable for 4 people. Include up-to-date furnishings and equipment. Sketch the vessel.

FOR PARENTS

Ask your child what he or she would like to do when grown up. Is the choice in a traditional field or a new occupation? Talk about the requirements necessary to prepare for the intended employment. Tell about the training requirements of the job that you hold. Share the advantages and disadvantages of a job like the one you hold.

INCH BY INCH

Author: Lionni, Leo
Illustrator: Lionni, Leo
Publisher: Astor-Honor, 1960
Suggested Grade Level: K-3
Classification: Recreational and Motivational Materials
Literary Form: Picture book
Theme: It is possible to measure almost anything inch by inch.

About the Book

STUDENT OBJECTIVES:

1. Describe an inchworm.

2. Explain the technique of measuring an object.

3. Measure 10 objects with a tape measure.

SYNOPSIS: An inchworm is almost gobbled up by a robin, but the robin discovers that the inchworm has a talent—measuring—and uses his abilities to measure other birds.

ABOUT THE AUTHOR-ILLUSTRATOR: Leo Lionni, May 5, 1910-1986.

Leo Lionni was born in Amsterdam, Holland, and according to him, he always knew he would be an artist because he spent his early years within 2 blocks of 2 of the best museums in Europe! He enjoyed his science classes in school and loved the study of nature.

Lionni received a doctorate in Italy and spent many years in the business and art worlds as a graphics designer working for and directing large businesses before illustrating his first children's book, *Little Blue and Little Yellow*, in 1959. He had shown a draft of it to a publishing friend, who liked and published it. It is the story of two patches of color who become friends.

Lionni was frequently asked if all his stories taught a lesson, and he answered that his works were all fables. Four of his books were named Caldecott Honor books: *Inch by Inch*, *Swimmy*, *Frederick*, and *Alexander, the Wind-Up Mouse*.

SELECTED ADDITIONAL TITLES BY THE AUTHOR-ILLUSTRATOR:

Biggest House in the World
Color of His Own
Cornelius
Fish Is Fish
Geraldine, the Music Mouse
Greentail Mouse
In the Rabbitgarden
Let's Make Rabbits
Mouse Days
On the Beach There Are Many Pebbles
Pezzettino
Theodore and the Talking Mushroom
Tico and the Golden Wings
What? Pictures to Talk About
When?
Where? Pictures to Talk About
Words to Talk About

Using the Book

Suggested Approach to the Book

Model Lesson #1

- Introduce the author-illustrator, Leo Lionni, as a talented artist who worked in different art media that he matched to the story, including drawings, crayon, collage, and gouache painting. The pictures in *Inch by Inch* are illustrations in the collage technique. The word *collage* is a derivative of the French word, *coller*, which means to glue or paste.

Model Lesson #2

- Read *Inch by Inch* and share Lionni's dramatic collage art with the class.

Model Lesson #3

- Some questions to share with the class:

    1. Describe the inchworm.
    2. What does a robin look like?
    3. What useful thing can an inchworm do?
    4. How many inches is a robin's tail?
    5. What other measurements of birds did the inchworm take?
    6. What did the nightingale want measured?
    7. What did the inchworm do to keep from being eaten?
    8. How else could the inchworm have escaped?

Model Lesson #4

- Art appreciation through picture books: Compare the following chameleon books by 2 authors who are noted for their use of collage art:

    Carle, Eric, *Mixed-Up Chameleon*
    Lionni, Leo, *Color of His Own*

Library Media Center Connections

1. Display all the Leo Lionni titles that are available in the library and have all the students classify them according to art technique: drawings, crayon, collage, and gouache.

2. Ask each student to choose a favorite picture book artist and compare the art media used in that artist's picture books. Are the materials the same as Leo Lionni's?

3. Label and classify the art media of both artists on an information chart supplied by the teacher by artist, book title, and art media used. Take the information back to class for the teacher to graph the choices.

Theme Reading Connections: Measurement

Branley, Franklyn M., *How Little and How Much*
Myller, Rolf, *How Big Is a Foot?*
Schlein, Miriam, *Modern Way to Measure*
Tresselt, Alvin, *How Far Is Far?*

Activities to Connect Literature and Curriculum

ART

Examine the title page of *Inch by Inch*. Find the inchworms. Create a bulletin board using the collage technique. Include all the birds mentioned in the story as well as snails, butterflies, grass, and flowers. Be creative in the use of collage. Brainstorm in class the different ways that a collage may be created.

Make inchworm bookmarks. Use the same inchworm design for a reading incentive mascot. Record the names of library book titles that have been read on paper inchworms and integrate them as part of the collage bulletin board described above.

Give each student a 2-inch square of cardboard to take home. Tell the students to draw a 1-inch square within the 2-inch square in pencil on the cardboard. They should fill the 1-inch area with items that produce a 3-dimensional textured surface. For example, use rice, seeds, beans, or cereal to cover the 1-inch area. The students should then bring the project back to school. Assemble all the squares into a classroom inchworm.

LANGUAGE ARTS

Write and illustrate another version of *Inch by Inch*. Create a large animal who can measure only "Foot by Foot." What would it look like? Name some items that it would be comfortable measuring. Make a cover for your story and decorate it in the collage technique.

What is a fable? What would you say is the moral to *Inch by Inch*? Plan to read some additional fable stories including selections written by the Greek slave, Aesop.

MATH

Select 5 items in the classroom that you believe measure 1 inch. Record the names of the items selected and then measure and record the actual measurement. Starter ideas would include an eraser, a paper clip, or the spine of a textbook.

Inch by Inch was busy measuring for the birds. Your job is to measure 50 objects in your school, classroom, and playground with a partner. Keep a source sheet to list the item measured and the measurement. A metric lesson may also be integrated into this activity. Use 15 minutes of the math lesson time on 2 different days to complete the lesson. Establish time and space constraints before the activity begins.

SCIENCE

Establish a worm terrarium in the classroom for observation purposes.

Design an ecosystem beginning with an inchworm. What food does he eat? The bird eats the worm. What happens next? Cluster the system on the blackboard for visual impact. Extend the thinking as far as possible with the class.

Beyond the Book

Guided Reading Connections across a Curriculum Rainbow: Insects

Adler, Irving, and Ruth Adler, *Insects and Plants*
Fischer-Nagel, Andreas, and Heiderose Fischer-Nagel, *Life of the Ladybug*
Fisher, Aileen, *When It Comes to Bugs*
Hoberman, Mary Ann, *Bugs: Poems*
Holly, Brian, *Bugs and Critters*
Hornblow, Leonore, and Arthur Hornblow, *Insects Do the Strangest Things*
Kirkpatrick, Rena, *Look at Insects*
Merrians, Deborah, *I Can Read about Insects*
Naden, C., *I Can Read about Creepy Crawly Creatures*
Peet, Bill, *Gnats of Knotty Pine*
Podendorf, Illa, *Insects*
Poulet, Virginia, *Blue Bug* Series
Reidel, Marlene, *From Egg to Butterfly*
Selsam, Millicent E., and Ronald Goor, *Backyard Insects*
Settel, Joann, and Nancy Bagget, *How Do Ants Know When You're Having a Picnic?*
Seymour, Peter, *Insects: A Close-Up Look*
Zim, H. S., and Clarence Cottam, *Insects*

Enriching Connections

FOR GIFTED STUDENTS

Begin an insect collection. Collect, mount, and identify available specimens. Can you name some ways that insects are helpful in our world? Read about insects in several encyclopedias and resource books to give you ideas.

Develop an insect "Trivial Pursuit Game." Divide the class into 2 teams and play "Insect Trivial Challenge."

Create an inchworm maze puzzle. Place the inchworm on the outside of the maze and provide a way for it to find its way into the garden. Locate the garden in the center of the maze. Include some predator birds and other threats and rewards in the puzzle. If the inchworm meets a bird in the maze, the game is over. The teacher will reproduce copies of the inchworm mazes so that students may exchange puzzles.

FOR PARENTS

Ask your child to come with you into the backyard and bring a yardstick to measure. Choose an area where plants are growing. Measure and mark a 3-foot-by-3-foot area. Examine the soil, grass, and plants to determine how many insects are living in the area. Sketch the area on paper and show where plants are growing. Mark each area where a living organism is observed. How many were identified in 9 square feet?

*   *   *   *   *   *   *   *   *   *   *

PROFESSIONAL READING

Bader, Barbara. *American Picturebooks from Noah's Ark to the Beast Within*. New York: Macmillan, 1976.

Baskin, Barbara H., and Karen H. Harris. *Books for the Gifted Child*. New York: R. R. Bowker, 1980.

Butler, Andrea, and Jan Turbill. *Towards a Reading-Writing Classroom*. Rozelle, New South Wales: Primary English Teaching Association, 1985.

California State Department of Education. *Recommended Readings in Literature, Kindergarten through Grade 8*. Sacramento, Calif.: California State Department of Education, 1986.

Carpenter, Humphrey, and Mari Prichard. *The Oxford Companion to Children's Literature*. New York: Oxford University Press, 1984.

Coody, Betty. *Using Literature with Young Children*. Dubuque, Iowa: William C. Brown, 1973.

Cook, Elizabeth. *The Ordinary and the Fabulous: An Introduction to Myths, Legends, and Fairy Tales*. New York: Cambridge University Press, 1978.

Cullinan, Bernice E. *Literature and the Child*. San Diego, Calif.: Harcourt Brace Jovanovich, 1981.

De Montreville, Doris, and Elizabeth D. Crawford, eds. *Fourth Book of Junior Authors and Illustrators*. New York: H. W. Wilson, 1978.

De Montreville, Doris, and Donna Hill, eds. *Third Book of Junior Authors*. New York: H. W. Wilson, 1972.

Faggella, Kathy. *Crayons, Crafts and Concepts*. Bridgeport, Conn.: First Teacher Press, 1985.

Fisher, Margery. *Who's Who in Children's Books*. New York: Holt, Rinehart and Winston, 1975.

Forte, Imogene. *Puppet Factory*. Nashville, Tenn.: Incentive Publications, 1984.

Freeman, Judy. *Books Kids Will Sit Still For*. Hagerstown, Md.: Alleyside Press, 1984.

Freericks, Mary, and Joyce Segal. *Creative Puppetry in the Classroom*. Roywaton, Conn.: New Plays Books, 1979.

Fuller, Muriel, ed. *More Junior Authors*. New York: H. W. Wilson, 1963.

Glazer, Joan I. *Literature for Young Children*. Columbus, Ohio: Charles E. Merrill, 1986.

Grun, Bernard. *The Timetables of History: A Horizontal Linkage of People and Events*. New York: Simon and Schuster, 1982.

Haglund, Elaine J., and Marcia L. Harris. *On This Day: A Collection of Everyday Learning Events and Activities for the Media Center, Library, and Classroom*. Littleton, Colo.: Libraries Unlimited, 1983.

Hardiman, George W., and Theodore Zernich. *Art Activities for Children*. Englewood Cliffs, N.J.: Prentice-Hall, 1981.

Holtze, Sally Holmes. *Fifth Book of Junior Authors and Illustrators*. New York: H. W. Wilson, 1983.

Hopkins, Lee Bennett. *Books Are by People*. New York: Citation Press, 1969.

Hopkins, Lee Bennett. *Pass the Poetry, Please!* New York: Harper & Row, 1987.

Kohl, Mary Ann F. *Scribble Cookies*. Mt. Ranier, Md.: Gryphon House, 1985.

Kunitz, Stanley J., and Howard Haycraft. *Junior Book of Authors*. New York: H. W. Wilson, 1951.

Lanes, Selma G. *The Art of Maurice Sendak*. New York: Abrams, 1980.

Lima, Carolyn W. *A to Zoo Subject Access to Children's Picture Books*. New York: R. R. Bowker, 1986.

Norton, Donna E. *Through the Eyes of a Child*. Columbus, Ohio: Charles E. Merrill, 1983.

Paulin, Mary Ann. *Creative Uses of Children's Literature*. Hamden, Conn.: Library Professional Publications, 1982.

Pearson, P. David, and Dale D. Johnson. *Teaching Reading Comprehension*. New York: Holt, Rinehart and Winston, 1978.

Polette, Nancy. *3 R's for the Gifted: Reading, Writing, and Research*. Littleton, Colo.: Libraries Unlimited, 1982.

Polette, Nancy, and Marjorie Hamlin. *Exploring Books with Gifted Children*. Littleton, Colo.: Libraries Unlimited, 1980.

Poltarnees, Welleran. *All Mirrors Are Magic Mirrors: Reflections on Pictures Found in Children's Books*. La Jolla, Calif.: Green Tiger Press, 1972.

Purves, Alan C., and Dianne L. Monson. *Experiencing Children's Literature*. Glenview, Ill.: Scott Foresman, 1984.

Renfro, Nancy. *Bags Are Big*. Austin, Tex.: Nancy Renfro Studios, 1986.

Rudman, Marsha Kabakow. *Children's Literature: An Issues Approach*. New York: Longman, 1984.

Schimmel, Nancy. *Just Enough to Make a Story*. San Francisco, Calif.: Sisters' Choice Press, 1984.

Smith, Carl B., and Peggy G. Elliot. *Reading Activities for Middle and Secondary Schools*. New York: Teachers College Press, 1986.

Somerfield, Muriel, Mike Torbe, and Colin Ward. *A Framework for Reading*. Portsmouth, N.H.: Heinemann, 1985.

Stott, John C. *Children's Literature from A to Z*. New York: McGraw-Hill, 1984.

Sutherland, Zena. *The Arbuthnot Anthology of Children's Literature*. New York: Scott Foresman, 1976.

Sutherland, Zena, and May Hill Arbuthnot. *Children and Books*. New York: Scott Foresman, 1977.

Toney, Sara D. *Smithsonian Surprises*. Washington, D.C.: Smithsonian Institution Press, 1985.

Wankelman, Willard F., and Phillip Wigg. *A Handbook of Arts and Crafts for Elementary and Junior High Teachers*. Dubuque, Iowa: William C. Brown, 1982.

Weisburg, Holda K., and Ruth Toor. *Elementary School Librarian's Almanac*. West Nyack, N.Y.: Center for Applied Research in Education, 1979.

Whitehead, Robert. *Children's Literature: Strategies of Teaching*. Englewood Cliffs, N.J.: Prentice-Hall, 1968.

CALDECOTT MEDAL BOOKS

1987   *Hey, Al.* Arthur Yorinks. Illustrated by Richard Egielski. (Farrar)

1986   *Polar Express.* Chris Van Allsburg. (Houghton)

1985   *Saint George and the Dragon.* Retold by Margaret Hodges. Illustrated by Trina Schart Hyman. (Little)

1984   *The Glorious Flight.* Alice Provensen and Martin Provensen. (Random)

1983   *Shadow.* By Blaise Cendrars. Translated and illustrated by Marcia Brown. (Scribner)

1982   *Jumanji.* Chris Van Allsburg. (Houghton)

1981   *Fables.* Arnold Lobel. (Harper)

1980   *Ox-Cart Man.* By Donald Hall. Illustrated by Barbara Cooney. (Viking)

1979   *Girl Who Loved Wild Horses.* Paul Goble. (Bradbury)

1978   *Noah's Ark.* Peter Spier. (Doubleday)

1977   *Ashanti to Zulu.* By Margaret Musgrove. Illustrated by Leo Dillon and Diane Dillon. (Dial)

1976   *Why Mosquitoes Buzz in People's Ears: A West African Tale.* Retold by Verna Aardema. Illustrated by Leo Dillon and Diane Dillon. (Dial)

1975   *Arrow to the Sun.* Gerald McDermott. (Viking)

1974   *Duffy and the Devil.* By Harve Zemach. Illustrated by Margot Zemach. (Farrar)

1973   *The Funny Little Woman.* Retold by Arlene Mosel. Illustrated by Blair Lent. (Dutton)

1972   *One Fine Day.* Nonny Hogrogian. (Macmillan)

1971   *A Story—A Story.* Gail E. Haley. (Atheneum)

1970   *Sylvester and the Magic Pebble.* William Steig. (Windmill)

1969   *The Fool of the World and the Flying Ship.* By Arthur Ransome. Illustrated by Uri Shulevitz. (Farrar)

1968   *Drummer Hoff.* By Barbara Emberley. Illustrated by Ed Emberley. (Prentice-Hall)

1967   *Sam, Bangs, and Moonshine.* Evaline Ness. (Holt)

1966   *Always Room for One More.* By Sorche Nic Leodhas. Illustrated by Nonny Hogrogian. (Holt)

1965   *May I Bring a Friend?* Beatrice Schenk De Regniers. Illustrated by Beni Montresor. (Atheneum)

1964   *Where the Wild Things Are.* Maurice Sendak. (Harper)

1963   *The Snowy Day.* Ezra Jack Keats. (Viking)

1962   *Once a Mouse.* Marcia Brown. (Scribner)

1961   *Baboushka and the Three Kings.* By Ruth Robbins. Illustrated by Nicholas Sidjakov. (Parnassus)

1960   *Nine Days to Christmas.* Marie Hall Ets. (Viking)

1959   *Chanticleer and the Fox.* Adapted from Chaucer and illustrated by Barbara Cooney. (Crowell)

1958   *Time of Wonder.* Robert McCloskey. (Viking)

1957   *A Tree Is Nice.* By Janice Udry. Illustrated by Marc Simont. (Harper)

1956   *Frog Went A-Courtin'.* Illustrated by Feodor Rojankovsky. Retold by John Langstaff. (Harcourt)

1955   *Cinderella.* Illustrated by Marcia Brown. Retold from Perrault. (Scribner)

1954   *Madeline's Rescue.* Ludwig Bemelmans. (Viking)

1953   *The Biggest Bear.* Lynd Ward. (Houghton)

1952   *Finders Keepers.* By William Lipkind. Illustrated by Nicholas Mordvinoff. (Harcourt)

1951   *The Egg Tree.* Katherine Milhouse. (Scribner)

1950   *Song of the Swallows.* Leo Politi. (Scribner)

1949   *The Big Snow.* Elmer Hader and Berta Hader. (Macmillan)

1948   *White Snow, Bright Snow.* By Alvin Tresselt. Illustrated by Roger Duvoisin. (Lothrop)

1947   *The Little Island.* By Golden MacDonald. Illustrated by Leonard Weisgard. (Doubleday)

1946   *The Rooster Crows.* Maud Petersham and Miska Petersham. (Macmillan)

1945   *Prayer for a Child.* By Rachel Field. Illustrated by Elizabeth Orton Jones. (Macmillan)

1944   *Many Moons.* By James Thurber. Illustrated by Louis Slobodkin. (Harcourt)

1943   *The Little House.* Virginia Lee Burton. (Houghton)

1942   *Make Way for Ducklings.* Robert McCloskey. (Viking)

1941   *They Were Strong and Good.* Robert Lawson. (Viking)

1940   *Abraham Lincoln.* By Ingri D'Aulaire and Edgar Parin D'Aulaire. (Doubleday)

1939   *Mei Li.* Thomas Handforth. (Doubleday)

1938   *Animals of the Bible.* By Helen Dean Fish. Illustrated by Dorothy P. Lathrop. (Lippincott)

AUTHOR/TITLE INDEX

SUBJECT INDEX